THE LINGUISTICS DELUSION

THE LINGUISTICS DELUSION

Geoffrey Sampson

SHEFFIELD UK BRISTOL CT

Published by

Equinox Publishing Ltd
UK: Office 415, The Workstation, 15 Paternoster Row, Sheffield, South Yorkshire S1 2BX, UK
US: ISD, 70 Enterprise Drive, Bristol, CT 06010, USA

www.equinoxpub.com

First published 2017

British Library Cataloguing-in-Publication Data
A catalogue record for this book is available from the British Library.

ISBN 978-1-78179-577-4 (hardback)
978-1-78179-578-1 (paperback)

Library of Congress Cataloging-in-Publication Data
Names: Sampson, Geoffrey, author.
Title: The linguistics delusion / Geoffrey Sampson.
Description: Sheffield, UK; Bristol, CT: Equinox Publishing Ltd, 2017. | Includes bibliographical references and index. | Description based on print version record and CIP data provided by publisher; resource not viewed.
Identifiers: LCCN 2017005213 (print) | LCCN 2017035610 (ebook) | ISBN 9781781796061 (ePDF) | ISBN 9781781795774 (hardcover) | ISBN 9781781795781 (softcover)
Subjects: LCSH: Linguistics.
Classification: LCC P121 (ebook) | LCC P121 .S2765 2017 (print) | DDC 410.1--dc23
LC record available at https://lccn.loc.gov/2017005213.

Typeset by Forthcoming Publications Ltd (www.forthpub.com)
Printed and bound by Lightning Source

For Alexander and Isabel

... like the baseless fabric of this vision,
The cloud-capp'd towers, the gorgeous palaces,
The solemn temples, the great globe itself,
Yea, all which it inherit, shall dissolve;
And, like this insubstantial pageant faded,
Leave not a rack behind ...

Shakespeare, *The Tempest*

Contents

Acknowledgements

Many people have made helpful comments on talks and manuscripts of mine which have turned into one or another of the chapters in this book. Some were audience members otherwise unknown to me or anonymous journal referees, but four individuals I can identify by name are Gerald Gazdar, Kees Hengeveld, Abby Kaplan, and Daniel Silverman. If I have overlooked others whom I ought to have named, I ask them to forgive my lapse.

In this book it is more than usually necessary to point out that those I thank cannot be blamed for the conclusions I have drawn. These are entirely my responsibility.

I am grateful to rights holders for permission to reprint material already published elsewhere, as follows:

Cambridge University Press, for material from *Language and Cognition* 8.587–603, 2016; the Linguistic Society of America, for material from *Language* 90.e144–8, 2014; John Benjamins Publishing Co., for material from *Language and Dialogue* 3.437–56, 2013, and 6.329–36, 2016; de Gruyter Mouton, for material from *Linguistic Typology* 20.561–7, 2016; the publishing office of the *Journal of Chinese Linguistics*, for material from that journal, volumes 41.255–72, 2013 and 43.679–91, 2015; Oxford University Press, for chapter 1 of G.R. Sampson, D. Gil, and P. Trudgill, eds, *Language Complexity as an Evolving Variable*, 2009; the Adam Mickiewicz University, Poznań, for material from *Poznań Studies in Contemporary Linguistics* 50.169–78, 2014; Informa plc, for material from the *Journal of Quantitative Linguistics* 23.342–60, 2016.

Chapter 1

Introduction

This book is a critique of the academic discipline of linguistics.

Some subjects taught in university departments have existed as recognized disciplines for centuries, but "linguistics" is new. I had never heard the word when I became an undergraduate; many educated adults who are not professional academics are unfamiliar with it today. The detailed history of linguistics as a university subject is known to me chiefly in the British context, but I believe Britain is not unrepresentative. When I graduated in Oriental Studies from Cambridge University in 1965, ours was the first year to be given the option of sitting a finals paper in "general linguistics" (I took that option). Students of "Modern and Mediaeval Languages" (that is, European languages) may have had the option earlier, but I think only a year or two earlier. Whatever else it is, linguistics is not a discipline that has earned a place in the map of learning through recognition by many generations of thoughtful and educated people of its intellectual standing.

Language has of course been studied for a very long time – as long, probably, as Mankind has had resources to spare for intellectual pursuits after the practical needs of food and shelter were provided for. In Europe, throughout the Middle Ages and long afterwards schooling was centred largely on the classics. The motive for learning about the Ancient Greeks and Romans was that they founded the civilization to which modern Europeans are heirs, so that study of their history, institutions, and ideas held lessons of potential value to subjects of modern European states; but those lessons had to be absorbed through the medium of languages which are so complex that language study alone accounted for a high proportion of all the effort put into classical studies. In recent centuries modern European languages, too, came to be seen as valid subjects for degree-level study. For a long while it was assumed that only languages of literate societies could be worth learning about, but by the late nineteenth century

Western researchers were finding intellectual value in examination of unwritten Asian, African, and Native American languages, which were often studied as an aspect of anthropology. There is nothing new about studying languages.

"Linguistics", though, is a discipline which claims to study *language in general*, rather than particular languages or families of languages; and that is a new development.

The germ of the modern discipline of linguistics is commonly identified with a series of courses given by Ferdinand de Saussure at the University of Geneva between the years 1908 and 1911, which his students compiled after his death into a book published in 1916 under the title *Course in General Linguistics*. But while Saussure may have introduced the concept of "general linguistics" as a subject in its own right, the practical development of such a subject got under way only considerably later. In the academic world, new disciplines become recognized through the creation of professorial chairs, university departments, and degree titles. In Britain the first professor of general linguistics was J.R. Firth in 1944, but for some time he was a one-off case, working in a very unusual, specialist academic environment (London University's School of Oriental and African Studies). It was in the 1960s – that decade when the world was crazily haring after innovation in every aspect of life – that the subject really took off, with new departments and degree schemes popping up in one university after another. (At first, the term used was Saussure's "general linguistics", in order to make an explicit contrast with the study of particular languages; later, as the new subject became widely established, the "general" was dropped and the subject was simply called linguistics.) At the oldest university in the English-speaking world, Oxford, I was told that I myself was the first person in its long history to be given a job with "linguistics" in the title, when I was elected to a college research fellowship in that subject in 1969. (More than one of my senior colleagues were puzzled to know what might lie behind this novel academic terminology.) Soon, perhaps half the universities in Britain were offering degrees in linguistics.

Fifty years later, it is plain to those with eyes to see that the subject has lost its way. An academic discipline which was founded a century ago, and took off in numbers and popularity half a century ago, ought presumably by now to be offering us worthwhile new insights into its subject-matter. We are not getting that from linguistics.

Many observers are vaguely aware of this failure, without pinning down where the problem lies. The heart of the problem is that linguistics sees itself as a science – the soundbite which it has used since the 1960s to define itself is “the scientific study of language”. That is a delusion. Human language is not the kind of thing that can be studied by the methods of science.

“Science” was originally a very general word, deriving from Latin *scientia*, “knowledge”, but at least since the nineteenth century it has had a better-defined, more specific application. The man who showed us what distinguishes the sciences from other areas of intellectual activity was Sir Karl Popper, initially through a 1934 book translated into English in 1959 as *The Logic of Scientific Discovery*. For Popper, the hallmark of the sciences is that they propose general theories which make themselves vulnerable to refutation, by yielding testable predictions about empirical observations which anyone is free to make. A scientific theory cannot be proved true, but it can be disproved if some of its predictions are falsified. (Popper was particularly keen to contrast genuine sciences in this sense with bodies of discourse which he regarded as pseudosciences – his examples were the Marxist theory of history, and Freudian psychoanalysis – which he saw as not admitting any possibility of refutation, since their exponents would in practice reinterpret any apparently adverse evidence in a way that turned it into a confirmation of the theories’ predictions.)

In other words, a true science draws a boundary round some set of imaginable future observations, and says “you may observe things falling within this boundary, but you will never observe anything outside it – if you do, the theory is wrong and must be given up”. The narrower the boundary, relative to the total universe of imaginable possibilities, the more contentful and better the theory. A good theory is highly “falsifiable” – to be falsifiable sounds like a bad thing, but in science it is a good thing: a theory which is potentially falsifiable (but which has not been falsified) tells us something, an unfalsifiable theory is empty. Thus, a theory of gravity which predicted “An object released near the Earth will fall towards its centre” would be an acceptable scientific theory, though a fairly weak one: it rules out the possibility of the object hanging motionless in mid-air, or moving in some other direction. A theory which predicted “…will fall towards its centre at a constant positive rate of acceleration” would be better: it excludes everything excluded by the earlier theory, and also excludes downward motion at a fixed speed, or at a speed which changes irregularly. A theory predicting that the released body will “move in accordance with its intrinsic nature” (which is rather like what some Ancient Greeks believed about motion) would not rank as a scientific theory at all, because we are not told what kinds of movement would refute it. (Unless we are told more, we would have to look at how the body actually does move in order to know what motions accord with its intrinsic nature.)

Popper's criterion for distinguishing science from non-science is not the be-all and end-all. As always, matters are more complicated. For instance, Popper's departmental colleague Imre Lakatos pointed out (Lakatos 1970) that scientific theories in practice are not (and should not be) abandoned at the first whiff of counter-evidence, because it will not be clear whether the surprising observation exposes a fault in the theory itself or arises from some interfering factor. What we have to assess is not a single theory in isolation, but an evolving sequence of theories resulting from successive modifications in response to evidence: do the theories evolve in a direction that gives them increasing content, or do they become ever emptier? As Lakatos put it, are they "progressive" or "degenerating" research programmes? But in broad outline Popper's idea about the difference between sciences and non-scientific subjects is accepted by everyone who recognizes science as a significant factor in the progress of civilization.

The trouble with applying this idea to the study of language is that human language behaviour is a very open-ended activity. As with some other aspects of human life, as fast as one tries to draw boundaries round sets of "things that can happen", to contrast them with other imaginable "things that can't happen", we find that human behaviour breaks through the boundaries. The planets in their orbits obey the same fairly simple laws of motion year in, year out, enabling astronomers successfully to predict things like eclipses over long periods of time – they can often match records of eclipses centuries past with "retrodictions" of when the laws say eclipses should have occurred. Human life has none of that changeless quality. The life of a 21st-century Englishman would in various respects be incomprehensible to an inhabitant of the Victorian age, and only by studying history can we understand many aspects of the lives of our ancestors.

Germans divide academic subjects into *Naturwissenschaften* and *Geisteswissenschaften* – literally, natural studies versus spiritual studies. The Newtonian laws of motion are a natural study, but human language behaviour is clearly a product of the human spirit (even though, in English, "spirit" and "spiritual" have religious or spooky connotations which are not present in the German word). No-one suggests that scientific knowledge is the only valid knowledge there is. Subjects like history, or ethics, are very significant fields of enquiry, but they are *Geisteswissenschaften*: they are not domains where one can usefully posit refutable scientific theories. History has trends, and we can gain insight into past times by reading a good historian's analysis of historical trends, but history does not have scientific laws. The study of human language, necessarily, must be more like history than like physics.

I said that no-one sees the sciences as having a monopoly on valid knowledge, but that is not strictly true. The 1960s, which saw the discipline of linguistics take off, was the tail-end of a period when intellectual life in general had been heavily influenced by doctrines such as logical positivism, which did come close to asserting that any statement is either scientific or it is meaningless. Few philosophers are impressed by logical positivism today. But the claim of linguistics to be scientific is this discipline's *raison d'être*, so it cannot be given up. Often the claim is maintained very explicitly. Consider for instance the preface included in successive editions of a standard modern linguistics textbook (my copy is the third edition, O'Grady et al. 1997 – the book is currently up to its sixth edition). William O'Grady and Michael Dobrovolsky begin their preface by writing:

> Thanks to the application of rigorous analysis to familiar subject matter, linguistics provides students with an ideal introduction to the kind of thinking we call "scientific". Such thinking proceeds from an appreciation of problems arising from bodies of data, to hypotheses that attempt to account for those problems, to the careful testing and extension of these hypotheses.

Words like "rigorous", "hypotheses", "testing" make it very obvious that linguistics is claimed to fall on the "science" side of the "science"/"arts" divide.

That claim is mistaken. Linguistics is not a science. I am not sure that it ought to rank as a "subject" at all, in the sense of a body of knowledge coherent and reliable enough to justify teaching it to undergraduates and awarding them degrees in it. But if it is a subject, linguistics is certainly not a scientific subject.

The word for the attitude which insists that studies of humane, cultural matters can and should be theorized as if they were natural sciences is *scientism*. The term was introduced from French into English (in this sense, at least) by the social philosopher Friedrich Hayek, who (after emphasizing his admiration for scientific method when applied within its proper domain) wrote

> we shall, wherever we are concerned, not with the general spirit of disinterested inquiry but with slavish imitation of the method and language of Science, speak of "scientism" or the "scientistic" prejudice… [I]n the sense in which we shall use these terms, they describe, of course, an attitude which is decidedly unscientific in the true sense of the word, since it involves a mechanical and uncritical application of habits of thought to fields different

> from those in which they have been formed. The scientistic as distinguished from the scientific view is not an unprejudiced but a very prejudiced approach which, before it has considered its subject, claims to know what is the most appropriate way of investigating it. (Hayek 1955: 15–16)

Linguistics has always been soaked in what Hayek called scientism. So much so, that we might have a better understanding of the nature of human language nowadays, if "linguistics" as an independent discipline had not been created.

Indeed, although the evolution of academic linguistics since the 1960s has laid increasing emphasis on the claimed "scientific" status of the discipline, in practice it has become *less* scientific than it originally was. For anyone who wants to learn in detail about a language or languages other than the commonly studied Western European ones, a knowledge of phonetics is very useful, and when linguistics first got going, phonetics formed a large part of it. Western European languages exploit only a small part of the total spectrum of sounds which human mouths are capable of making and which are used in languages of other parts of the world. In Britain, at least, people who studied language as a general phenomenon used standardly to be given phonetics courses which not only taught them theoretically about the full range of speech-sounds, but also included practical training in recognizing exotic speech-sounds and in producing them accurately. Plenty of that went on decades before linguistics degrees had been invented, and I was still given such training as an undergraduate in the 1960s. We know that this approach worked: there is experimental evidence (Ladefoged 1967: 133–42) showing that linguists who have not undergone this kind of training are unable to identify speech sounds with the same degree of precision. Understanding how the human vocal organs act to produce various kinds of speech-sound, and how those sounds are embodied as different patterns of air-pressure waves, is a thoroughly scientific subject. But, as linguistics won greater recognition as a freestanding discipline, it came to treat phonetics as not truly included within its purview. Phonetics is a practical, empirical subject, and linguisticians wanted to focus on grand theories at a considerable remove from the detailed realities of individual human beings speaking and listening to speech. John Ohala (2005) has discussed how language facts which have straightforward explanations in terms of the physical anatomy of the vocal organs are nowadays treated by linguisticians in terms of abstract theoretical concepts having no basis in phonetic reality. Today, a degree syllabus in linguistics will typically contain only a smattering of phonetics, and no practical ear-training at all.

Incidentally, a point of terminology. I have used the word "linguistician" to label someone who pursues the subject I am criticizing. When linguistics was new, that word was commonly used. An older generation of academics, who tended to feel that the established language subjects already covered the ground pretty adequately without leaving a gap large enough to require the creation of a new one, used the term "linguist" for practitioners of those established subjects, and assumed that if the new subject was called linguistics its practitioners must be linguisticians. Those who pursued the new subject tended to reject that term, and insist that they too should be called linguists. "Linguist" was henceforth to be a word with two meanings: on one hand someone who is skilled in or knowledgeable about some particular language or languages, and on the other hand someone who studies general linguistics. The newcomers on the whole won that argument, and it is a while now since I heard anyone use the word "linguistician". But in the context of the present book, which is pitting the claims of traditional language scholarship against those of general linguistics, it will be convenient to have separate words for followers of the separate approaches. Accordingly, people who pursue linguistics will here be called linguisticians.

One benefit of the scientific method, in domains where it applies, is the humility it enforces on practitioners. Someone who goes off on a flight of theoretical fancy will soon be brought down to earth if his theory is wrong, when some of its predictions turn out to be mistaken. This enforced humility is a valuable counter-weight to the pomposity which is a besetting sin of the academic profession, whose members spend their working lives lecturing to young people and assessing their work. Humanities subjects, though, lack the concept of "crucial experiment". Historical generalizations, for instance, may be assessed as plausible and convincingly argued or as fanciful and overblown, but this is a matter of judgement and discretion, depending on the wisdom of those making the assessment. Unless a generalization rests on basic facts that are simply mis-stated (Queen Anne did not die in 1704, she died in 1714), no-one can ever say "This historical theory has been refuted, end of story". The danger this creates is that scholars might feel free to make names for themselves by dreaming up theories in an irresponsible fashion, reckless about whether there is good reason to accept the theories. Long-established humanities subjects have depended on cultivating the kind of wisdom that enables people to distinguish reasonable ideas from implausible puffery. Linguistics has never cultivated this sort of wisdom.

One of the very worst features of academic linguistics is its irresponsibility. It makes reckless assertions, not really caring whether or not they are true.

For instance, for many decades it has been an accepted truism of the subject that "all languages are equally complex". Students of my generation often made their first acquaintance with the subject via Charles Hockett's 1958 textbook *A Course in Modern Linguistics*. According to Hockett, if a language is relatively complex in one aspect of its structure, this will be balanced out by relative simplicity in some other aspect; overall complexity of different languages is equal, because "all languages have about equally complex jobs to do" (Hockett 1958: 180–1). Similar statements go back to the earliest days of academic linguistics. Henry Sweet (who was the real man behind Eliza Doolittle's teacher "Professor Higgins" in the musical *My Fair Lady*) wrote in 1899 that "If a language is very regular and simple in one department, we may expect it to be irregular and complex in another". The same point has been repeated again and again in the literature of linguistics. According to Robert Dixon (1997: 118), "It is a finding of modern linguistics that all languages are roughly equal in terms of overall complexity". He is echoed by Benjamin Fortson (2010: 4): "A central finding of linguistics has been that all languages…are equally complex in their structure." (A "finding", no less – it sounds pretty scientific.) None of these writers, Sweet, Hockett, Dixon, or Fortson, quoted anything that one could call serious evidence to support this large claim, and so far as I know nobody else ever did so, but it became a received truth of linguistics. Undergraduates who took just one or a few linguistics courses as part of their degree syllabus were very likely to be taught about the equal complexity of all human languages.

This doctrine always seemed to me a politically correct fiction rather than a considered factual generalization. The phrase "politically correct" only made its appearance in the 1980s, but linguisticians throughout the twentieth century had been keen to promote the obscure languages and cultures of undeveloped tribal societies as being fully as entitled to consideration as the great written languages of Western civilization. Worthy of respect they may be – that is an ethical rather than factual issue; but for many linguisticians it seemed a short step from saying that languages are all worthy of respect to saying that they are equally structurally complex, which is a factual claim. Linguisticians wanted the claim to be true, so they announced that it was, and taught generations of students to repeat this in their essays and exam scripts. The idea was treated as an uncontroversial axiom.

I found this so questionable that in 2007, together with a colleague based in Leipzig, I organized a meeting in that city to examine the equal-complexity doctrine. One man who came to Leipzig objected to the doctrine on the ground that there is no satisfactory way to compare languages in terms of their overall complexity – he thought it was meaningless to say either that languages are, or that they are not, equally complex, which is a reasonable line to take. Most speakers, though, did believe that comparisons are possible, and they urged that some languages are indeed more complex than others. (Incidentally, the more complex languages by no means coincide with the more technically advanced cultures; if anything, the correlation goes the other way.)

We published a selection of the solidest and most interesting papers from the Leipzig meeting in book form, and in due course our book was reviewed by *Language*, the world's premier learned journal of linguistics (see Sampson, Gil, and Trudgill 2009, reviewed by Faarlund 2010). The central point made by the reviewer was that we were "pushing at an open door": few linguisticians were likely to disagree with our view that languages differ in complexity. And indeed, over the following years, discussion of the differential complexity of languages became a routine element of linguistic discourse. According to Ray Jackendoff and Eva Wittenberg (2014: 66), languages "obviously" differ in syntactic complexity. Numerous academic conferences and books were dedicated to particular aspects of this idea. To date I have seen no publications arguing that the idea is mistaken.

It is pleasing, of course, to discover that others agree with one's own point of view. But in another way this episode was shocking. Apparently, for many decades, linguisticians all over the world had routinely been teaching a doctrine which, once it was openly challenged, few or none of them turned out actually to believe in. (It still is being taught. At the time of writing, an educational organization called the Centre for Languages, Linguistics, and Area Studies, an offshoot of the British Higher Education Academy, is continuing to publicize a list of "83 points on which linguists seem to agree and which are important for education". One of the 83 points is a cautiously worded restatement of the equal-complexity doctrine.)

One might perhaps feel that this doesn't really matter too much. After all, an arts subject like linguistics is not comparable to subjects like medicine or engineering, where teaching false facts could lead to patients dying or bridges collapsing.

But it does matter. It is true that most humanities students are not acquiring bodies of knowledge which, as graduates, they are going to apply to practical problems, as doctors or engineers do. But what they are doing (or should be doing) is learning to practise the skills involved in absorbing and making sense of complex bodies of information, and using these to produce reasonable answers to questions which are too subtle and debatable to have unique "right answers". This has traditionally been seen as a main justification of university-level teaching of the humanities, and these skills are fundamental to many of the roles which holders of BA degrees commonly go on to fill. Undergraduates study mediaeval history, or analytic philosophy – or perhaps linguistics – in order to hone habits of critical thought which, as graduates, they may apply to the similarly intractable domains of public administration, or political journalism, or business management. (Or indeed to the role of citizen and voter – what is voting, if not making a reasonable choice in the face of overwhelmingly complex arguments for and against rival parties?) Being taught to parrot ideas which your teachers have been parroting for decades, but in which they have so little solid belief that they abandon them at the first breath of challenge, is the worst imaginable training for exercising these graduate-level skills.

What's more, the equal-complexity doctrine has been repeated in so many textbooks because it looks like a humanly significant finding. Language is one of the most – perhaps *the* most – distinctive property of our species. People want to know how language works, because it might shed light on our human nature. If languages of all human groups were indeed measurably equal in complexity, that might seem to open up whole avenues towards a new understanding of what kind of creatures we are. Since languages differ in so many respects, what mechanisms achieve identity in this particular respect? Might it depend on genetics? Or on properties of the communication task which languages execute? Or what? Someone who spends some time pondering that question, and then hears that it is a non-question because linguisticians only *said* languages are equal in complexity, they did not seriously *believe* it, might feel that "irresponsible" is a mild adjective to apply to this academic subject.

I have voiced some harsh criticisms of academic linguistics here, and I shall continue to do so as this book develops. But before going further, let me make two important provisos.

In the first place, I certainly do not believe that linguistics is uniquely valueless as a subject. My impression is that several of the disciplines which students can take degrees in nowadays but which were not recognized as separate subjects sixty or seventy years ago may be fairly rubbishy. For that matter, there is a lot going on in some older-established subjects which is hard to take seriously. Some of the writing I have read emanating from university departments of English Literature in recent decades, for instance, is astonishingly empty or, if it appears to mean anything at all, then utterly question-begging (cf. Sampson 1989). And, if the reader suspects I am discussing a provincial problem specific to Britain or to the English-speaking world, it is worth adding that blatant scientism in the humanities – writing that is peppered with equations and pieces of scientific terminology that look impressive to outsiders but in reality mean nothing whatever – has been taken to far worse extremes in France than, I believe, in any English-speaking country. (See Sokal and Bricmont 1999.) But linguistics, particularly as practised in English-speaking countries, is a subject I know, so it is a subject I am entitled to criticize in detail.

Also, very importantly, I certainly do not want to suggest that all the academic work going on nowadays within Departments of Linguistics is worthless. By no means: there is plenty of good work going on, discovering and recording facts about language which are true and well worth knowing.

On the other hand, I am not sure that any of this worthwhile work could not have occurred just as readily within previously existing academic units, if Departments of Linguistics had never been created. (After all, two of the "bibles" of pre-1960s linguistics, books by Edward Sapir and by Leonard Bloomfield both with the title *Language*, were written respectively by a director of anthropology for a national museum, and a professor of Germanic philology.) The boundaries between disciplines are fairly artificial, so that a lot of what is studied in any one university department might equally well be studied in some other department. But what the creation of linguistics departments and linguistics degrees has done is to reorient our perceptions of language as a topic of study, in terms of which aspects of the study are central and which peripheral. And as I see it, it is the aspects of language study that academic linguistics has taught us to see as central which are most misguided. Here and there in a typical university linguistics department there will be scholars who are busy developing bodies of knowledge and thinking which genuinely rank among the valuable achievements of 21st-century scholarship. But an undergraduate degree-syllabus in Linguistics will not contain much of that material. It will focus largely on the aspects which I criticize in this book, because those are the aspects which the novel discipline treats as central.

Institutionalizing an academic subject creates a powerful pressure to believe and to teach that the subject has abundant content. The famous mathematician G. H. Hardy wrote that "It is one of the first duties of a professor…in any subject, to exaggerate a little…the importance of his subject" (Hardy 1940: 66). That was true when Hardy was writing during the Second World War, but it is far more true in the 21st-century world of university league tables and research assessment. Members of any academic unit, as a matter of survival, have to convince the world (and hence, first, convince themselves) that whatever corner of the map of learning they are responsible for is a large and important terrain. Thus creating departments and chairs of general linguistics, alongside long-established departments and chairs of particular languages, brings into being a cadre of people with a professional need to believe that apart from what can be said about individual languages, dialects, language-families, and so forth, there is also a great deal to be said about human language in general, and what is to be said about language in general is important rather than trivial.

But the truth is that while there is indeed an enormous amount to be said about any particular language, about language in general there is less to be said than present-day linguisticians believe. Less is not nothing; but the result of elevating general linguistics into an independent discipline has been to foster a belief that the languages of the world have far more in common than they really do, and a tendency to overlook or make little of the respects in which individual languages are unique cultural constructs. I do not say that no 21st-century linguisticians are resisting that tendency – one notable exception to it is the German grammarian Martin Haspelmath (see e.g. Haspelmath 2015); but exceptions are rare. Linguistics trains those who study it to see what is in reality a rich panoply of deep intellectual diversity as little more than a set of minor variations on a familiar European theme.

And this matters, because language is so crucial an element of what makes us human that promulgating a distorted model of the nature of human language leads to a distorted idea of human nature itself. Creating a new subject of general linguistics was far from a harmless academic error.

By this point, readers may be itching to say "You are an academic yourself – what are you doing running your own subject down in this way?"

Well, I suppose a scholar who came to see his subject as empty or damaging might have a public duty to say so, though it is asking a lot to expect anyone to condemn his bread and butter. But as it happens, that is not my situation. Normally in academic prose one avoids writing about oneself, but in this case I probably should say a little, to avoid the imputation of hypocrisy.

As an undergraduate I studied a traditional language-literature-and-history degree syllabus (in my case the language was Chinese), but I have mentioned that for finals I sat one paper in general linguistics. Like many other students and young academics of my generation, I swallowed the Kool-Aid. I knew I wanted an academic career, but the prospect of researching to become an authority on some special area of Chinese history, Chinese literature, or the like felt fuddy-duddy and unappealing. Linguistics by contrast was an exciting young person's subject which was promising to open totally new horizons in our understanding of human cognition. How could one turn down the chance of being part of a movement like that? So, by the time I was ready to apply for university posts, I was committed to the new subject. I spent several years as a graduate student in the USA, where most of the impetus behind the subject was coming from, and then gradually climbed the academic ladder, eventually being appointed to the Chair of Linguistics in a leading British civic university in 1984.

Climbing the ladder involved publishing books and journal articles; as I thought and wrote about my subject, I found myself increasingly sceptical about various of its claims. The new horizons were failing to emerge from the haze. Some of my publications were attempts to advance the state of knowledge about some particular language-related topic. Others, though, set out to persuade my fellow linguisticians that in one or another respect our discipline was making unjustifiable claims for itself.

Naively, in the early years of my career I assumed that if my arguments and evidence were strong enough, colleagues would be persuaded and the discipline of linguistics would draw in its horns accordingly. I was too young and inexperienced to reckon with the fact that the first law of any human institution is to survive and if possible expand. An academic discipline is an institution, and hence will never be in the business of voluntarily retreating from territory it has claimed as its own. My writings were well received, in the sense that reviewers and others saw them as intellectually interesting and worth reading. But that is not at all the same thing as influencing the shape of a discipline. Of course, linguistics rolled on, unaffected by any views of mine.

Happily, when I eventually came to the conclusion that academic linguistics was a hopeless cause, I was able to shift into a different subject. After lecturing on linguistics for the first half of my teaching career, I spent the second half in a computer science department. In my later years as a university professor, I was teaching computing students about electronic business and about the aspects of law relevant to the information-technology profession (and of course writing books and articles about those subjects). These are not topics which raise troubling questions about whether they are worth undergraduates' while to study.

I never ceased to be intensely interested in language and languages, so even in my years as a professor of computing I continued to research various linguistic topics. And I kept up with what was going on within linguistics as an organized discipline – which is what gives me the confidence to write about that discipline here.

(In the interest of full disclosure I ought to add that, after reaching retirement age in Britain, I accepted a research post in the Linguistics department of a South African university. I had no teaching duties there, so there was no issue of conscience about misleading the young. I was encouraged to take the position by being told that the department in question had set its face against current linguistic orthodoxy – I hoped there might be opportunities to help foster better ways of studying language. In practice things did not work out like that, and after a few years I resigned from the post.)

One major reason why the public gives more credence to implausible academic ideas than they often deserve is that educated people in other walks of life have little concept of how dramatically professional academics' "terms of trade" have changed over the past forty years. Previously, university dons had little motive, beyond personal vanity, to press their ideas further than the evidence would take them. Nowadays, the circumstances of university employment create strong motives for academics to devise novel theories and use the techniques of public relations to insist that their theories are important and correct, almost irrespective of their true worth. When commercial firms do this sort of thing, people know to make allowances for their overblown claims. Academics, though, are still taken to be the disinterested seekers after truth that they used to be not long ago, so their pronouncements are treated with more respect – often, with too much respect.

Until the present generation, the "tone" of British academic life was set by the ancient universities of Oxford and Cambridge. By the 1960s dozens of other universities existed, but they occupied lower rungs of a universally acknowledged hierarchy. They were staffed largely by Oxbridge graduates, and they aimed to reproduce Oxbridge standards so far as the available resources allowed. (A number of the universities created in the 1960s adopted the collegiate structure which had developed organically in mediaeval Oxbridge, for instance.) At least on the humanities side there was no external source of intellectual authority. When I was an undergraduate in the early 1960s, some of my teachers quite explicitly saw American academic research as a bit of a joke.

As already mentioned, I spent some years at the outset of my career as a fellow of one of the Oxford colleges. It had been founded and endowed in the fourteenth century, and we worked and (if unmarried) lived in elegant buildings dating mainly from the seventeenth and eighteenth centuries. As holder of a temporary junior post I had no seat on the College council, but the bulk of my colleagues, who had permanent teaching roles, ran the affairs of the College as they collectively saw fit and were beholden to no outside agencies. Some of them researched and published on their subjects, because they wanted to rather than because they were told to, but for all of them their chief activity was teaching undergraduates, which was done largely through weekly one-to-one tutorial meetings. These highly intelligent men put in long hours teaching, and there was good reason for them to see this as a worthwhile use of their time and energy: they were helping to mould the minds of the future leaders of society. Even now, and still more then, most individuals prominent in British public life had spent their undergraduate years at one or other of the Oxbridge colleges, and they and their tutors got to know each other pretty well after three years of individual tutorials. Some students graduated and were never heard of again, but any tutor could expect that a proportion of his pupils would make their mark on the world. It would be no small thing, I imagine, to reflect in later life that it was you who taught the Chancellor of the Exchequer to avoid the fallacy of the undistributed middle.

In these circumstances, banging the drum for some half-baked intellectual theory would have seemed embarrassingly gauche. Oxbridge dons were above that kind of thing. We lunched and dined together on a daily basis, and on special occasions it was not unusual for our dinner guests to include people such as a past prime minister, a member of the royal family, or others prominent in the great world outside. A don who spent his time talking up his particular academic specialism excessively might have found it hard to live with the smirks of the more urbane colleagues surrounding him on High Table.

To some extent that milieu still exists at Oxbridge, but it certainly no longer sets the tone of academic life more widely. Oxford and Cambridge now form a much smaller fraction of the British academic profession, and most members of the profession were educated elsewhere (and in any case Oxford and Cambridge themselves have had to adapt heavily in the face of novel external pressures). The average British academic today is more likely to see the pinnacle of his profession as associated with leading American universities than with Oxbridge. And, crucially, that average British academic is not a member of a self-governing society which sets its own working conditions. He or she is an employee, and is made to feel like an employee. Universities are becoming poorer year by year, and to keep afloat they have to compete for funds doled out by government agencies. The main way in which an individual academic can improve his institution's financial standing is by winning research grants which are distributed on a competitive basis by bodies such as the national Research Councils and their European counterparts. Not only do these grants include elements to cover a university's general running costs, but the relative success of an institution in attracting research grants is a chief factor in deciding its level of overall public funding.

One might think that, at least in the arts, much research scarcely needs special funding – access to a library and time to write are the only necessities. That is true, and a great deal of the most valuable scholarship has appeared in books written by individuals who never applied for a research grant in their lives. But, today, that kind of research no longer "counts" – it does not depend on winning competitions, so it is given little weight in allocating university funding. Essentially it is seen as self-indulgent. To be a good citizen in today's academic world, a don must devise programmes of research which require funding to employ research assistants, to pay for equipment and travel, and so forth, and must "sell" these programmes to his academic peers, writing grant proposals that will be accepted in the face of truly fierce competition. The managerial types who hold the reins of power in a modern university ensure that the academics serving under them are clearly aware that this is what is required.

(Teaching undergraduates is a low priority by comparison, because the managers know that – provided the students are kept happy, which realistically depends only to a limited extent on the intellectual substance of their courses – there is little an academic can do in his or her teaching role that will affect university income. Consequently, undergraduate teaching is often done in groups too large for teachers to learn the students' names, and a great deal of it is farmed out to the most junior staff, and to graduate students – whom the undergraduates find more congenial as teachers anyway. It tends not to be seen as something for established academics to take pride in.)

In this situation, it becomes important to develop theories which research assistants can be employed to explore and extend, and to persuade the academic community that the theoretical framework one is working in is one which has to be taken seriously. The referees who will judge your grant applications will be drawn from the community of academics pursuing your subject at other institutions, so you need them to come to your particular applications with a prior assumption that this general kind of work makes sense and is valuable. Part of what I shall be arguing in this book is that (as already suggested) there just is not a great deal to say about languages at a theoretical level. Individual languages can be described, as they have been for many centuries past, but there are not many deep "general linguistic" principles to be uncovered: different languages are different. In the professional environment I have sketched, though, that message is disastrous. It says that there is little scope for spending public money on linguistic research – but academics' careers depend on convincing people that public money needs to be spent on it. So the message cannot be allowed to be true.

The consequence is that academics (in all subjects) have been pushed into adopting some of the behaviour patterns of commercial advertising. Without always realizing it, they have come to find it natural to exaggerate the virtues of their particular line of work and to minimize or suppress its limitations or counterarguments, to an extent that would have felt unnatural and shameful to their predecessors of forty years ago. Writing about the changes since his own days as vice-chancellor of the University of London, Noel Annan (Lord Annan) put it bluntly: "The dons had become liars" (Annan 1999: 294). The development is still recent enough that the public often fail to realize that they need to treat academic pronouncements nowadays with the cautious scepticism which everyone sees as appropriate for literature circulated by car or detergent manufacturers.

Excessive cracking up of one's own work is understandable, if regrettable. But things are worse than that. One senior linguistician with nothing to lose, Esa Itkonen, has commented that open criticism of the current orthodoxies of the subject can "jeopardize a person's career prospects" (Itkonen 1996: 471) – the heretic might be denied a university post. One hears of cases where a linguistician with a stellar reputation has withheld the oxygen of publicity from an intellectual opponent by threatening to withdraw from an academic conference if his opponent is invited to share the platform – knowing that the hapless conference organizer has to take the threat seriously, because he depends on the star name to attract a worthwhile audience. I have not knowingly encountered tricks quite as underhand as that myself (though there have been puzzling occasions when I wondered what was going on behind the scenes). But I have for instance had the experience, on being invited to expound some of my ideas about language to an academic audience in an Asian country, of being physically shouted down by an "orthodox" Western linguistician who apparently felt that loudness of voice would serve better as a rhetorical strategy than reasoned debate.

Another tactic is to treat a dissident scholar as an unperson, as in the old Soviet Union, so that orthodox linguisticians carefully refrain from mentioning his writings for fear that open-minded readers might be led to read them and perhaps find them convincing. (I have had some of that, in situations where the omission was too artificial to be other than deliberate.)

So the reader should not feel that a theoretical edifice which is being worked on by hundreds of professional academics in many countries of the world must necessarily have substance to it. The substance might be little more than academics' need to justify their salaries in 21st-century university circumstances. One can persuade oneself, sincerely, to believe all kinds of things if one is aware that the reward of disbelief may be unemployment.

If the discipline of linguistics has so little to be said in its favour, one might wonder how it continues to flourish as widely as it does. It was never the case that all universities contained a linguistics department, and there are probably fewer of them today than there were in the immediate aftermath of the 1960s wave of enthusiasm. But the many linguistics departments that still exist are fairly secure. In the 21st century, decisions about which subjects should be offered in a university are made not in terms of their intellectual solidity but of which will be cost-effective, by attracting a market of student takers. Linguistics departments are well placed there, for two reasons.

One became apparent to me in the days when I still taught linguistics to undergraduates, and sometimes out of curiosity would ask a first-year student what had led him or her to opt for our subject. An answer which recurred was "I did languages at school but I didn't like literature". Secondary-school pupils who study languages to university-entrance level normally combine them with study of the literature of the respective languages, and evidently these students hoped that linguistics would be "languages minus literature".

As a depressing, negative way for a youngster to choose how to spend three of the best years of his or her life, this struck me as hard to beat. But, in those days and even more so in the 21st century, now that students are forced to obsess about "what will look good on my CV" and how they will pay off their student loans, it is understandable that they look for safe or easy study options rather than ones which will make their hearts sing. I do not suppose this source of recruits will dry up.

The other draw card in the linguistics hand has to do with the fact that English is now unchallenged as the language of international communication. Foreign countries are full of teachers of English, whose governments are willing to pay for them to upgrade their skills by spending some time in an English-speaking country. They will not pay for language teachers just to be tourists for a year, but often they will pay for the teachers to come in order to acquire something that can be seen as an advanced professional qualification. And the financial arrangements that apply to universities (in Britain, at least) mean that foreign students are a more lucrative proposition than students who are British citizens. The consequence is that most or all departments of linguistics offer one-year master's degrees in "applied linguistics", meaning studies which are claimed to use linguistics in order to help people be better language-teachers. For some universities, their applied-linguistics master's is quite a significant component of their overall business model.

If your job is teaching a foreign language, it is obvious that immersing yourself in that language for a while by living where it is spoken must be hugely valuable. Whether the master's studies add much to that value was never very clear to me. Teachers of "applied linguistics" publish research, but I never noticed them spending much time researching how far their courses do improve language-teachers' performance in practice. (The men who taught me various languages other than my own seemed to manage pretty well without applied-linguistics qualifications, which did not exist at the time; though, since I was never taught by someone with such a qualification, I cannot compare.) But the system certainly has a positive effect on the viability of university linguistics departments.

Some of the chapters following this Introduction are adapted from material I have published previously, as articles in learned journals or contributions to multi-author volumes. For present purposes these chapters are partly rewritten, in order to marshal the ideas they contain into a coherent critique of the discipline. I have added wording to spell out the links between the contents of individual chapters and the overall thesis of the book, and cut out wording that was closely tied to the circumstances of the original publication and irrelevant in the present context. Where I saw ways of improving my original argument, I adopted them.

In order to offer readers some signposts, I have grouped the chapters that follow into sections, and each section is equipped with its own brief introduction.

I should mention in advance that among other references to various languages, in a few chapters I discuss features of the Chinese language in some detail. Obviously I know that most readers will not be familiar with Chinese, and I word these passages accordingly. But a discipline which claims to be discovering general truths applicable to all human languages must be tested against more languages than just English – though English is the only language some linguisticians discuss. (There are linguisticians in the 21st century for whom the subject seems to be not just "languages minus literature", but minus languages too.) Compare the fact that many people enjoy reading books or watching television programmes about the animal kingdom: they would be less interested, if the books and programmes only really covered *Homo sapiens* and implied that other species are all much the same as us.

Chinese is by far the world's "biggest" language. Just the Mandarin dialect alone has two to three times as many native speakers as any other language (the runner-up is Spanish, with Hindi and English a little behind). Taking (more realistically) Chinese as a whole, the ratio approaches four to one. Chinese also has a recorded history several times as long as English, and it is probably the world's "first language" in that respect too (the one or two living languages which might challenge Chinese are spoken by small numbers today). Whether or not he thinks of it this way, whoever theorizes about human language in general is in effect discussing the Chinese language, plus some minor ones – so it feels strange that linguistics often contains ideas that are hard to apply to Chinese. I make no apology for doing a little to redress the balance.

There is an obvious danger with a book like this that the overall impression created will be drearily negative. To an extent this may be unavoidable: there really is a lot wrong with academic linguistics. But no-one wants to read one or two hundred pages of unrelieved negativity. Accordingly, I have included material in the book intended to illustrate the fact that language can be discussed in a worthwhile fashion. Language and languages are fascinating topics, even if linguistics is not. If a few chapters here are less tightly related to the central thesis of the book than others, they earn their place by offering content that is positive, I hope instructive, and, perhaps, enjoyable.

I

LANGUAGE OVER-THEORIZED

The fundamental problem with academic linguistics is linguisticians' claim that human language behaviour can be the subject of falsifiable scientific theories. Indeed, they sometimes claim that the discipline has achieved considerable success in developing such theories. But human language behaviour is too open-ended for the scientific method to apply.

One important way in which "scientism" manifests itself in linguistics is through the idea that a human language can be treated as a set of potential grammatical sentences. For those who accept that idea, a theory of a human language – a "generative grammar" – will be something that yields predictions about which sequences of words are grammatical in the language and which sequences are ungrammatical. (Conventionally, linguisticians distinguish the two kinds of word-sequence by marking ungrammatical sequences with an asterisk.) A grammar, in this sense, is a potentially falsifiable theory: if its predictions are not testable by observation of real-life usage, then they are testable by reference to the native speaker's intuitive responses to various word-sequences.

This move has only worked because the linguisticians who made it simultaneously redefined the concept of "creativity" – in a way that few seemed to notice. If one steps back and asks whether it is realistic to think of a human language as a fixed set of grammatical sentences (even if the set may be infinitely numerous), there is plenty of evidence to show that this is not realistic. In the everyday sense of "creative", language is too creative an activity for that. But linguisticians use the word "creative" differently, so this issue did not hold many linguisticians back.

By now, generative linguistics no longer has the field to itself. Even schools of linguistics which see themselves as its rivals, though, have imbibed this same scientistic assumption – as have approaches in linguistics that never had much to do with grammar.

Chapter 2

Two Ideas of Creativity

Discussion of the scientific status of linguistics is often clouded by an ambiguity in the terms "creative", "creativity". Linguisticians have taken to using these words in a way that is very different from the way they are used in everyday English, and this idiosyncratic usage is responsible for serious misunderstandings about the nature of human language.

Many people see academic discourse about language as having undergone a "revolution" in the 1960s, and one leading feature of that "revolution" was said to be a new awareness that language behaviour is *creative*. What is meant, by those who say this, is that the grammar rules of a human language allow an infinitely numerous range of distinct grammatical sentences, so that most sentences we utter or hear have never been uttered or heard by us (or perhaps by anyone) before. Many sequences of words are "ungrammatical", but the sequences which are grammatical are endlessly numerous. Human languages are contrasted in this respect with the signalling systems used by some animal species, which are said to comprise small finite ranges of possible signals.

Thus, Sir John Lyons's *Chomsky* (1970) was a concise summary of the linguistic theories of Noam Chomsky, the man commonly seen as the leading linguistic "revolutionary". Lyons's book was addressed to the educated general reader, by an author with wide intellectual horizons who was broadly sympathetic to his subject without being an uncritical acolyte. After drawing attention to "duality of structure" in human language (the fact that languages characteristically have structure at both phonological and syntactic levels), Lyons wrote:

> The second general property of human language to be mentioned here is its *creativity* (or "open-endedness"). By this is meant the capacity that all native speakers of a language have to produce and understand an indefinitely large number of sentences that they have never heard before, and which may indeed never have been uttered before by anyone.

A generation later, O'Grady et al. (1997), already quoted in chapter 1, was an undergraduate textbook of linguistics, compiled from a position of judicious theoretical neutrality rather than promotion of any particular theoretical "party line". (It appeared in a series edited by two one-time departmental colleagues of mine, Geoffrey Leech and Mick Short, neither of whom could possibly be accused of wearing partisan blinkers.) In their opening pages O'Grady et al. wrote:

> human language must be *creative*... Creative systems are found in all aspects of language, including the way in which sounds are combined to form words...[they give examples of what one might call "grammatical but non-occurring" wordforms such as *prasp* or *flib* versus "ungrammatical" forms such as **psapr* or **bfli*]... Nowhere is the ability to deal with novel utterances more obvious than in the production and comprehension of sentences...much of what you say, hear, and read in the course of a day consists of sentences that are new to you. [They give examples of well-formed versus starred sequences of English words, e.g. *Bob holidayed in France* versus **Jerome midnighted in the streets*.]

So far as I know, Noam Chomsky was the first linguistician to use the term "creative" in this way (e.g. Chomsky [1965b] 1971: 153–4; 1966: 11). Linguisticians have continued to do so ever since. I myself have not taught linguistics since 1990, so in order to confirm that the usage remains current I googled, and quickly found a webpage "Linguistics 101: An Introduction to the Study of Language" by Jennifer Wagner, an Australian doctoral student who teaches first-year linguistics.[1] Her first paragraph says:

> Words in languages are finite, but sentences are not. It is this creative aspect of human language that sets it apart from animal languages, which are essentially responses to stimuli.

I have little doubt that essentially similar remarks could be found in linguistics books and articles published in any one of the past fifty years or so.

To see why this is a very unusual way to use the term "creative", consider another kind of human activity where, equally, the range of distinct potential examples of the activity is infinitely large: multiplying numbers together. I have just multiplied the integers 4792 and 5306 to generate the equation:

$$4792 \times 5306 = 25426552$$

1. See <ielanguages.com/linguist.html>, accessed 18 July 2015.

This is almost certainly the first time in my life I have carried out that particular multiplication, and possibly no-one has ever carried it out before. (With four-figure numbers, perhaps the chances are that there have been a few precedents in the long history of human arithmetical activity, but if I had used six-figure numbers, as I easily could have, I suggest it would be quite unlikely that anyone had previously multiplied together just the same pair of numbers.) There is an infinitely large range of distinct multiplications which, in principle, I am competent to carry out, provided we ignore time and memory constraints. (In practice I could probably never finish accurately multiplying million-digit numbers together, or checking such a multiplication carried out by someone else, but similarly I could never utter, or understand, a million-word sentence.) Although the range of well-formed multiplications is infinitely large, there are also the arithmetical equivalents of "starred sentences"; for instance,

*4792 × 5306 = 25426553

is an invalid equation. The parallels between multiplications, and grammatical sentences as discussed by linguisticians in connexion with the concept of linguistic creativity, are really quite striking.

Nowadays, we have machines to carry out multiplications for us. But, almost within living memory, people were employed to execute such tasks. Was that type of work regarded as "creative"? It was not. On the contrary, carrying out arithmetical operations was and is seen as a clear case of uncreative, mechanical work. Some creative intellectuals did such work as an ancillary part of their activities, for instance a physicist or an astronomer might have needed to carry out tedious arithmetical operations in order to check how well some innovative hypothesis agreed with observational data. But the creative aspect of such a person's work was not seen as residing in his arithmetic. Clear examples of creative activity, as that term is understood outside the discipline of linguistics, are activities like writing fiction or poetry, producing paintings or other kinds of artwork, composing music, and so forth. Developing novel scientific hypotheses, or inventing new areas of mathematics, would also be good examples.

What makes these activities "creative", in the ordinary as opposed to the linguistic acceptation of the word, is not to do with the mathematical fact that the range of possible examples is infinitely numerous (though that may well be true). Rather, the key point is that valuable examples of the activity commonly extend our idea of that range. A creative painter will produce a canvas which in one respect or another is at least a little different from anything one might have imagined on the basis of familiarity with the previous history of painting – and yet which, once painted, can be recognized as a worthwhile addition to that history. The activity of multiplying integers does not have that quality, which is why we think of it as uncreative. Any worthwhile instance of multiplication will conform perfectly to the (infinitely large) range of potential multiplications we have implicitly grasped when we learned multiplication at school. Any attempt to go outside that range and produce an "innovative" kind of equation, say:

4792 × 5306 = pelargonium

is not creative, it is just silly.

As a statement of how the term "creative" has traditionally been used, this is uncontroversial. (I made these points at length as long ago as Sampson 1979: 101–7, in an analysis that was received warmly by philosophers though it was rejected out of hand by linguisticians, who in those days were in such triumphalist mood that they seemed deaf to any questioning of the assumptions of the dominant linguistic ideology.) The trouble with linguisticians' commandeering of the term for a very different, weaker sense is that, if one accepts their redefinition, the English language is left with no obvious word to mean "genuinely creative, creative in the traditional sense".

If it is agreed that we are faced with two very different senses of "creativity", in order to move the discussion forward we need to adopt terms to identify the respective senses unambiguously. Let me describe activities which characteristically produce examples drawn from a fixed and known (even if infinitely large) range as "F-creative", and activities which characteristically produce examples that enlarge our understanding of the range of possible products of the activity as "E-creative". (F chosen as standing for "fixed", E for "enlarging" or "extending".) Then I hold that, outside the discipline of linguistics, people who describe an activity as "creative" normally mean E-creative, but that when linguisticians say that human language behaviour is "creative", they mean that it is F-creative.

Categories of behaviour which are (merely) F-creative are good candidates as subjects for scientific theorizing. As we have seen, a scientific theory must identify a class (which may well be infinitely numerous) of distinct potential observations and must assert that members of that class, and *only* members of that class, can occur; the content of the theory depends on the complementary class of "potential falsifiers" – logically possible observations which are predicted never to occur, so that the theory is refuted if they do occur. Linguisticians' descriptions of language behaviour as "creative" fit this model very well: notice how O'Grady et al. (like many other linguisticians) illustrate the "creativity" of language by contrasting sets of word-sequences, and phoneme-sequences, which they regard as possible in English with other, "starred" sequences which they regard as not possible.

Behaviour which is E-creative, on the other hand, is not a candidate for Popperian scientific theorizing. If it is normal and expected that future examples will fall outside any class that might be hypothesized on the basis of past examples, then there is no point in putting forward a falsifiable theory: we know in advance that it will be falsified. In such a domain, the enterprise of scientific theorizing would not make sense. And indeed we do not commonly find people claiming to propound scientific theories of poetry, or of graphic arts.

If this contrast between two ideas of creativity is well-founded, two questions arise. Why has it seemed important to linguisticians to urge that human language is (merely) F-creative? And does the deeper concept of E-creativity not apply to language?

The original impetus behind linguisticians' insistence on the F-creativity of language behaviour seems to have stemmed from Noam Chomsky's opposition to a model of language which he attributed to the psychologist B. F. Skinner, in a famous negative review (Chomsky 1959b) of Skinner's 1957 book *Verbal Behavior*. As Chomsky described Skinner's view, this claimed to explain language behaviour as a set of responses which individuals learn to utter or execute in reaction to particular features of their environment because similar stimulus–response pairings have been positively reinforced in the past. (Stimuli, and responses, can both be either linguistic or non-linguistic: on this view, we are trained to say given things in response to non-linguistic stimuli, and also to act in given ways in response to linguistic stimuli.) I am not sure that Skinner's idea was really as crude as Chomsky portrayed it as being, but, leaving that issue aside, if anyone really did hold the view which Chomsky attributed to Skinner, we can all agree that that view was absurdly mistaken. To quote just one of Chomsky's counter-arguments ([1959b] 1967: 160):

> Suppose, for example, that while crossing the street I hear someone shout *Watch out for the car* and jump out of the way. It can hardly be proposed that my jumping…was conditioned (that is, I was trained to jump) precisely in order to reinforce the behavior of the speaker.

Many things we say have no particular relationship with our environment at the time we say them, and much of the language we hear evokes no particular action from us at the time (and is not intended by the speaker to do so). As portrayed by Chomsky, Skinner's stimulus–response theory of verbal behaviour is fairly ridiculous.

(Having said that I am unsure whether Chomsky's account of Skinner's linguistics was fair, for ease of exposition I shall assume that it was fair, and shall use simple phrases such as "Skinner's model" where a more careful treatment might add a qualifying phrase like "as described by Chomsky".)

The link with F-creativity arises from the fact that, if Skinner's model were correct, it would seem to follow that the ranges of distinct verbal stimuli and verbal responses offered by a language would both have to be finite. If acquiring a language means being trained through reinforcement to associate particular responses with particular stimuli, then an individual only has time to learn some finite number of associations (a fairly small finite number, one might think). So the fact that grammars of human languages allow in principle for infinitely large ranges of semantically distinct sentences is a large nail in the coffin of Skinner's model. As Chomsky wrote ([1959b] 1967: 157–8):

> It is simply not true that children can learn language only through "meticulous care" on the part of adults who shape their verbal repertoire through careful differential reinforcement...a child will be able to construct and understand utterances which are quite new, and are, at the same time, acceptable sentences in his language. Every time an adult reads a newspaper, he undoubtedly comes upon countless new sentences...which he will recognize as sentences and understand...

Notice how the quotation from Jennifer Wagner above contrasts the F-creativity of human languages with animal languages for which, she says (probably correctly), a Skinner-type model is adequate.

To stress that a human language is more than a finite list of possible utterances would have been worthwhile, then, if linguisticians before Chomsky had mostly believed in the simple kind of stimulus–response model which he attributed, correctly or otherwise, to Skinner. Did they? I am sceptical. I came to linguistics early enough to have read a fair amount of older linguistics before I got round to reading Chomsky; I had never heard of B. F. Skinner before Chomsky's writings introduced him to me as a kind of intellectual Aunt Sally figure. Reading, then and later, the well-known linguisticians of the first half of the twentieth century who presumably defined the Ancien Régime that Chomsky's "revolution" was destined to overturn, it has rarely seemed to me that they expressed a belief in a Skinner-type model, either explicitly or even by implication.

Probably the single leading figure among that group of linguisticians was Leonard Bloomfield. Lyons (1970: 31–2) quotes a number of passages from Bloomfield's *Language* to show that Bloomfield embraced a version of

J. B. Watson's "behaviourist" approach to psychology, but it would be quite a stretch to argue that these passages committed Bloomfield to anything like the Skinner model (and Lyons does not argue that). Indeed, Lyons comments that Bloomfield's behaviourism had no appreciable effect upon syntax or phonology in his own work or in that of his followers. The only respect in which Lyons identifies behaviourism as affecting Bloomfield's model of human language was that it hindered him in developing a satisfactory account of meaning in language. (That would be more of a criticism, if subsequent linguisticians had ever improved on Bloomfield in that respect. On the emptiness of modern "linguistic semantics", see e.g. Sampson 2001: 180–207.)

In the preface which Chomsky added to his Skinner review when it was reprinted in 1967 (see my list of references, beginning on p. 203), Chomsky claimed that Skinner's book was an unusually careful and thoroughgoing example of a widely held view about the nature of human language – "a paradigm example of a futile tendency in modern speculation about language and mind". The implication was that, if readers agreed that Skinner was wrong about language, they would have to agree that almost everyone else then writing about the subject was wrong too, leaving only Chomsky and those who thought like him as having ideas worth taking seriously. But this is like arguing that, because Islamic State with its public beheadings and stonings is clearly barbaric, anyone else who aims to conduct his social life in accordance with religious tenets must be dismissed as beyond the pale.

(Incidentally, any reader who finds the tone of the present book excessively censorious might care to read Chomsky's Skinner review, and reflect that this was widely acknowledged as a valuable and important contribution.)

In practice, those who come to linguistics nowadays, as students or as general readers, are introduced to Skinner's stimulus–response model of language behaviour only so that they can then be told that linguistics has shown that it was wrong. Without that, I doubt whether a picture of language akin to the Skinner model would ever occur to many people. The idea of language behaviour as F-creative is being put forward as a means of curing a problem which people don't have.

But the "cure" is not just redundant, it is damaging. The problem with describing language behaviour as "creative", meaning by that F-creative, is that it gets in the way of thinking about whether language behaviour might be E-creative.

People routinely agree, of course, in seeing the activity of literary composition as E-creative. But the creativity there is at a different level from what linguisticians are commonly concerned with, and linguistic theory has little to say about it.[2] Many linguisticians might happily accept that a given English-language novel has assembled English prose in such a way as to express something about human feelings, human relationships, or other topics in a fashion unlike anything found in previous novels – the novelist has been genuinely E-creative. But linguisticians would nevertheless expect that each of the individual sentences in the novel, as specimens of English syntax, will be drawn from a fixed (though infinitely numerous) range of grammatical sentences defined by the novelist's linguistic competence – the novelist's syntactic behaviour will be only F-creative. Chomsky's *Syntactic Structures* began, after a brief introduction, by saying:

> I will consider a *language* to be a set (finite or infinite) of sentences, each finite in length and constructed out of a finite set of elements. All natural languages in their spoken or written form are languages in this sense... The fundamental aim in the linguistic analysis of a language L is to separate the *grammatical* sequences which are the sentences of L from the *ungrammatical* sequences which are not sentences of L and to study the structure of the grammatical sequences. (Chomsky 1957: 13)

This passage expresses very clearly the idea that human languages are *not* E-creative, though they are F-creative (the material omitted and indicated here by an elision mark includes a statement that a human language has infinitely many sentences). If the syntax of a human language were E-creative, there could be no particular set of word-sequences which would count as the complete set of grammatical sentences of that language. Any attempt to identify such a set would quickly be refuted by the occurrence of sentences having novel structures. A "generative grammar" is a system of rules which generates "all and only" the grammatical sentences of a language, as an algebraic equation may generate the set of points comprising a circle or some other curve. It is central to the generative approach to syntax to hold that a person's linguistic competence defines a fixed class of grammatical sequences, and is not E-creative. A person

2. Though this may be changing, with scientism spreading to literary studies too. An academic journal with the title *Scientific Study of Literature* has been appearing since 2011, and as I write, the Linguist List announces a new book from Oxford University Press entitled *Cognitive Literary Science* (see <linguistlist.org/issues/28/28-64.html>, accessed 5 January 2017).

may produce utterances which fall outside that class, as "performance errors", and from time to time the grammar of a language alters – historical language-change occurs. But these are complicating factors overlaid on languages or idiolects which are basically F- but not E-creative.

In my experience as a teacher of linguistics during the 1970s–80s, quite a common reaction on the part of students or other newcomers was to say something like "It's too rigid – real-life usage is often more unpredictable and open-ended than that". And the standard response by an orthodox linguistician would be along the lines "Well, you can't fault Chomskyan linguistics for failing to recognize the creative aspect of language behaviour – Chomsky is the very man who has drawn attention to the creativity of language use". I doubt whether such a response ever fully satisfied the enquirer, but if the enquirer was an undergraduate he would probably reflect that he needed the teacher to award him marks towards a degree, and accordingly would learn to stop pressing this objection. From our point of view, the two people are simply talking past one another. The objector is complaining that linguistics fails to recognize that language behaviour is E-creative, the respondent is explaining that linguisticians have emphasized that language behaviour is F-creative. But both use the word "creative", so neither appreciates that the objection has not been addressed.

This equivocal use of an ordinary English word has in practice done a great deal, I believe, to deflect criticism which might otherwise have made it very difficult for linguistics to win converts and achieve the standing it has come to enjoy in the past half-century. Because, if one explicitly asks "Are human languages syntactically E-creative?", it is hard to assert confidently that the answer is no.

To my mind, the answer is yes. Anna Babarczy and I have discussed the fact (Sampson and Babarczy 2014) that the concept of "starred sentence" (or "ill-formed word-sequence") seems to have been alien to those who discussed grammar, even formally, before the 1960s. We argued, at length and by reference to concrete data (and I shall argue further in chapter 3 of this book), that the idea of separating the possible sequences over the vocabulary of a human language into a class of grammatical sentences and a complementary class of starred sentences does not make sense. Putting words together in novel syntactic structures, and making sense of novel structures that we hear or read, are normal parts of the activity of using a human language. Sometimes – often – we may say or write sentences which conform perfectly to grammatical patterns that could be abstracted from language examples we have encountered in the past, but those utterances have no special privileged status with respect to our linguistic competence. The more innovative examples are not to be classed as "performance errors".

Others have eloquently expressed essentially the same point of view. John Taylor (2012: 285) writes:

> speakers are by no means restricted by the generalizations that they (may) have made over the data. A robust finding from our investigation is that speakers are happy to go beyond the generalizations and the instances that they sanction. Speakers, in other words, are prone to *innovate* with respect to previous usage, using words in ways not already sanctioned by previous experience, extending the usage range of idioms and constructions...

If someone believes that syntax in some human language truly is F- but not E-creative, he should presumably expect linguisticians to be able to make progress in developing a scientific theory of the syntax of that language. Such a theory would be what linguisticians call a grammar of the language, and in the early years of generative linguistics they did indeed see defining the grammars of human languages as a plausible goal for the discipline, as suggested in the above quotation from *Syntactic Structures*. In the domain of scientific theorizing of course one does not expect to hit on the perfect, watertight theory immediately – a science proceeds by progressive refinement, whereby a theory that succeeds in accounting for much of the available data nevertheless has exceptions and in due course is replaced by a theory which improves on its predecessor in terms of data coverage, only eventually to be replaced in its turn. But in a successful science there is a sense of converging towards the truth, even if the truth is never perfectly attained.

Is this the pattern we find in the enterprise of developing generative grammars for English and other human languages? By now it has long been notorious that it is not. As David Graddol (2004) put it, "No one has ever successfully produced a comprehensive and accurate grammar of any language". It is not just that the grammars which have been produced are not perfectly watertight: there is little sense of convergence towards the ultimate goal. Indeed, after some years, linguisticians tacitly recognized this by abandoning the attempt to produce comprehensive grammars.

If one bears the distinction between E- and F-creativity in mind, the lesson one might draw from this experience is that human languages are indeed syntactically E-creative. Successive attempts to develop accurate generative grammars of a human language could not define increasingly close approximations to the set of all and only the grammatical sentences of the language, because there is no such set to be defined.

Perhaps surprisingly, that is not the lesson which most linguisticians seem to have drawn. Many of them continue to discuss formal grammar rules, but commonly they write papers arguing for or against particular rules which might be appropriate to define specific constructions or to account for specific sets of example sentences in a language. In other words, they debate the nature of fragments of an overall structure of grammar rules which many if not all of them now recognize can never exist. It would be for the linguisticians to say how this activity makes sense. To a believer in grammatical E-creativity, it smacks of the work of the Academy of Lagado.

One reasonable way in which someone might perhaps argue against grammatical E-creativity would be by suggesting that *nothing* in human life is genuinely E-creative: "E-creativity" is a hypothetical concept with no application to reality, and if we have no good scientific theories about the arts, that is only because they are too complicated or we have not tried hard enough.

I am not sure how many people would find this point of view plausible, but Noam Chomsky does seem to hold it. He has argued (1976: 9–11, 24–5, 124–5; 2009a: 184–5) that the ranges of artistic styles, scientific hypotheses, and so forth available to humanity are rigidly limited – so limited that in some of these areas we may already have exhausted all the possibilities. For Chomsky, this idea links to his theories about the genetic determination of human cognitive systems. But people who do not go along with those ideas might nevertheless argue that a human being is a material entity of finite complexity, so there must necessarily be *some* definable limits on the diversity of outputs that entity is potentially capable of producing.

This is an aprioristic, philosophical kind of objection to the concept of E-creativity, whereas most people who see domains such as the arts as E-creative do so because of the empirical fact that new things have continued to appear in these domains for centuries past and further innovations seem to keep on coming. To the aprioristic point, the best reply is that plenty of highly regarded thinkers have argued philosophically in favour of the reality of E-creativity. Karl Popper was one of them; according to W.W. Bartley (1978: 676):

> The chief ideas of Popper's philosophy all relate to the basic theme that something can come from nothing. Scientific theories introduce new forms into the universe and cannot be reduced to observations: there is no such thing as scientific induction. The future is not contained in the present or the past. There is indeterminism in physics; and there is indeterminism

> in history, *ipso facto*, and also because new scientific ideas affect history and thus the course of the physical universe. There is genuine emergence in biology. Value cannot be reduced to fact. Mind cannot be reduced to matter. Descriptive and argumentative levels of language cannot be reduced to expressive and signal levels. Consciousness is the spearhead of evolution, and the products of consciousness are not determined.

Popper saw not just the human mind but even Nature as E-creative ("genuine emergence in biology"). The E-creativity of biological evolution was the main point of the earlier philosopher Henri Bergson's most widely read work, *L'Evolution créatrice* (1907). Or again, an area of human life where continuing original innovation is a matter of great practical significance is economics: I shall point out in chapter 5 that rejecting the concept of E-creativity would contradict an assumption which is crucial for current economic theory. Anyone is free to argue that the idea of E-creativity is untenable, but they cannot do so merely by saying, dismissively, that its untenability is self-evident: others see it as clearly applicable. And if the arts, economic life, and even biological evolution are E-creative phenomena, why would one reject the idea that human grammatical behaviour is also E-creative?

Linguisticians do not explicitly reject that idea. They never consider it, because it is concealed from them by the concept of F-creativity. If one is concerned to arrive at truth, rather than merely to win arguments for one's own side right or wrong (which is not respectable academic behaviour), hijacking of key terms is not a helpful move.

To establish that grammar is indeed E-creative, so as to change the mind of a reader who consciously accepts linguisticians' belief that it is not, would be a large undertaking. But it may not be necessary. My aim in this early chapter has simply been to make the point that E-creativity and F-creativity are two different ideas, and that linguisticians' use of "creative" to mean F-creative has functioned so as to eliminate from consideration the question whether human language might be E-creative. If readers allow themselves to face that question explicitly, I believe many of them may find they already share my answer to it.

Chapter 3

Grammaticality Meets Real-Life Usage

For those who lay stress on the "scientific" status of linguistics, a centrepiece of the discipline is the study of grammar (or syntax, as American linguisticians prefer to call it). A "grammar" of a language, which defines the class of "all and only" the grammatical word-sequences of the language, looks like the very model of a Popperian scientific theory: if sentences occur which are not within the set defined by the grammar, the grammar must be wrong. A few such anomalies would not imply junking the grammar wholesale, of course: if many of the predictions about other grammatical and ungrammatical sequences still seem right, then (as in any science) one would look for limited modifications to the grammar which cure the anomalies without changing the correct predictions.

And linguisticians see their discipline as involving scientific theorizing also at a deeper level. Once we have grammars (or even just partial grammars) of a range of languages, we can see (they claim) that these resemble one another more than we have any *a priori* reason to expect. We can develop scientific theories of "language universals", which draw a narrow boundary round the diversity of grammars – again, these theories are scientific because they could potentially be refuted by finding languages whose grammars fall outside the boundary. To many present-day linguisticians, the alleged existence of language universals represents the chief claim linguistics has on the attention of the public at large. The universals show (it is claimed) that the mechanisms of human cognition are innately determined in much more detail than people have traditionally supposed – which, if true, is certainly something worth knowing and pondering.

It all rests on the grammars of individual languages. But there is a problem about the phrase "if sentences occur" in my opening paragraph. What does "occur" mean in practice? Word-sequences which would decide between rival linguisticians' grammars of a given language are often quite unusual sequences, so that even if they are in fact grammatical one might have to listen to a very great deal of speech, or read a great deal of writing, before encountering an example. With the research techniques that were available when linguistics took off in the 1960s, this was often scarcely feasible.

Many linguisticians held that this did not matter, because it was not going to be necessary to observe linguistic data "in the wild". A native speaker of a language can judge whether a given sequence of words of his language is grammatical or not. A linguistician's grammar stands or falls by whether the sequences it allows match native speakers' grammaticality judgements – does the native speaker put asterisks on the same sequences as those excluded by the linguistician's grammar?

This approach proved hugely problematic. Different speakers of the "same language" often made conflicting judgements about the same word-sequences, and anyway it was not clear what it meant for a native speaker to judge a sequence as "not good in my language". After twenty years or so, the computer revolution made a more objective style of research possible. When I began working with computers in the 1960s, few linguisticians had access to such equipment. But by the 1980s, while home computers were not yet common, anyone in a university who wanted to use computing equipment could easily do so, and linguisticians were beginning to produce what became known as "corpora", large electronic samples of real-life spoken or written usage, and "treebanks" – corpora annotated with information about the phrase and clause structures of their successive sentences. With a computer it takes seconds to search databases of grammatical tree structures which it might take weeks to search by hand, so the problem about crucial structures being too infrequent to check began melting away.

Once we had the ability to study real-life usage, it became clear that the problem with the earlier linguistic methodology went much deeper than some native speakers' grammaticality judgements being mistaken. The truth is that "grammaticality" is a fictitious concept. Natural human languages do not have grammars. There is no particular set of word-sequences (whether finitely or infinitely large) that constitutes "all and only" the grammatical sentences of a particular language or a particular speaker's idiolect. Consequently there are no things which could appropriately be called grammaticality judgements: there is no "grammaticality" for there to be judgements about.

The grammatical habits of a language-community could be compared to the tracks that might develop in grassland among settlements of a pre-modern society lacking the institution of private land ownership. There will be some broad, well-trodden highways, corresponding to the most usual sentence structures, other narrower tracks, corresponding to less common turns of phrase, and other cases again where one or two people have walked and scarcely left a disturbance in the grass. Even if no-one has ever yet happened to walk from point *A* to point *B*, nothing prevents someone doing so tomorrow. And, if he or she finds that route convenient, perhaps others will follow – the new route might eventually become a major thoroughfare.

Logically there must exist a distinction at any given moment between routes which have at some past time been taken by at least one person, and routes which no-one has ever walked. And similarly, since only a finite number of English-speakers have ever lived, there must be a distinction between those strings of English words which have been uttered at least once in the history of the language, and those which have never yet been uttered. But these are not interesting distinctions of principle. New sentences are constantly being assembled and uttered, and although some of these will conform perfectly to patterns found in many previous utterances, others will deviate from prior experience, in minor or perhaps in major ways. As John Taylor put it (p. 32), "Speakers…are prone to *innovate* with respect to previous usage, using words in ways not already sanctioned by previous experience". For an innovative utterance to work, its hearer(s) need to grasp more or less what the speaker intends by it. But, evidently, hearers often do.

A map of the kind of grassland territory I have described would include the broadest, most-frequented tracks, but it would need to impose some essentially arbitrary cut-off between paths well-defined enough to chart and routes too occasional to be recorded. Likewise, a grammatical description of a natural language will identify the best-established sentence structures, but could not hope to cover every structure that some speaker has occasionally used, or might use in the future. Any grammar must limit itself to describing usage down to some frequency threshold, and that threshold will be governed by practical issues such as the quantity of time and manpower available for compiling the description. There is no "natural" place to set the threshold. "Starred sentences" are a myth.

An unorthodox point of view can be persuasive only with a concrete example, so let me give one. My wife and I recently addressed the problem of one of our cats stealing the other's food, by buying a new type of feeding-stations with lids that open and close automatically under the control of the individual pet's microchip. The makers, Sureflap, are an English firm founded recently by a Cambridge physicist, and the manual provided is well written. So I was initially surprised to encounter a section headed "Learning your pet into the feeder" and beginning "When learning your pet into the feeder, make sure all other pets are kept away". (It explains how to get the mechanism to respond to a particular pet.) Surely these word-sequences are not English? – *learn* does not take an animate object, or an *into* phrase. But the activity described is novel, and the writer has used English in a novel way to refer to it. I might have preferred to write "Teaching the feeder to recognize your pet" – but that would not be quite right, because the change to the feeding-station is instantaneous, brought about by a single press of a button, it is the cat which has to be gradually taught to exploit its resulting behaviour. Perhaps there would be some other form of words which would have been faithful to that reality and yet deviated less from established usage; but the manual writer chose the words I quoted, and he or she is doubtless as much an English native speaker as I am, so who am I to say the wording is not English? It did not seem so previously, because no English-speaker had found occasion to use *learn* that way. But now someone has had a reason to use *learn* with that grammar, and I and other native speakers can certainly understand what is intended. If Sureflap prospers, in years to come perhaps no-one will bat an eyelid at this way of using *learn*.

Many linguisticians have a concept of "grammaticality" according to which, at a given time, some fixed (but infinitely numerous) class of word-sequences are "grammatical" in a given idiolect, though from time to time the rules of the language or idiolect change so that new word-sequences become grammatical. They would describe the *learn your pet* usage as one that is currently ungrammatical (for most speakers) but which may be destined to become grammatical, under the influence of things such as the Sureflap manual. I do not believe in this concept of "grammaticality". Putting words together in novel ways in order to express novel ideas is part of competent language behaviour. Perhaps the *learn your pet* example seems a rather extreme case – but it might strike us that way only because it was encountered in print, and it could well be that innovation, or major innovation, occurs most often in speech. In any case, grammar that departs from prior norms is normal.

The idea that some sequences of words of a language are "grammatical" and the rest "ungrammatical" is not a self-evident one. So far as I am aware it never occurred before the passage in Noam Chomsky's 1957 book quoted on p. 30 above – though from then on it was accepted by the discipline remarkably uncritically. We saw in chapter 2 that earlier grammarians discussed the grammatical structures which do occur in a language without feeling a need to contrast them, explicitly or implicitly, with "starred sentences". Chomsky was misled, at the outset of his career, by a false analogy between human languages and computer programming "languages". A programming language, such as Java or Perl, really is defined by a fixed, clearcut generative grammar – if it were not, it could not be used with computers. But human languages are very different kinds of thing from programming "languages", in this (and other) respects. Computers are excellent tools for recording and studying speakers' and writers' language behaviour, but as a source of models for the workings of the human mind they are seriously misleading.

(Most of Chomsky's early writings about language were published in computer science journals. In 1958, for instance, he wrote (Chomsky and Miller [1958] 1965: 157) that "one possible method for describing a grammar is in terms of a program for a universal Turing machine" – and the phrase "one possible" did not mean that Chomsky and his co-author George Miller had any doubt about the relevance of this mechanical concept to human language behaviour, they took that relevance for granted and were interested only in whether the kind of machine in question could be defined more narrowly.)

Some linguisticians responded to the lack of an empirical basis for grammaticality by saying in effect "If the empirical evidence conflicts with the concept of grammaticality, too bad for the evidence". Orthodox linguisticians believed they could classify word-sequences in their own language as grammatical or otherwise just by thinking about them, and they said that those classifications themselves, rather than observation of concrete facts about what language-users say or write, were the proper data for grammar theories. But a speaker's judgements are not empirical data (if you judge word-sequence XYZ to be good English, I might disagree but there is nothing I could point to in order to show that you do not have that judgement). So linguisticians who made this move were embracing a thoroughly "degenerate research programme".

If the existence, in human languages, of a distinction between grammatical and ungrammatical word-sequences were more than a dogmatic article of faith, it would have to have some observable correlates. The question is what these might be.

One way in which grammaticality could very convincingly be shown to be a real property would be through successful construction, for one or more human languages, of generative grammars which came close to the ideal of covering all the sentence structures actually used in practice while failing to cover numerous word-strings that are never uttered or written. But that goal proved much less achievable than linguisticians initially hoped. Robert Stockwell et al. published an attempt at a generative grammar of English in 1973, but they summarized the conclusion they eventually reached about the feasibility of the task by quoting the seventeenth-century grammarian James Howell (spelling modernized):

> the English…having such varieties of incertitudes, changes, and idioms, it cannot be in the compass of human brain to compile an exact regular syntaxis thereof.

Likewise Maurice Gross (1979) wrote interestingly about the failure of a more-than-ten-year effort by a team of French linguisticians to produce a satisfactory generative grammar for that language. Cedric Boeckx has even claimed (2006: 220) that the "early goal" of "a grammar that would describe all the well-formed sequences and none of the ill-formed ones… was abandoned as soon as it was formulated", as if the goal was given up for some principled reason (though the truth, I believe, is that attempts faded away after various linguisticians had discovered from experience that the task was impossible). Boeckx's remark greatly exaggerates the speed with which linguisticians came to see the task formulated by Chomsky in 1957 as hopeless. The State-sponsored "Alvey Natural Language Tools Grammar" of English was being developed at Cambridge University into the early 1990s. But no linguisticians today, I believe, still see developing a generative grammar for a human language as a realistic goal.

One factor which those who believe in grammaticality point to as explaining the futility of trying to compile adequate generative grammars is the contrast between "competence" and "performance", and this might offer an alternative approach to finding an empirical basis for "grammaticality". Even if a native speaker's mental linguistic competence implies some limited, definable class of word strings as "all and only" the grammatical sentences of his language, the utterance-patterns produced in practice will be affected by various extra-linguistic performance factors, such as slips of the tongue, memory limitations, and so forth, and these might interfere so unsystematically with the class of sentences defined by competence that the class of utterances actually produced will not be definable by any finite system of rules.

It is tempting to dismiss this move as one which renders the idea of grammaticality unrefutable, and hence a mere empty dogma. That may be correct; but it could be unfair. If performance factors interfere with linguistic competence in ways that are essentially random from a grammatical point of view, then one might expect to find a frequency difference between structures that are grammatical in a language, and those which are ungrammatical but occur nevertheless as a consequence of "performance factors". Structures of the former type ought to recur repeatedly in a sufficiently large corpus, while the latter would be "one-offs" or at least recur very rarely. Some sort of discontinuity ought to be visible in the spectrum of frequencies of different grammatical structures. Observation of such a discontinuity would provide empirical evidence that "grammaticality" is a real property despite the fact that its extension cannot be defined.

I have been arguing for thirty years, first in Sampson (1987), and most fully in the book *Grammar Without Grammaticality* already mentioned, that such discontinuities do not exist. In the data that Anna Babarczy and I examined, constructions occurred at all frequencies from very common down to one-offs. The tracks in the grassland turned out to vary smoothly from very wide to evanescent, as it were, with nothing akin to the sharp contrast we find in modern societies between recognized public rights of way and occasional routes taken by trespassers. The grammaticality concept seemed to have no leg to stand on.

We dealt in that book with most of the criticisms that had been levelled against this point of view as expressed in my earlier publications. One criticism, though, did have some force: the "SUSANNE" treebank we had used was one for whose compilation we were ourselves responsible, and this appeared to create a danger that we might have built into our data the conclusion that we wanted to prove. There was a good reason for using SUSANNE: the project which created it gave an unusually high priority to precision and refinement of the annotation scheme (as has been noted by independent third parties, e.g. Lin 2003: 321), while some other treebank projects have instead prioritized quantity of material annotated. Nevertheless, I accept that the danger appeared to exist (though I do not myself believe it was real).

Another criticism which I would also have accepted as fair (though to my knowledge no-one made this criticism) was that research of this kind ought not to consider exclusively English. Apart from the fact that it is unhealthy for research on general linguistics to limit itself to looking at a single language, English with its very limited system of grammatical inflexion could be a language in which the bounds of grammaticality are unusually vague.

And of course for research on frequencies, a larger data-set will always be better than a smaller one. The SUSANNE treebank contains only 130,000 words, so that a discontinuity occurring anywhere on the frequency spectrum below 1 in 130,000 words would be invisible in that data-set.

Accordingly, in this chapter I aim to settle the matter, by using a treebank compiled by researchers unconnected with myself, larger than SUSANNE, and representing a language other than English: namely version 2.0 of the NEGRA Corpus of German newspaper prose, compiled at the Universities of Stuttgart and the Saarland and containing about 20,000 sentences comprising 355,000 "tokens" (words, punctuation marks, etc.).[1]

German is arguably a particularly suitable language for this investigation. In the first place, having more inflexion than English, it makes grammatical structures relatively explicit and hence, perhaps, more open to clearcut delimitation. But, also, it is a socially "disciplined" language in a way that English has never been. English might be described as an anarchic language: no organ of the British State has ever claimed a right to regulate the language, and I believe the same is true in other English-speaking countries. National and provincial governments in German-speaking Europe, on the other hand, regard themselves as "owning" the German language. One noteworthy way in which this attitude manifested itself recently was that these governments jointly imposed a set of language reforms (on which see Johnson 2005), including regulations which instructed schoolteachers about precisely how they should in future mark down deviations from the new norms in pupils' written work. The reforms led to a series of controversies fought out in law courts, in a way that simply could not happen in Britain. Between 1997 and 1999 German orthography in the province of Schleswig-Holstein changed three times, with schools legally required to modify their teaching accordingly (Johnson 2005: 111–15).

A striking feature of these reforms was that many of the changes were of a kind whose English-language equivalents would be below the radar even for educated English speakers. The school I attended in the 1950s would certainly by 21st-century standards be seen as traditional in its syllabus and teaching methods, and it put a great deal of effort into training pupils to write well, but at no time in my schooldays did I hear any suggestion that there were specific rules for the use of punctuation marks such as commas – in English there are no definite rules. Pupils were expected to absorb good punctuation practice tacitly through the activities of reading, writing, and having their prose criticized. German, on the other hand, has explicit syntax-based rules for punctuation. One feature of the 1996 reforms, for instance, was to make commas newly optional before co-ordinating conjunctions (Johnson 2005: 72). If a contrast between

1. See <www.coli.uni-saarland.de/projects/sfb378/negra-corpus/>. I thank Tania Avgustinova of the University of the Saarland for making the NEGRA treebank available to me.

"grammatical" and "ungrammatical" structures were a reality for any human language, one would surely expect it to be a reality for German.

Furthermore, all material in the NEGRA Corpus is taken from a single publication, the *Frankfurter Rundschau* daily newspaper. For many research purposes this would be a drawback, making the corpus less representative than it might be, but for present purposes it is if anything a positive factor. Newspaper publishers commonly require their journalists to conform to a set house style, so a single-newspaper corpus offers a specially stiff test of my contention that there are no definite boundaries between the grammatical and the ungrammatical.

The NEGRA treebank exists in alternative forms, of which I used the one called <negra-corpus.penn>. To give an impression of the nature of the analysis, Figure 1 shows the structure assigned to the short sentence *Schade jedoch, daß kaum jemand daran teilhaben kann.* (This is NEGRA sentence 5, which translates as "All the same, it's a pity that scarcely anyone is able to share in it.")

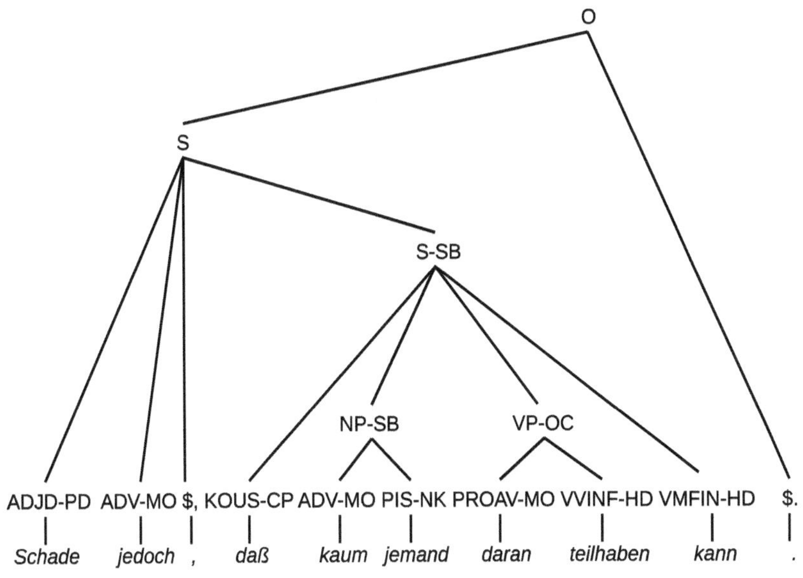

Figure 1

Where a node label contains a hyphen, the symbol after the hyphen identifies the function of the constituent (e.g. subject, direct object) within its containing construction. The function-tagset has 45 members.

Symbols preceding hyphens, or occurring as sole node-labels, are drawn either from a 57-member set of wordclass tags, or from a 25-member set of construction-type labels. For the full tagsets the reader is referred to the NEGRA documentation, but the tags occurring in Figure 1 are defined in Table 1.[2] (Because German grammar differs from that of English, the wordtag categories in particular often have no direct English equivalents, and since the NEGRA documentation defines them in German I have taken the liberty of modifying some of the definitions in order to clarify the categories for English-speaking readers.)

Table 1

wordtags:	
$.	sentence-final punctuation
$,	comma
ADJD	adverbial or predicative adjective
ADV	adverb
KOUS	conjunction introducing finite subordinate clause
PIS	indefinite pronoun functioning as NP
PROAV	preposition–pronoun portmanteau
VMFIN	finite modal verb
VVINF	full infinitive verb
construction-tags:	
NP	noun phrase
O	root node
S	sentence
VP	non-finite verb phrase
function-tags:	
CP	complementizer
HD	head
MO	modifier
NK	noun kernel modifier
OC	clausal object
PD	predicate
SB	subject

2. The category which is tagged PROAV in the treebank is listed in the NEGRA documentation as “PAV”.

One can think of a grammatical tree-structure such as Figure 1 as a set of constructions: ways in which a grammatical category is realized as a sequence of smaller categories, until one gets down to the level of parts of speech of individual words. In English, a clause can be realized by a noun phrase functioning as subject, followed by a verb; or as subject noun phrase followed by verb followed by direct-object noun phrase; or in several other ways. A noun phrase can be realized as an article followed by a noun, or as article + adjective + noun, or… And so forth.

A linguistician's grammar, if it were possible to devise one, would be a system that identified what constructions the language possesses, so that a structure like Figure 1 (and hence, in particular, the word-sequence running across the bottom of the Figure) would be grammatical, provided each pairing it contained of a mother-node label with a sequence of daughter-node labels corresponded to some construction recognized by the grammar. There might be some extra constraints of one kind or another, but by looking at the statistical distribution of the various constructions contained within a sizeable treebank it ought to be possible to determine whether there is any particular boundary to grammaticality in the relevant language.

In registering NEGRA constructions I modified the raw NEGRA data in three ways. Most importantly, although functiontags are for convenience shown in the treebank as parts of node-labels, logically (as the NEGRA documentation rightly says) they apply not to nodes but to the lines linking mother to daughter nodes – they label the relationship between a constituent and its containing construction. (The fact that *the dog* is subject in *the dog barked* is a fact about the relationship between the noun phrase *the dog* and the clause as a whole, rather than about the relationship between the noun phrase and the individual words it comprises.) Consequently, in listing constructions I included functiontags where they occur in the labels of daughter nodes, but deleted them from the labels of mother nodes. Secondly, NEGRA leaves root nodes unlabelled, but for practical convenience I gave root nodes a distinctive label of their own, namely "O". And lastly (although there happens not to be an example in Figure 1), some NEGRA parse-trees include pairs of nodes bearing "trace" labels showing where a constituent occurs in a different surface-structure construction from the construction in which it plays a logical role. (An English example would be *John was expected to refuse*: logically speaking, *John* is subject of *refuse* – what was expected was that John would refuse – but in the surface grammar *John* appears only as subject of *was expected*. NEGRA would use a pair of trace nodes linking *John* to the empty subject position before *refuse*.) NEGRA trace labels use digits to show how they pair off, in trees containing more than one pair, but if two constructions differ only in containing traces labelled with different digits, that does not make them "different grammatical constructions" in any meaningful sense. Therefore in my investigation all trace labels were replaced by the same invariant symbol.

The tree of Figure 1, then, comprises five constructions:

O	→	S $.
S	→	ADJD-PD ADV-MO $, S-SB
S	→	KOUS-CP NP-SB VP-OC VMFIN-HD
NP	→	ADV-MO PIS-NK
VP	→	PROAV-MO VVINF-HD

The construction O → S $. is the most frequent in NEGRA as a whole: it is instantiated 12,750 times. At the other end of the frequency scale, there are almost 19,000 *hapax legomena* – construction-types instantiated just once each.

(A few examples of the latter are listed, with the wording realizing them, their NEGRA sentence numbers, and English translations, in Table 2. In this table, immediate constituents are single words except as indicated by square brackets, e.g. in sentence 4878 the label AP-MO applies to the phrase *zu schlecht*, the label VVPP-HD to the word *erschlossen*. The symbol **T0** in sentence 700 is a trace label, showing the logical position of a phrase *als ein zum Trocknen aufgehängtes T-Shirt*, "than a T-shirt hung up to dry", which logically belongs with *größere*, "greater", but in the surface grammar has been shifted after the noun.)

Table 2

NP → PIAT-NK AP-NK ADJA-NK NN-NK
keine [*größere* **T0**] *rechtliche Qualität* (Sentence 700)
no greater legal status [than…]

VP → AP-MO VVPP-HD PP-MO
[*zu schlecht*] *erschlossen* [*für die Schüler*] (Sentence 4878)
too poorly accessible for the pupils

PP → ADV-MO APPR-AC ART-NK ADJA-NK NN-NK CAP-MNR
rund um den ehemaligen Schrottplatz [*nördlich des Höllweges und westlich des Park-and-ride-Platzes*] (Sentence 19114)
all round the former scrapyard north of the Höllweg and west of the park-and-ride area

Figure 2 plots construction-type frequencies against the numbers of different construction-types instantiated at the given frequencies (i.e. the frequencies of construction frequencies). Both axes are scaled logarithmically. To make the figures at higher frequencies meaningful, zero figures are averaged with the nearest non-zero figure. (Precise details of the derivation of Figure 2 from the NEGRA data can be read off from the software used, available at <www.grsampson.net/SNegFofs.html>.)

The plot of Figure 2 extends smoothly and log-linearly from a handful of high-frequency constructions on the right to large numbers of low-frequency construction-types and hapaxes on the left. I see no hint of discontinuity. There is no suggestion of a large gap or U-shaped trend indicating bimodality, and hence a possible contrast between grammatical constructions versus one-off or a-few-off quirks of performance. Reading from right to left, where do "grammatical" constructions end and ungrammatical oddities of performance begin?

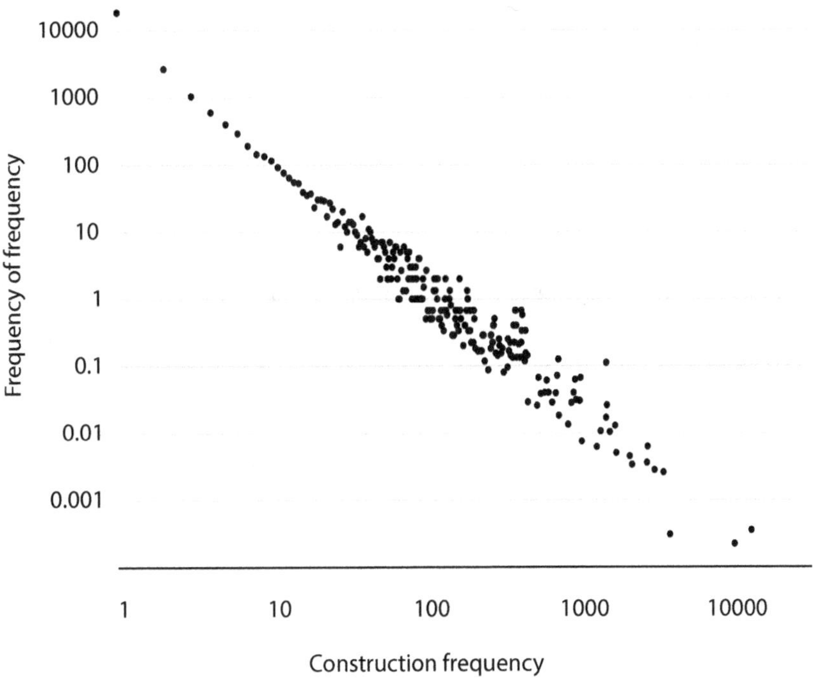

Figure 2

Christopher Culy (1998) responded to the original version of my argument, which used English-language data, by claiming that it is possible to devise probabilistic generative grammars which yield frequency-of-frequency distributions not dissimilar to Figure 2. But (apart from the fact that Culy's plots did not look *very* like Figure 2, or like the plot based on English data which he had seen), as a would-be defender of "grammaticality" Culy was missing the point. If it were possible to produce successful generative grammars for English, German, or other human languages, they would be excellent evidence in themselves for the reality of "grammaticality". We would not care what plots of frequency data looked like. It is worth examining data like those of Figure 2 just because, as everyone now accepts, producing accurate generative grammars has turned out to be a hopeless task. If frequency data had revealed a discontinuity between high-frequency grammatical constructions and one-off or rare oddities of performance, that might have been a way to show that grammaticality is a real thing even though no-one can manage to capture it in a generative grammar. But there is no discontinuity. So far as I can tell, we have no evidence of any kind for grammaticality. It really is just an unsupported dogma.

It might be, of course, that other evidence, of kinds that have not occurred to me, is waiting to be uncovered and put forward. But linguisticians who defend the grammaticality concept never put such evidence forward. In my experience they show little interest in empirical evidence – they rarely work with real-life data such as treebanks. Some present-day linguisticians seem as resistant to the idea of dealing with data held electronically as an Edwardian lady might be to the possibility of doing her own housework. They see it as enough to assert that native speakers of a language have "grammaticality intuitions".

If there is no such thing, in reality, as an "ungrammatical sentence", where do the reactions that linguisticians call "grammaticality intuitions" or "grammaticality judgements" come from? There is no doubt that speakers who are asked "Can you say XYZ in your language?" often feel able to give a yes or no response (though there are also plenty of cases where they feel puzzled to know how to answer). What is more, there are often clear patterns in the responses to related word-strings – informants do not just answer yes or no at random, as one might perhaps expect they should if the "grammaticality" concept corresponded to nothing at all in reality. Linguisticians sometimes point to research establishing such patterning (e.g. Schütze 1996; Kepser and Reis 2005) as confirmation that, despite appearances, intuition-based grammar development is a genuine empirical science.

But someone who is asked "Can you say XYZ?" has to decide how to interpret the question – its meaning is not self-evident. There are plenty of ways to interpret such a question which do not involve postulating a distinction between "well-formed" or "grammatical" word-sequences and ill-formed or ungrammatical sequences. For instance, one obvious interpretation would be "Can you imagine circumstances in which you might want to say XYZ?" If XYZ asserts something which is obviously false or absurd, the answer is likely to be no – not because XYZ is "ungrammatical", but because people do not normally want to assert absurdities.

This point has been overlooked from a very early stage in the history of generative linguistics. Noam Chomsky's *Aspects of the Theory of Syntax* (1965a) claimed that the machinery of language competence included a complex system of "selection rules" and "subcategorization rules", whose function was to disallow sentences such as the English examples:

> the boy may frighten sincerity
> John amazed the injustice of that decision
> the book dispersed

These sentences are certainly odd, but not because they are "ungrammatical". Sincerity, and the injustice of a decision, are abstractions, which as such feel no emotions; it is obviously impossible to frighten or amaze an abstraction. To "disperse" means for an aggregate of physically separate items to spread apart and become sparse; a book is not such an aggregate, it is a single physical object, so it cannot disperse. These examples conform perfectly to the norms of English grammar, contrary to Chomsky's statement (1965a: 76) that they "deviate...from the rules of English". They correspond in my grassland analogy to broad, well-trodden highways. It is just because the examples are grammatically normal that we can easily see what they mean – and hence see that they assert absurdities.

It is true that, if the absurdity of a proposition is *too* obvious, linguisticians will not be tempted to call a sentence asserting the proposition "ungrammatical". We could not imagine wanting to say *My daughter is 500 years old*, or *I ate a lorry*, but because anyone can immediately see why these assertions are absurd they do not look for explanations in terms of grammar. On the other hand, one has to ponder a little about the precise meaning of *disperse*, or about the fact that *sincerity* refers to an abstract character-trait rather than to a bearer of the trait, in order to see that the propositions in question are impossibilities. Only brief pondering is needed, but many linguisticians have not done even that much before leaping to the conclusion that there must be something about the English language which disallows those examples.

After the publication of *Aspects*, selection and subcategorization rules became part of linguisticians' standard grammatical apparatus for many years. I do not know how far they are still accepted by linguistic theorists today, but I do know that invalid leaps from "speakers don't say XYZ" to "there must be some principle or mechanism in speakers' minds that renders XYZ ungrammatical" are as widespread today as they ever have been.

Bernd Heine and Heiko Narrog's *Oxford Handbook of Linguistic Analysis* (Heine and Narrog, 2nd edn 2015) is a standard collection of articles about (mainly) the grammatical aspects of modern theoretical linguistics, from one of the world's leading academic publishers. It is reasonable to assume that the approaches espoused by its various authors are representative of the best-established styles of linguistic research in the early 21st century. Yan Huang's chapter in that *Handbook*, entitled "Neo-Gricean pragmatic theory of conversational implicature", remarks that "we can say *They summered in Scotland* [but] cannot say **They falled in Canada*", and he explains this by postulating a universal linguistic principle which he calls "pre-emption": the fact that *fall* has the verb sense "drop down" blocks it from being used as a verb similar to *summer* meaning "spend the relevant season".

But we need no linguistic principle to explain the difference between the *summered* and *falled* examples. That difference arises because there are (or at least have been) recognized, established social institutions, among people whose circumstances allow(ed) it, of spending whole summers, or whole winters, away from home in places with pleasanter weather: hence "to summer" and "to winter". In spring and autumn the weather is not extreme, so there was never an institution of spending those seasons away from home. In Britain we call the season following summer *autumn* rather than *fall* as in American English, but (although "pre-emption" would be irrelevant to *autumn*, since this word has no alternative meaning) we too do not say things like *They autumned in Canada*. *They falled…*, or *they autumned…*, are not "ungrammatical": they are just not customary, for a good non-linguistic reason. (If a new custom arose of spending the autumn season away, presumably for some non-weather-related reason, then Americans and Britons probably would begin using *to fall/to autumn* in that sense. Certainly no linguistic "pre-emption principle" would stop them doing so.)

The same principle explains the difference between O'Grady et al.'s examples *Bob holidayed in France* and *John midnighted in the streets* (p. 24). We have a social institution which consists of spending a week or two relaxing away from home, and so we have a word for that institution, but we have no recognized institution of spending midnight at some special place. If for some reason we were to develop the latter kind of institution, very likely the *John midnighted…* example would become normal.

In the examples discussed above, there were at least good reasons why speakers find them odd, though linguisticians were wrong to locate the oddness in the structure of the language. In other cases it seems that linguisticians have answered "no" to the question "can you say XYZ?" merely because they were not imaginative enough to think of circumstances in which they might want to say it.

Anna Babarczy and I discussed a case (Sampson and Babarczy 2014: 81–2) where, beginning in the 1970s, linguistician after linguistician asserted that a particular type of clause is ungrammatical in English, as a preliminary to proposing theoretical mechanisms that could be used to disallow it, despite the fact that the clause-type is in reality perfectly normal and commonplace. Again this approach remains alive and well in the 21st century. Another chapter in Heine and Narrog's book is Vilmos Ágel and Klaus Fischer's "Dependency grammar and valency theory", which notes a difference between the grammars of English and Hungarian: in Hungarian it is acceptable, but in English unacceptable (they claim), for the verb *lie* (tell an untruth) to take a complement clause expressing the content of the lie. What sort of "unacceptable" would that be? I googled *lied that* and was offered "about 328,000 results", beginning with *Have you ever lied that you had a boyfriend…* and *Kelly Baker lied that a young member of her family had cancer…* There were a few irrelevant examples using *lied* as the noun meaning a type of song, but the great majority directly refuted Ágel and Fischer's claim.

Linguisticians who make ungrammaticality claims that are at odds with observable usage sometimes explain this in terms of idiolect differences: perhaps the usage is grammatical for many fellow-speakers, "but I can't say it". That is analogous to someone who always walks home from work by one route, ignoring another street which would serve equally well to get home by, and who explains this by saying "I can't walk down that street". Of course he *could* walk that way, he has just got into a different habit. What is described as an "ungrammaticality judgement" would in this case be better described as a perception of novelty.

Undoubtedly there are many other factors that may give rise to the feelings which theoretical linguisticians think of as "grammaticality judgements". William Labov (1975) recounted a now-famous anecdote about fieldwork in Philadelphia, where people use the phrase *any more* in an unusual way: elsewhere in the English-speaking world, one expects to hear *not* (or some other negative word) in the vicinity of *any more*, but

Philadelphians say things like *John is smoking a lot any more*. However, Labov's Philadelphian informants assured him in all sincerity that this usage was impossible, they would never produce it themselves and could not imagine what it might mean if someone else said it – yet some of those same individuals were then overheard saying things like *John is smoking a lot any more*. In this case, what seemed to be going on was that the informants firmly believed that a turn of phrase which they regularly and systematically used was impossible and meaningless, because they knew that it was not current in a higher-prestige majority dialect.

Doubtless there are other factors again which can contribute to speakers' intuitive judgements of the status of particular word sequences. But none of these factors, so far as I am aware of them, suggests that grammaticality judgements are usable as data for a scientific theory of anything, and certainly none of them justifies a model of language which divides the class of all possible strings of words of a language into a set of "grammatical" sheep and a complementary set of "ungrammatical" goats.

The case against "grammaticality" seems overwhelming. But that raises a large question about how the concept can have been accepted so widely for so long. Charles Hockett (1968) argued a contrary point of view, but although he was one of the best-known linguisticians of his day his book was politely ignored. Another leading name in mid-twentieth-century linguistics, Fred Householder (1973: 371), discussed how difficult it is in practice to come up with clear cases of "starred sentences" in English, but again his objection achieved no traction. Yet it was not as if the arguments against grammaticality are particularly convoluted or depend on obscure data. Most of the points I have made above could have been made by any linguistician at any time. My analysis of the NEGRA data did depend on the availability of electronic treebanks, which are a fairly new thing, but I believe few linguisticians will have been surprised by the findings summarized graphically in my Figure 2.

Indeed I have the impression that even linguisticians whose work depends on a belief in grammaticality know quite well that the picture of human language offered by Figure 2 is a fair one. My reason for saying that is that, although I have been putting forward the view argued in this chapter for thirty years now, and plenty of linguisticians have argued against my view, so far as I am aware no defender of "grammaticality" has ever voiced the kinds of objection that I would expect them to make, if they believed that the model of language expressed in a diagram like Figure 2 was misleading.

Defenders of grammaticality could argue that the treebanks I have used as data sources are too small to provide good evidence against the grammaticality concept. Or they might suggest that the fuzzy continuity of a plot like Figure 2 merely shows that the parsing schemes embodied in the relevant treebanks – the shapes of the tree structures assigned to particular sentences, and the range of grammatical categories from which node-labels are drawn – are ill-chosen. On the face of things, these might seem quite reasonable objections. Creating treebanks is such a labour-intensive activity that reliably analysed treebanks are inevitably smaller than one would like, but the consequence is that a hypothetical discontinuity in frequency statistics would be invisible in the SUSANNE treebank unless it occurred at a higher point on the frequency spectrum than 1 in 130,000 words, and even in the NEGRA treebank it would need to occur somewhere above 1 in 355,000 words. These frequencies are not all that low. Someone might well urge that a discontinuity is there, but that to observe it one would need a treebank of millions of words, or hundreds of millions of words. Furthermore, correct labelled trees for language examples are not self-evident. A treebank development project has to evolve an explicit parsing scheme for itself; normally such a scheme will try to agree with consensus views about grammatical structure wherever possible, but that principle is far from enough to settle every question that arises, and the parsing schemes of different treebank projects differ in many respects. (There are features of the NEGRA parsing scheme for German that I find surprising – but if one wishes to avoid the suspicion of circularity arising from using one's own analyses as data, the only alternative is to use someone else's analyses.) It seems quite possible that a statistical discontinuity between "structures which are grammatical" and "performance oddities", which would emerge clearly from a "correctly" analysed treebank (whatever "correct" might mean in this context), could be blurred if the same language samples are analysed in line with an "incorrect" parsing scheme.

So far as I am aware, proponents of grammaticality have never made either of these objections, reasonable though they might appear. (Perhaps they will start doing so now, but it is more instructive to look at how my intellectual opponents argued before I told them what objections might have force.) The counter-arguments I have encountered have been pitched at a more aprioristic level. This could just be because the objectors are aware that making good the kinds of objection I have outlined would require them to descend from the realm of abstract theorizing and get their hands dirty working with detailed empirical language data, which is something they would find uncongenial. However, I suspect that a main reason is that, in their hearts, even believers in grammaticality know that displays like Figure 2 are in fact a fair representation of how human languages are. They accept that, however much one were to increase the quantity of data examined, and whatever reasonable parsing scheme one were to use, the picture would not change radically.

So one is left with the question why so many academics have accepted such an implausible concept of grammar. This question is answerable, but to answer it one must draw attention to issues which professional academics commonly prefer to leave undiscussed.

One is the reckless quality of many linguisticians' writings, which I criticized in chapter 1. Linguisticians want theories of grammar to be scientific, so they declare that they are, and they do not worry too much about conflicting evidence.

And the other issue is the modern pressure on academics, on which I also remarked in chapter 1, to bring in outside funding for their research. In linguistics, this pressure creates a powerful motive for believing in grammaticality. If a language is defined by rules of grammar which imply a clearcut distinction between "grammatical" and "ungrammatical" sequences of words, and which can be inferred from judgements about the status of individual word-sequences, then this creates a fertile research field. A high proportion of "theoretical" articles in linguistics journals, for many years now, have dealt with formalizing grammatical rules to define some aspect of the structure of some language, or with what such rules suggest about universal features or constraints that are alleged to apply to the grammars of all human languages. On the other hand, if there is no grammaticality and human languages are not defined by specific sets of grammar rules, then much of theoretical linguistics becomes an empty non-subject. If languages do not have grammar rules, then there is no room for universal properties applying to the rules of all languages. There is just much less to say about human language in general than theoretical linguisticians suppose, and hence less scope for proposing projects that might appeal to research sponsors.

It is not so much that present-day theoretical linguistics consists of theories which are false. Depending on precise wording, some of them may be false, but many will be neither false nor true: there is nothing in the real world to which they apply, accurately or otherwise. In the phrase which, among genuine scientists, counts as the ultimate condemnation, these theories are "not even wrong".

Small wonder then if, for many 21st-century linguisticians, grammaticality simply cannot be allowed to be unreal. If it is unreal, much of the discipline, and many university posts for linguisticians, lose their *raison d'être*. To imagine that considerations like this do not have a powerful influence on climates of academic opinion would be naïve. There is no implication of conscious dishonesty here. People are good at not permitting dangerous ideas to rise to the conscious surface of their mind. I shifted subjects, but not all linguisticians are prepared to face that kind of intellectual retooling. So they resist recognizing the unreality of "grammaticality".

Academic research should be about establishing truth, however, not about providing careers for academics. Grammaticality is an academic counterpart of the "caboose" which once brought up the rear of every goods train on the American railway network. (The British term was "guard's van", but American trains still had cabooses when guard's vans were no longer in use in Britain.) By the 1980s, as I understand it, cabooses had in many cases lost their original safety function, and for a while they served only to create jobs for the railwaymen who rode in them. Eventually, like comparable make-work arrangements in other industries, cabooses were swept away. It is high time for grammaticality, grammaticality judgements, and associated areas of linguistics to follow the caboose into history.

Chapter 4

Rigid Strings and Flaky Snowflakes

Everyone agrees nowadays that Noam Chomsky's is, by a clear margin, the single most significant name in the discipline of linguistics. A *New York Times* interview published as I write introduces Chomsky simply as "the founder of modern linguistics" (Tanenhaus 2016). Chomsky is quoted more often than any other individual by linguisticians themselves. And among those who observe the discipline from outside, Chomsky will often be the only linguistician whose name they know. (If they know two names, the second is quite likely to be that of Chomsky's acolyte Steven Pinker, who expounded Chomsky's ideas, in prose far more accessible to the layman than Chomsky's own writings, in his 1994 book *The Language Instinct: the new science of language and mind.*) Chomsky has long been seen as someone who has "revolutionized the scientific study of language" and has "spoken with unrivalled authority on all aspects of grammatical theory" (Lyons 1970: 9). He has even been described, more generally and more grandly, as someone "who will be for future generations what Galileo, Descartes, Newton, Mozart, or Picasso have been for ours" (Barsky 1997: 3).

Clearly, a critique of the discipline must examine and assess the "Chomsky phenomenon". That is my task in this chapter. Chomsky's writings on language are numerous and, to many readers, often rather confusing. What are the intellectual contributions which have led him to be seen as the pre-eminent master of linguistics?

There are four main ideas, which came to the fore roughly in the following order (though they are heavily interrelated, and I lay no great stress on the issue of chronological sequence):

A. The "Chomsky Hierarchy". Formal "languages", as classes of well-formed strings of words, are definable by formal grammars of various types, and a number of the grammar types are related to one another hierarchically: e.g. the class of languages definable by "context-free phrase-structure grammars" is a proper subset of the class definable by "context-sensitive phrase-structure grammars". So it seems to be a meaningful and perhaps interesting question where on this "Chomsky hierarchy" the grammars of human languages lie.

B. Transformational Grammar. Contrary to what appeared to be assumed by many linguisticians who approached the subject before Chomsky, adequate grammars of human languages need to contain, in addition to structure-defining "phrase-structure rules", also structure-changing rules which Chomsky called "transformations". Within academic linguistics, at least during the early decades of Chomsky's fame, *B* was the aspect of his thought that was seen as central, so that for instance undergraduate courses tended to focus on it.

C. Language Universals and Innate Ideas. All human languages, Chomsky has claimed, share many deep structural properties which are contingent (one can easily imagine language-like systems which have different properties, but no human groups could use such languages). The respects in which human languages differ from one another are so trivial, relative to these linguistic universals, that a Martian visiting Earth would see the human race as all speaking a single language though with minor dialect differences (e.g. Chomsky 1991: 26; 2009b). Indeed, the differences among humanly usable languages not only concern unimportant matters of detail but are numerically limited: Chomsky has sometimes claimed (e.g. 1981: 11) that there are probably only finitely many possible human languages.

Furthermore, he says that the evidence available to an individual child about his elders' language typically lacks data allowing the structural universals to be inferred from observation (the "stimulus" is "impoverished"); the fact that children do all grow up as competent speakers can only be explained by postulating that our genetic inheritance includes a detailed blueprint for human language structure, just as it includes detailed information controlling the development of our complex human anatomy. As Chomsky put it (1980: 134), "we do not really learn language; rather, grammar grows in the mind". Some of Chomsky's interpreters, e.g. Hornstein and Lightfoot (1981: 9), have seen this idea of the "poverty of the stimulus" as the central core of Chomsky's thought.

For Chomsky, language is in this way a particularly clear case of a more general thesis, that human cognition is largely determined by innate structuring, which controls and limits the range of ideas, theories, or even artistic styles which Mankind can create, just as genetics uncontroversially controls our anatomical development (cf. the references on p. 33). Even if I were placed in a precipitous mountain environment where the ability to fly would greatly improve my survival chances, I could not grow a pair of wings, because my genetics does not allow for that possibility. Likewise, if the correct scientific theory of some phenomenon happens not to be a theory allowed by our cognitive genetics, then we will never be able to understand that phenomenon.

Aspect *C* of Chomsky's thought has had immense impact on the intellectual world far beyond the discipline of linguistics. Chomsky is asserting that the cognitive life of human beings, which many of us see as the core of our selves, is controlled in a way fundamentally different from what thinkers at least in the English-speaking world have traditionally supposed. Any reflective person who believes that Chomsky has good reason to make this assertion is likely to find it intensely significant.

D. The Snowflake Analogy. In recent years Chomsky has argued that the main structural features of human languages are not only common to all languages but are a matter of "(virtual) conceptual necessity" (see e.g. Chomsky 2005: 10, or references in Postal 2003). An analogy he has taken to using is that "Language is something like a snowflake, assuming its particular form by virtue of laws of nature…once the basic mode of construction is available" (Berwick and Chomsky 2011: 30; cf. Chomsky 2007: 20). Individual snowflakes are actually very diverse in their detailed shapes, but at a gross level they all share a common pattern, hexagonal and symmetrical; and they share this pattern not, obviously, because they contain complex chromosome-like machinery which includes something like a hexagonal blueprint, but because from the physical chemistry of water molecules and the laws of physics it follows necessarily that ice crystals will grow that way. Chomsky's suggestion is that, likewise, if we understood clearly the constraints (notably, "principles of computational efficiency") which any language has to resolve, we would see that the panoply of structural linguistic universals, which *prima facie* seem contingent and surprising, in reality just have to be that way.

These are the ideas about language which have made Chomsky famous; how solid are they? Let me take them one by one.

A. I know that the existence of a hierarchy of formal grammar- and language-types, classically set out in Hopcroft and Ullman (1969), is soundly established mathematically, and that this hierarchy has had considerable significance for the field of computer science, in connexion with compiler design. But I do not know that it ought to be called the "Chomsky hierarchy". The main reason for that name is probably that the hierarchy was drawn to the attention of non-technical readers through Chomsky's *Syntactic Structures* (1957). That book, though, discussed the hierarchy only sketchily and informally, referring for fuller information to a manuscript by Chomsky, *The Logical Structure of Linguistic Theory*, which was not published until 1975. (On the un-rigorous nature of *Syntactic Structures* see Pullum 2011.) Chomsky (1975) is a long book full of algebraic notation which may look impressive to the mathematically naïve, but which when carefully examined turns out to be mathematically semi-literate, containing various expressions which are meaningless, or say something other than what the author evidently wants to say, or at best choose a gratuitously obscure way of saying something which a competent mathematician would express straightforwardly (Sampson [1979b] 2001: 153–6). It is very hard to see how the same individual could have been responsible for the sound maths of the "Chomsky hierarchy" and the lamentable maths of *The Logical Structure of Linguistic Theory*.

In his early career Chomsky collaborated with Marcel-Paul Schützenberger (see e.g. the opening line of Schützenberger 1963: 246; Chomsky and Schützenberger 1967). Schützenberger was a distinguished pure mathematician, and although based in Paris was affiliated during part of that time with the IBM research centre in New York State, where compiler design was an important topic. Neither Chomsky nor Schützenberger, so far as I know, have ever specified the division of labour in their collaboration, but the best guess must be that Schützenberger was responsible for the maths of the "Chomsky hierarchy", so-called, and Chomsky was responsible for drawing links between the abstract hierarchy and human language. Chomsky (1959) cited unpublished work by Schützenberger. By the time of Chomsky (1963), which unlike *Syntactic Structures* did spell out the mathematics of the hierarchy, almost every theorem was explicitly attributed to publications by Schützenberger or other writers.

But if Chomsky's contribution was to relate the categories of the abstract formal-language hierarchy to aspects of human language (an issue of no mathematical or computer-science interest), that was the least valuable aspect of the collaboration. No-one before Chomsky suggested that human languages can usefully be treated as formal languages, i.e. fixed sets of sentences, and indeed they cannot be: the concept of a "starred sentence" or "ill-formed string", which is indispensable in formal language theory, is more or less alien to human languages. As we have seen, there is no particular rigid class of strings of English words which comprises "all and only" the well-formed sentences of English, because putting words together in new patterns is a normal part of the activity of speaking or writing English.

Already before the end of the 1960s, Hopcroft and Ullman (1969: 8) noted that hopes of linking human languages to the formal-language hierarchy had not borne fruit. What was valuable under heading *A* may not have had much to do with Chomsky, and what Chomsky does seem to have been responsible for is a seriously misleading model of human language.

(Incidentally, Schützenberger's influence on Chomsky seems to have extended beyond providing a mathematical framework for discussing formal grammar. Readers of Chomsky have often been puzzled by passages in which he dismisses Darwinian evolution as a serious biological theory, without ever – so far as I have seen – explaining clearly what he sees as wrong with Darwinism. Schützenberger on the other hand has presented objections to Darwinism, e.g. Schützenberger 1996, which, whether ultimately convincing or not, are explicit and well-argued. Chomsky's obscure objections seem to chime with Schützenberger's clear ones, so I take it that the former are echoes of the latter.)

B. There are two main problems about "transformational grammar". First, whereas the point of the "Chomsky hierarchy" was to define classes of language which are proper subsets of more inclusive classes (e.g. some languages can be defined by context-free grammars, but many cannot be), such exploration as there has been of the generative power of transformational grammar suggests that it is capable of defining *any* definable language, in other words it fails to make a falsifiable claim. Respectable areas of science have often begun as ideas which were intuitively appealing but vague, and were only later sharpened up into substantial, consistent and falsifiable theories. But it would be very hard to defend Chomsky's grammatical research programme in that way. Its high point of apparent non-vagueness probably came with the technical-looking "X-bar theory" of the 1970s–80s; Kornai and Pullum (1990) showed how empty that theory was in reality. I am not aware that anyone since has even attempted to develop a more falsifiable descendant of transformational grammar.

Second, much of the persuasive force of Chomsky's *Syntactic Structures* book stemmed from the fact that it proposed a specific grammatical rule to define the range of possible English auxiliary-verb constructions, and this rule was strikingly successful in reducing an apparently messy aspect of English syntax to neat simplicity, as scientific laws should do.

(In *Syntactic Structures* the rule was called "Auxiliary Transformation", though later the name commonly used was "Affix Hopping".) However, the concept "transformational rule" was defined too informally in *Syntactic Structures* to enable readers to check that Affix Hopping was the kind of rule allowed by Chomsky's theory of transformational grammar. Later, when a more explicit formalization of that theory was published, it turned out that Affix Hopping was *not* a valid transformation (Sampson [1979b] 2001: 152–3). In other words, what linguistics departments internationally had been teaching as one of the best arguments for Chomsky's theory was in reality a standing contradiction of that theory.

C. To most of us who are reasonably familiar with a few of the world's many languages, the idea that they are all so similar that someone could think of them as essentially the same language seems bizarre. On the contrary, they feel exceedingly diverse. (Admittedly I claim no insight into what our world might look like through Martian eyes.) Point *C* depends very much on identifying some explicit list of properties which are universally shared and yet non-trivial (in the sense that there is no logical reason why any system usable as a language would necessarily have to be that way). Chomsky and some of his acolytes have made large claims about the size of this list, for instance Neil Smith (1999: 42) wrote that "A glance at any textbook shows that half a century of research in generative syntax has uncovered innumerable such examples", and he was echoed by Cedric Boeckx (2015: 430–1), "Fifty years of intensive research have revealed an astounding array of properties that must be part of UG [i.e. Universal Grammar]... The degree of details with which UG principles are formulated requires advanced training in linguistics...and never fails to impress or overwhelm the non-specialist." But if one presses for specifics, it is not easy to pin them down. I trawled through the literature of generative linguistics to identify specific claims about language universals; I could not find all that many, and none of those stand up (Sampson 2005). Evans and Levinson (2009) have compared this aspect of the linguistics literature with the facts of human languages, and are *under*whelmed; they conclude that "there are vanishingly few universals of language...diversity can be found at almost every level of linguistic organization".

Ljiljana Progovac is a linguistician who takes generative linguistic theory much more seriously than I do, but, reviewing a new book which develops Chomsky's remarkable idea that "sophisticated Martian scientists would consider...all human languages as one and the same", she comments drily that "The burden has to be on [Chomsky and his co-author] to at least identify a method by which one can prove or disprove claims of this kind… Simply making claims about things and hoping to be right is not nearly as useful as generating specific and testable hypotheses" (Progovac 2016: 996).

One might naturally expect that a linguist for whom the idea of languages sharing universal properties was important would frequently refer in his writings to features of different languages. Non-Chomskyans who write about general linguistics commonly do stud their writings with examples cited from languages other than English, whether because they make particularly clear illustrations of some general point or because they seem *prima facie* to contradict some general statement and hence require explanation. There are strikingly few examples in Chomsky's writings taken from languages other than English.[1] Presumably it is easier to believe in the similarity of all languages if you only ever consider one of them.

What is true is that in recent centuries many languages have been remoulded to make them structurally more equivalent to the languages of European civilization. This has led to a situation in which, if one is familiar only with major present-day "standard languages", one might well get the impression that all human languages are just alternative means of clothing the same range of thoughts in speech-sound. But that has nothing to do with genetics. It is a consequence of the cultural dominance of the West in this period. A human group which aspired to the status of independent nationhood would simply not be taken seriously in the 21st century if it could not render official documentation produced by international bodies into its own language, and since languages are very adaptable things, non-European languages have often been structurally Europeanized. (Cf. pp. 160–2 below.) But if one turns to colloquial non-European languages spoken far from centres of power (e.g. Gil 2001), or languages of influential non-European societies before the period of Western dominance (e.g. Sampson and Babarczy 2014: 13–19), in some cases they are very different from European languages in terms of the logic of the thoughts they encode. (See also Calvet 1998: 106, Deutscher 2000.) We cannot conclude, because in the last hundred or two hundred years many people all over the world have learned to become rather like us, that being like us is the only pattern biologically available to humanity. (Cf. Henrich et al. 2010; Sampson 2007.)

1. In the area of grammar rather than phonology, the only exceptions I can think of are a one-word German example, and an example quoted from a French grammarian, in Chomsky (1965a: 170–4, and 233–4 n. 35).

As for "poverty of the stimulus": what exactly are the features of language which everyone gets right although most people hear no relevant evidence while learning to speak their mother tongue? Almost all the repeated discussions of this idea, by Chomsky and by his followers over decades, have focused on the same single example, which relates to the English rule for question-formation. (Geoffrey Pullum and Barbara Scholz 2002: 39 cite a long list of these passages in publications which appeared between 1965 and the date when they were writing.) Chomsky (e.g. 1976: 30–3) offers two alternative hypotheses which a child might entertain about the question-formation rule, and he says that if the choice between them were to be determined by experience, the child would need to hear a specific, rather complex kind of question. This specific question-type, Chomsky believes, is so rare that in practice few children will ever hear an instance. But children all do acquire the correct rule, so the choice must have been determined by innate linguistic knowledge.

The statement about rarity is a factual claim, but Chomsky has never cited evidence. He just said things like "you can go over a vast amount of data of experience without ever finding such a case" (Piattelli-Palmarini 1980: 115); "It is quite possible for a person to go through life without having heard any relevant examples that would choose between the two principles" (Chomsky 1972: 30); the belief that each child hears relevant evidence "strains credulity" (Chomsky 1976: 213). And this style of argumentation has become very influential in linguistics. For instance, Mark Baker (2015: 936) sees it as "hard to imagine" that every language-user whose behaviour demonstrates mastery of given features of a language has been exposed to and has registered evidence for those features. According to Cedric Boeckx (2015: 430) "It should be obvious to anyone that the linguistic input a child receives is radically impoverished and extremely fragmentary when compared with the subtlety and complexity of what the child acquires."

To be fair, in the days when Chomsky made the statements I quoted from him, it was not very easy to check what range of grammatical structures occur in casual chat such as young children are exposed to (which would have made some of us cautious about venturing any frequency predictions). But we have good data sources nowadays. Using such a source, I calculated (Sampson 2002; 2005: 79–81) that a child in an English-speaking environment could expect to hear the allegedly rare question-type not just once in a lifetime, but *at a minimum* once every ten days or so on average – possibly more often. The "stimulus" for language-acquisition is not impoverished, it is very rich.

D. The first thing to say about *D* is that, if the snowflake analogy is right, it thoroughly undercuts *C*. If complex properties of some aspect of human behaviour have to be as they are as a matter of conceptual necessity, then there is no reason to postulate complex genetically inherited cognitive machinery determining those behaviour patterns. Even if human groups everywhere are wont to say that three plus four is seven (in whatever words they use for counting), we are not tempted to search for a specific 3 + 4 = 7 gene in the nucleotide sequences of the human genome. In other words, if his recent snowflake idea were correct, Chomsky would be refuting everything in his earlier writing that led him to be seen as a serious thinker beyond the narrow discipline of linguistics. Even some generative linguisticians (e.g. Culicover 1999: 138) have remarked on this odd development.

But anyway, what is snowflake-like about real-life human languages? In some Australian languages, a speaker has to use an entirely separate vocabulary, not one-to-one equivalent to his usual vocabulary, when in the presence of his mother in law. In Biblical Hebrew, prefixing the word for "and" to a verb in either of the two "tenses" changes its meaning to the other tense, so "and + I went" means "and I shall go", and *vice versa*.[2] In Classical Chinese, active verbs need not have subjects (not even "understood subjects"). How do things like these square with "(virtual) conceptual necessity"? They don't.[3]

Perhaps the kindest thing one can say about *D* is that, when Chomsky began writing about snowflakes, he was already an old man. Every such passage I have seen has been extremely vague, and if they say anything specific it seems quite wrong.

Chomsky is known to the public not just for his theories about language and cognition but well known also, perhaps better known, for his comments on current affairs. Chomsky's activities as a citizen may be logically

2. OK, this is a conventional oversimplification (see e.g. contributions by Robert Longacre and by Alviero Niccacci to Bergen 1994), but the full truth is no more snowflake-like than this.

3. Tree structure is important for the syntax of (probably) every human language, and I have explained elsewhere (Sampson 1980a: 133–65; 2005: 137–66) that this is a natural consequence of the very general fact that languages are gradually evolved cultural institutions. So one might perhaps see the centrality of tree structure in syntax as analogous to the hexagonality of snowflakes. But to say that a particular language has a grammar based on tree structures is to say very little. The rest of what there is to say about that language is not some minor details akin to dialectal idiosyncrasies: it is virtually everything that makes the language what it is.

independent of his linguistics, but as subsidiary indications of the quality of the man's mind we are entitled to take into account things like: his intemperate political positions, which according to W. D. Rubinstein (1981) and Werner Cohn (1988) have repeatedly included support for neo-Nazi groups; the eccentric way in which he responded to an invitation from the then editor of *Language* with a tirade denouncing that august and blameless journal for its "scandalous…lies" (Hill 2007: 636); or the fact that while levelling broadside after broadside against American capitalism as supremely evil, Chomsky himself uses tax-avoidance devices, five-figure speaking fees, and the like to ensure that a generous share of the good things which American society offers to its wealthy men comes the Chomsky family's way (Schweizer 2005: 16–38).[4]

Does all the above add up to the profile of an intellectual giant? Clearly not. It is the profile of a clown.

But the bigger clowns, perhaps, are the members of the linguistics profession who allowed Chomsky to lead them by the nose for decades. I include myself here: as an undergraduate I had the good fortune to be taught by a group of eminent and deeply serious scholars of Sinology, and for years after graduation it was just unimaginable to me that an academic with an international reputation in any subject, affiliated to a world-class institution, might have as little real achievement to his name as we have seen here. I took Chomsky at his own valuation. (In my case the light did eventually dawn; and in my defence, much less evidence was available than later emerged. It was ten years after I graduated, for instance, when *The Logical Structure of Linguistic Theory* was published and proved to be by no means the calibre of work which I and, I believe, many others had imagined it to be.)

As evidence against his account of human language has piled up, Chomsky has taken (e.g. 2002: 98–102) to defending his approach by referring to a highly controversial historical analysis by Paul Feyerabend (1975) of Galileo's astronomical thinking. According to Feyerabend's account (which Chomsky evidently takes as gospel), at the time when Galileo adopted the theory that the Earth goes round the Sun, the objective evidence available to him actually pointed the other way, in favour of the traditional idea that the Earth is the still centre. Galileo opted for the heliocentric theory against the evidence, because he "just knew" (my paraphrase) that it was

4. For links to numerous severe online critiques of Chomsky's role as commentator on public affairs, see Paul Bogdanor's webpage "The Chomsky Hoax" (<www.paulbogdanor.com/chomskyhoax.html>, accessed 14 February 2015).

right; and we can see (Feyerabend says) that it was good that he did so – that is how science advanced. The moral Feyerabend draws is that we should encourage an "anything goes" approach to science, and Chomsky appeals to this in dismissing the weight of linguistic counterevidence because, in effect, he "just knows" that his ideas are correct. As Chomsky puts it, "it is the abstract systems that you are constructing that are really the truth; the array of phenomena is some distortion of the truth". Some of Chomsky's followers have been taking this entirely seriously, for instance Robert Fiengo (2006: 471) asks "Why should we expect Chomsky to follow normal scientific practice…?"

If generally accepted, Feyerabend's prescription would spell the end of any ambition by society to increase the total of human knowledge. The elderly lady down the street, who is convinced that her neighbour is poisoning her by directing death rays at her teapot, would merit a Nobel Prize as much as an Einstein would. But, in the first place, there has been a chorus of replies to Feyerabend arguing that his account of Galileo's intellectual biography is wrong, and that in reality Galileo acted as a rational scientist is supposed to act. Feyerabend himself discussed Machamer (1973); more recently, see Fischer (1992). More important, even if Feyerabend were correct about Galileo, all that would mean is that Galileo was luckier than he deserved: he irrationally opted for an implausible theory that turned out to be right after all. Feyerabend wrote (1975: 155–6) "it is advisable to let one's inclinations go against reason *in any circumstances*, for science may profit from it", but that is a glaring *non sequitur*: science may equally (indeed more probably) be set back by it. Galileo might have "just known" something which turned out against the odds to be true, but Chomsky "just knows" many things about language which, when checkable, are wildly mistaken (the case of English complex questions was one example).

Whether Chomsky is right about the nature of human language and cognition is an easy question: he isn't. More interesting, to my mind, is the question how it could have come about that someone acquired such a towering reputation on such a flimsy basis.

To this there are many answers. Chomsky's name first became widely known when he was a leader of public opposition to the American war in Vietnam, at a time when reluctance to be called up to fight in that war was a chief concern of male student-age Americans. I was a graduate student in the USA myself at the time (though, as a foreigner, not subject to call-up), and it was noticeable how people's thinking slid in a quite natural way from "This man is telling the world why I shouldn't have to do what I very much don't want to do" to "This man's ideas must be good stuff". (Incidentally, on the unwisdom of US involvement in Vietnam I agreed with Chomsky. No-one manages to be wrong about absolutely everything.)

Then in due course Chomsky became an intellectual standard-bearer for the American Left in general, which meant that for a lot of people on that side of politics, even though they themselves had no special interest or competence in linguistics, it was necessary to maintain that Chomsky's professional academic work was outstandingly great, because this validated his status as a political commentator.

The fact that *The Logical Structure of Linguistic Theory* appeared in print very late, eighteen years after *Syntactic Structures*, helped Chomsky's cause. Many people who read *Syntactic Structures* and were impressed could see that it was sketchy, but any doubts this might have raised in their mind were assuaged by the knowledge that the big book existed in the background. If *Logical Structure* had already been available, some of those impressed by *Syntactic Structures* would have turned to *Logical Structure* for fuller detail, would have discovered its shortcomings, and news would have got around. As it was, by the time *Logical Structure* came out in 1975, the world had moved on and was no longer very interested in the body of ideas I labelled *A*; the focus had shifted to *B* and *C*. My impression is that very few people have actually read *The Logical Structure of Linguistic Theory*.

One-to-one discussion between undergraduate and teacher, which was a standard teaching style in the better British universities in the 1960s, was a system that encouraged questioning and criticism of received ideas. Nowadays, staff–student ratios have changed to the point that teachers rarely meet individual undergraduates, and students' written work is largely a matter of demonstrating that they know "what it says in the book". That has clearly made it easier for weak ideas to remain safe from being replaced by new and better ideas.

And another aspect of the changing nature of the academic profession has had large consequences for linguistics. Fifty years ago, there were no material pressures giving teachers of humanities subjects a motive to embrace any particular body of ideas, and the concept of competing to win research funding was more or less unknown. People in the "hard sciences" needed money for research, but arts dons (as already said) needed little more than time to write, access to libraries, and salaries (which were guaranteed until retirement). If anything, arts academics derived more kudos from exploding an established body of thought than by accepting and developing it. Nowadays, things are very different. In Britain the change was formalized by the 1985 Jarratt Report, which laid down as an explicit principle that an academic's duty is to the welfare of his employing institution, rather than to the welfare of his discipline – an idea which twenty years earlier would have seemed not just novel but disgraceful. I am not aware that the USA had a Jarratt equivalent, but the general working style which Jarratt promoted in Britain already seemed normal in the USA. Under the new dispensation, university finances depend heavily on the quantity of research funding attracted from outside sponsors; discipline competes with discipline, and research group with research group within a discipline, to win shares of the limited funds available. Because this began around the time when Chomskyan linguistics had become fashionable, many research groups acquired a strong motive for resisting any ideas that threatened to undercut it: if grant referees came to believe those ideas, the groups' future funding would be at risk.

Chomskyan linguistics, with its doctrine that there exists a complex range of universals and correspondingly complex innate cognitive machinery geared specifically to the task of language acquisition, creates a domain in which it is easy to carve out topics that research assistants can be paid to explore. If Chomsky is wrong, and human languages are just different from one another, with individual children acquiring their elders' language using the same general learning techniques with which we learn whatever else life happens to throw at us, then there is much less scope to devise technical linguistic research proposals. The outside world might be neutral between these alternative models of cognition, but university managers will certainly not be. These days, an academic who fails to produce research proposals knows full well that this will be directly reflected in his promotion prospects.

These novel pressures on academics have led to novel models of proper academic behaviour. Paul Postal has written (2014: note 2) about how, when he has drawn public attention to examples of grievously low scholarly standards in Chomsky's writing, he has sometimes been chidden by colleagues as if the ethical failure were his rather than Chomsky's. Once or twice I have had similar experiences. The subtext seems to be "Don't rock the boat, or there will be less money for linguistics"; the version of linguistics which has become established simply cannot be allowed to be wrong. If so, at least to a scholar of my generation that is profoundly shocking. True, we have no analogue of the Hippocratic Oath, but surely professional academics are expected to recognize truth as a higher value than money – or what is the good of us?

Finally, it is not an original observation that nowadays we inhabit a celebrity culture. People become "famous for being famous". One of Chomsky's most loyal acolytes, Neil Smith, has actually written that "Most people *need* heroes… I am happy to admit that Chomsky is a hero for me" (Smith 1999: 5). One might have thought that the academic profession is supposed to train people to see past the hype and the stardust in order soberly to evaluate the realities behind them; but academics are not insulated from trends in the wider societies they inhabit, and in a media-obsessed age it is quite possible for a giant reputation to rest on very little.

I was originally prompted to compile this survey of the "Chomsky phenomenon" by reading a recent book-length analysis of Chomsky's linguistics, by the philosopher Christina Behme (2014). Ms Behme painstakingly analyses Chomsky's pronouncements about language and cognition, and shows that one after another of them is intellectually indefensible. Indeed, she even shows that on occasion Chomsky explicitly contradicts himself. For instance, he has taken to defending himself against those who disagree with his idea that detailed language structure is innate by making assertions such as (2000: 66) "it is not clear what thesis is being proposed by [those] who reject what they call 'the innateness hypothesis'… I have never defended it and have no idea what it is supposed to be." (Ms Behme's p. 87 gives several similar quotations.) Yet he has also written (1976: 13) "Every 'theory of learning' that is worth considering incorporates an innateness hypothesis" (again Ms Behme quotes a range of similar remarks); and we are not dealing here with mere forgetfulness, or a change of mind over 24 years, because two pages earlier in the 2000 book just quoted Chomsky has associated himself with the idea that "properties of language and…aspects of the acquisition and use of language can be explained in terms of…assumptions about the innate structure of the language faculty". Even a Feyerabendian, I take it, would not see asserting contradictory statements as a worthwhile scientific move – or does "anything goes" go as far as that?

What motivated Ms Behme to write her book, it seems, was a concern that if other disciplines take the measure of this scholar who is being put forward by linguisticians as their intellectual champion, the result may be that linguistics as a whole finds itself rejected as unserious. That perhaps understates the danger. Chomsky, after all, is not just the best-known linguistician; it is common nowadays to see him described in terms such as "one of the greatest minds of the 20th Century" (in any discipline), or "arguably the most important intellectual alive" (quoted from the *New Yorker* and the *New York Times* respectively by Kennard 2013). If taxpayers come to understand what it takes nowadays to earn accolades like that, they might well wonder whether they can afford to maintain universities, or at least their arts faculties, at all.

Unfortunately, once people take to viewing academics as "heroes" or gurus, it is no longer clear that sober criticism of their ideas is effective. I do not disagree with the individual points Ms Behme makes in her book, or very few of them, but it seems to me that by taking Chomsky's writings seriously, and subjecting them at length and in a deadpan manner to close textual analysis, in practice she might just be helping to validate them. We can be sure that Chomsky or some of his supporters will produce a fog of logic-chopping replies to Ms Behme's criticisms. The average reader who lacks time or patience to follow and weigh up the arguments and counter-arguments clause by clause is likely to think "More long books about this man Chomsky – by Jove, what a mind he must have."

Chomsky was adequately refuted years ago, for readers willing to entertain the possibility of his being wrong. The time for that may be past. What we do with clowns is simply laugh at them.

Chapter 5

Economic Growth and Linguistic Theory

When one asks the linguisticians for empirical evidence that individual human languages have fixed grammars, or evidence that differences between languages are constrained within a fixed boundary, the answers they come up with are unsatisfactory. But linguisticians' belief in the scientific status of their discipline depends only to a minor extent, I believe, on concrete evidence. There is another kind of argument which is not often spelled out in so many words but which frequently seems to be lurking not far below the surface of linguisticians' writing. I suspect that in practice this argument has more influence than any empirical considerations on linguisticians' thinking about the foundations of their subject.

A paraphrase of this argument might run as follows. A human being must be a machine of some kind, admittedly an enormously complex machine but nevertheless finite in complexity. So, logically, it must be true that there are definable limits to the range of a human being's potential behaviour-patterns. In the case of language behaviour, that implies some limit to the range of utterances a speaker might produce or a hearer might understand. It could, admittedly, be that these ranges are massively more complex and subtler than is envisaged by linguisticians' current attempts to devise grammar rules – but that would be a difference of degree merely. Linguistics may be going astray in its theorizing about human languages, but the basic fact that a human language must be a definable entity with definable limits is not up for serious debate.

Likewise, Noam Chomsky's suggestion (p. 57) that the constraints on human linguistic variability are so tight that they permit only a finite number of possible different languages might be wide of the mark. But our ability to learn anything is a faculty embodied in finite structures of neural anatomy, so again there must be some definable limits to the diversity of languages that human children are capable of acquiring. The reasonable area for debate is about just how wide those limits are and what precisely they include and exclude, but one cannot reasonably deny that some such limits must exist.

To anyone convinced by arguments along these lines, the proposition that language behaviour is too open-ended to be the subject of scientific theorizing will not seem to be a meaningful objection. The implication of the term "open-ended" is that linguisticians' ideas about the bounds of grammaticality within a language, or about the limits to the diversity of languages, are not wrong as a matter of degree merely, because *no* such bounds or limits exist. That suggestion, to someone who has the arguments of the two preceding paragraphs at the back of his mind (as I believe many linguisticians do) could seem to amount to little more than romantic waffle.

One answer to this is to point out that what might strike linguisticians as waffle is treated as a fundamental axiom by practitioners of another discipline which is considerably better-established than linguistics.

Few present-day linguisticians, in my experience, show much interest in economic thought. That seems a pity: there are a number of interesting and enlightening parallels between the two subjects, and distinguished scholars were thinking about economics long before Saussure inaugurated linguistics as a discipline. Particularly relevant in the present context is endogenous growth theory (or in full, "post-neoclassical endogenous growth theory"), which was formulated by Paul Romer (e.g. Romer 1990) and others, and has come to be acknowledged as one of the largest – perhaps *the* largest – advance in economic thought in recent decades, solving an intellectual problem which dates back to the nineteenth century.[1]

Endogenous growth theory claims to solve a longstanding economic paradox. The classical economic principles developed by men such as David Ricardo and Alfred Marshall predict that any society should move towards an economic steady state in which Gross Domestic Product per capita is constant, or even shrinks as increases in population lead to diminishing returns from exploitation of non-labour resources. This contradicts the experience of much of the world over the past two hundred years, during which per-capita GDP has increased dramatically although populations have also risen. For some time economists have understood that the resolution of the paradox must have to do with the creation of new economically useful ideas, which enable greater value to be extracted from a given range of resources. Endogenous growth theory incorporates the process of idea creation into the economic machinery; it treats

1. An excellent exposition for a non-specialist readership is Warsh 2006; see also Helpman 2004.

manufacturing, and research to generate ideas which might improve future manufacturing, as alternative uses to which a given set of human and other resources can be put. Considered as economic goods, ideas have some distinctive properties; notably, they are "non-rivalrous": if I give you an apple I can no longer eat it, but I can give you my idea and still exploit that same idea myself. Taking these properties into account, the theorists demonstrate (via algebraic reasoning whose details will be of little interest to readers of a book about language) that a society of economically rational individuals in a free market will choose to deploy resources in ways that create sufficient new ideas to cause per-capita GDP to grow at an accelerating rate. This matches observed long-term trends in the advanced countries reasonably well (even if we have had recent experience of a hiccough in this growth).

One does not have to agree that economic growth is a good thing in order to see endogenous growth theory as a satisfying solution to what was previously a baffling intellectual puzzle. Voters in democratic countries commonly do see growth as good, and evaluate the politicians competing for their votes largely in terms of their ability to deliver growth; and writers such as Matt Ridley (2011) argue passionately that economic growth offers the only realistic solution to a large range of threats facing humanity. But the opposite point of view is also possible. Some people nowadays see the costs of growth, in terms of damage to the environment, as outweighing its benefits. In 2010 John Holdren, director of the White House Office of Science and Technology, advocated a "massive campaign…[to] de-develop the United States", i.e. to move economic growth into reverse (quoted in Ballasy 2010). This book is not the place for that debate. What no-one will deny is that the phenomenon of economic growth has immense practical significance for human life, for good and/or for ill.

Presenting endogenous growth theory as an innovation which began about 1990 arguably understates the extent to which it amounts to incorporation into mainstream English-speaking economics, and/or independent reinvention, of principles of the "Austrian" school of economics initiated early in the twentieth century by figures such as Ludwig von Mises and Joseph Schumpeter. However, my present aim is not to investigate the history of economic thought but to describe the current state of play. At the beginning of the 21st century, endogenous growth theory is generally accepted as the most persuasive explanation of the phenomenon of economic growth; so much so that it is serving as a basis for policy-making by practising politicians. (Nick Crafts (1996) opened an analysis of the policy implications of the theory by referring to a famous occasion when Gordon Brown, soon to be Chancellor and later Prime Minister, was lampooned in the press for referring in a public speech to its abstruse-sounding full name.) The theory could of course be wrong, but it cannot be ignored as merely an out-of-the-way eccentricity.

Endogenous growth theory makes one assumption which economists see as so uncontroversial that it is often left unstated: the theory takes for granted that the supply of new economically valuable ideas is unlimited, so that the quantity produced in practice depends only on the quantity of resources devoted to idea-creation. Paul Romer does recognize this as an assumption rather than a truism; in his first paper he argued that rejecting it "would imply that Newton, Darwin, and their contemporaries mined the richest veins of ideas and that scientists now must sift through the tailings and extract ideas from low-grade ore" (Romer 1986: 1020), which he saw as a *reductio ad absurdum*. In his more widely read 1990 paper, the point was dismissed in less than two lines: "there is no evidence from recent history to support the belief that opportunities for research are diminishing" (Romer 1990: S84). Romer's fellow economists, while often calling other aspects of his work into question, do not seem to have found this assumption problematic. At one point Romer (1994: 16–21) described resistance to the postulate of an unlimited supply of new ideas as a symptom of a widespread but irrational philosophical prejudice, but that prejudice appears not to be influential among the current economics profession.

Much linguistic theorizing is founded on the contrary assumption, that the potential products of human cognition are tightly constrained by our biology. Theoretical linguistics has by and large taken for granted that humanly learnable languages are a narrow subset of the class of recursively enumerable languages, and much of the effort devoted to the field has aimed to identify the precise boundaries of that subset.[2] In the semantic area, Jerry Fodor (1975) argued that natural-language vocabularies can be mastered by speakers only because all of them are based on a common, innately fixed "language of thought" which defines the set of all possible word-meanings, various subsets of which are encoded in the words of individual languages. Both of these points of view were restated for a new generation in Steven Pinker's *The Language Instinct* (Pinker

2. "Recursively enumerable" is a mathematical term, meaning roughly speaking that there is some finite way of defining the membership of a set, even though the set may have infinitely many members. If a language can be treated as an (infinitely numerous) set of grammatical sentences (strings of words), linguisticians assume that there must be some finite grammar defining which strings are grammatical, but the point alluded to here is that they also believe (pp. 57–8) that many definable "languages" would not be humanly learnable languages.

1994: see e.g. pp. 106–25, 81–2), the most widely influential book about linguistics of the last few decades. Anna Wierzbicka (1996) attempted to turn Fodor's abstract argument for the existence of a language of thought into a concrete description.

Although some linguisticians discuss this concept of constraints on cognition purely in connexion with language structure, many others explicitly see language as providing evidence for a much more general picture of the nature of human cognition. Ray Jackendoff (1993: chapter 13) used Universal Grammar as a precedent to argue for innate cognitive constraints on our ability to recognize music, or to extract meaning from visual stimuli. Pinker (1994: 412–15), citing the anthropologist Donald Brown, argued that innate cognitive constraints impose strikingly similar behavioural conventions and patterns on all human societies. Noam Chomsky has argued (1976: 124–5) that the rapid advances in scientific knowledge and innovations in the arts which have characterized the centuries since the Middle Ages were a temporary phenomenon reflecting a period when human beings were for the first time free to explore novel ideas and had not yet reached the limits of the cognitive possibilities biologically available to our species; "If cognitive domains are roughly comparable in complexity and potential scope, such limits might be approached at more or less the same time in various domains… It may be that something of the sort has been happening in recent history." Evidently, for Chomsky, Romer's remark about Newton and Darwin would be not a *reductio ad absurdum* but a plausible description of the current state of the sciences.

I have quoted a handful of linguisticians, but assumptions akin to those quoted about the supply of novel cognitive constructs being strictly limited are very widely shared by contemporary linguistic theorists. Not all linguisticians accept these assumptions, and not all economists accept endogenous growth theory, but they are part of the dominant consensus in the respective disciplines.[3]

Not too many linguisticians, perhaps, would go all the way with Chomsky in suggesting that the constraints on one important domain of language structures are so very tight as to permit only *finitely many* distinct possibilities. But if other linguisticians see cognitive constraints

3. In 2012 Robert Gordon attracted widespread attention among economists with a paper (Gordon 2012) which argued that the economic growth that has characterized the West for the past two hundred years may be a temporary blip that has now run its course – making a neat parallel to Chomsky's idea quoted in the preceding paragraph. Gordon's suggestion, though, is a minority view within his discipline (see e.g. Krugman 2012; Pielke 2012; *Economist* 2013).

as permitting infinitely numerous, though well-defined, ranges of alternatives, this would not alleviate the incompatibility with the economists' assumption. Economic activities are commonly about optimizing some parameter or parameters, such as profit, market share, work/life balance, or the like. When elements of a solution-space are enumerable, infinite cardinality is usually no hindrance to optimization. (There are infinitely many positive integers, but that creates no special difficulty for a decision about how many people to invite to a party.) Endogenous growth theory depends on the range of future ideas not being identifiable at any particular point in time. It assumes that an economic agent engaged in an optimization exercise will be working with a solution-space which omits numerous possibilities that will not occur to anyone until later, if ever.

Since Romer and his fellow endogenous-growth theorists are concerned with only one category of new ideas, namely economically valuable ones (as Ridley 2011: 269 paraphrases Romer, "recipes for rearranging atoms in ways that raise living standards"), and linguisticians do not discuss this particular category, it would be logically possible to deny that there is a contradiction. But neither linguisticians nor economists, surely, would want to suggest that human beings might have two separate faculties for idea-generation, one inexhaustible and specialized for economically useful ideas, and another drawing on a limited range of ideas relevant to other domains. Much more plausibly, either the economists or the linguisticians are mistaken in their assumptions about intellectual innovation. Romer's and Chomsky's respective comments about scientific progress, quoted above, make the incompatibility rather explicit.

It is perhaps no accident that linguistics is the discipline which poses a challenge to the endogenous growth theorists' assumption, because, apart from economics itself, linguistics may be the only area of social science which has been sufficiently formalized to enable the contrary of that assumption to be clearly stated. (This shared special status of the two subjects has been noticed from the economists' side e.g. by Friedrich Hayek 1967: 34–5.) Here and there one encounters informal hints in other fields of social study, for instance Vladimir Propp's claim that folk tales conform to certain limited patterns. But I know of no field other than linguistics in which it is meaningful and normal to raise questions such as whether a given class of potential cognitive structures is or is not recursively enumerable.

I am not saying here that linguistics depends on the assumption that human idea-generation is a bounded system, but economics assumes it is open-ended, so linguistics must be wrong. It could be the economists who have got things wrong. Indeed, there are plenty of voices these days urging that the discipline of economics, too, is going astray by claiming to be able to formalize mathematically various aspects of behaviour which in reality are too open-ended to be subject to formal analysis.[4]

But it would be foolish for linguisticians to assume without argument that they are the ones in the right. In any crude comparison of the respective quantities of intelligent brainpower devoted to the two disciplines, it is obvious that the overwhelming preponderance lies on the side of economics – not surprisingly, since that subject is so much more directly related to human welfare. Intellectual issues cannot be resolved by voting, of course, but the numbers ought at least to make linguisticians aware that bounded ideas are a concept which must be argued for rather than just assumed. And if so, I am not clear how it can be argued for. I have already mentioned the fact that many people, before they study linguistics, seem to find it natural to think of language behaviour as a largely open-ended phenomenon – though, when linguisticians tell them it is not, some of them will accept that the experts presumably know what they are talking about. (Undergraduates may have to accept it, if they want their degree.)

Linguisticians offer no resolution of the contradiction I have described, because few of them know of its existence. But it must be resolved somehow. My belief is that linguisticians are mistaken to see human idea-generation as a bounded phenomenon – and therefore mistaken to believe that most aspects of language study can be scientific disciplines.

Before closing this chapter, I ought to add that neither I, nor any economist I have read, can offer an answer to the puzzle of how finite creatures of flesh and blood can be capable of producing ideas in a truly open-ended fashion. All we can do is to observe that evidently it is so. To my mind, intellectual creativity is one of a number of deep mysteries about human cognition, to which it may be vain to seek answers. Linguistics has a history of underestimating the difficulty of such issues. Nineteenth-century philologists accepted that there was little hope of ever saying anything useful about how human language originated; more recently a number of linguisticians have theorized about how that might have happened, but their theories skate over the real problems without addressing them (Sampson 2014). The German physiologist and philosopher of science Emil du Bois-Reymond gave a well-known lecture in 1872 in which he

4. See for instance the open letter written by ten economists to the Queen in response to her famous question at the London School of Economics about why no-one saw the financial crisis coming, Hodgson et al. 2009. Paul Romer has himself made an important contribution to this debate, Romer 2015.

argued that there are some fundamental mysteries, particularly to do with cognition, about which "*Ignoramus* [*et*] *Ignorabimus*" – we do not know, and we never shall know (du Bois-Reymond 1872: 34). Likewise the philosopher Thomas Nagel wrote recently that "There are things that science as presently conceived does not help us to understand, and which we can see, from the internal features of physical science, that it is not going to explain" (Nagel 2012: 22).

Du Bois-Reymond, and Nagel, discussed mainly the phenomenon of consciousness, about which the philosopher David Chalmers has written that "We do not just lack a detailed theory; we are entirely in the dark about how consciousness fits into the natural order" (Chalmers 1996: xi). Du Bois-Reymond alluded to creativity only tangentially (it is not so salient a concept in the German language as it is in English), and he seemed to imply that if consciousness is inexplicable, creativity must be so *a fortiori*. I am not sure that follows logically, but it does seem likely that creativity is another *ignorabimus* phenomenon.

In previous ages, creativity was ascribed to divine inspiration. Possibly, explanations in such terms ought not to be dismissed as reflexively as they are by 21st-century academics.

Chapter 6

The "Cognitive" Alternative

Noam Chomsky's "generative" school of linguistics has so dominated the discipline in recent decades that there is a risk of giving readers the impression that this is the only style of linguistics currently extant. That is by no means true.

Back in 1980, when university arts faculties were in better shape than at present, I wrote a book *Schools of Linguistics*, which surveyed the main approaches that had been taken to the subject in its fairly short life (the generative school being just one of these). The book was well received in its day, and from time to time a fellow academic asks me whether I plan to write a new, up-to-date edition. The question arose during a recent visit to a distinguished Central European university, and I had to explain that unfortunately I would not be capable of it: "The most popular current alternative to generative linguistics seems to be what is called the 'cognitive' school, and I just don't understand what it is saying." To my surprise, the immediate response was "You're not the only one." It is not controversial, I believe, to say that "cognitive linguistics" is the principal counter-current that has emerged to challenge the hegemony of the generative school. Yet, while cognitive linguistics has succeeded in winning the loyalty of a sizeable number of converts, it remains rather opaque to many of us outside it.

Not long after returning from Prague, I got hold of a book which ought to be the ideal means of filling this gap in my knowledge: Vyvyan Evans's *The Crucible of Language* (Evans 2015). Evans is the best-known representative of the cognitive school. For years he was a Professor of Cognitive Linguistics (Evans must be one of very few individuals to have had the phrase included in his formal job title – though since changing universities in 2008 he is now simply Professor of Linguistics). He is co-editor of *Language and Cognition*, the journal of the UK Cognitive Linguistics Association. And he prides himself on writing in a non-technical style well judged to appeal to newcomers to his field.

Evans made a splash with his 2014 book *The Language Myth*, the central message of which was that language is not a genetically fixed instinct, as the generative school would have us believe; and in that he was correct. (I notice, though, that Evans's book has been criticized for condemning generative theories without demonstrating understanding of them (Toolan 2015: 473). I have always taken for granted that in order to refute Chomsky and Pinker it is necessary to take their ideas seriously, and to offer evidence and argument to show why those ideas are mistaken.) *The Language Myth* was an essentially negative book; now, in *The Crucible of Language*, Evans offers his positive account of how human language really works as a "cognitive" system. The book puts itself forward as an exposition of the new school of linguistics, addressed to readers who are not yet members of that school.

In itself the word "cognitive" tells us little – who could deny that language is an aspect of cognition? As Evans's new book develops, it appears that a more distinctive feature of his school has to do with what he calls "embodiment". A leading idea for cognitive linguistics, evidently, is that the ways in which we talk about abstract relationships of various kinds are derivative from turns of phrase referring to concrete spatial relationships – we interpret abstractions in terms of our bodily situation in the world. Evans draws attention, for instance, to the spatial metaphors in:

> Christmas is *fast approaching*. The price of shares has *gone up*. Those two have a very *close* friendship.

As his book continues, Evans reverts frequently to examples like these, and similar examples are assigned a central place in writings by other cognitive linguisticians. Members of this school seem to see "embodiment" as a crucial key to understanding how language works.

Clearly there is a lot of this sort of thing in English, and perhaps in other European languages; and that is not surprising. As languages, and the intellectual outlook of their speakers, co-evolve, it seems almost inevitable that concrete ideas would be encoded first, and it seems natural enough that words for them might often be re-purposed when a need arises to express more abstract ideas. Even for English, though, I am not sure that this is anything more than a fact about the past etymology of such usages. Whoever first talked, in some ancestor-language of modern English, about a festival "approaching" perhaps did think of himself as standing still while the event moved physically towards him – but I doubt that is true today, just as I doubt whether people who talk today about "embarking" on a project picture themselves as walking up the gangplank of a ship. These are just conventional ways of expressing abstract ideas.

What is more, if this idea that "human concepts are embodied" were as significant for our understanding of language and mind as the cognitive linguisticians believe, would one not expect comparable turns of phrase to be similarly salient in languages all over the world? Evans writes that his examples "point to something fundamental about the way we *all* think" (his italics). The non-European language with which I am most familiar is Chinese, and impressionistically it seems to me that spatial metaphors referring to non-spatial abstractions are strikingly less frequent in that language than in English, though they are not entirely absent. It would be a large undertaking to establish this difference reliably, but just looking at Evans's examples: English "approach" in "Christmas fast approaches", with its derivation from *proche*, "near", clearly has a basically spatial sense, but Chinese would just say *kuài dào* 快到, "quickly arrive", which feels relatively neutral between space and time. For a price to go up is *zhǎng* 漲, which etymologically refers to the flood tide; in English we say that the tide "comes in" or "rises", but the Chinese word includes no such explicit spatial reference. "Close friend" translates as *qīn yǒu* 親友, "intimate/ affectionate friend". Or to take another example which Evans makes much of a few pages later, the best my English–Chinese dictionary can do for "to be *in* love with" is *àizhe* 愛着, the verb "love" with the durative suffix. This contrast between more figurative and more literal turns of phrase runs through the respective languages more generally, I believe. But if concepts are spatially "embodied" much more in some languages than in others, can that "embodiment" really be a central key to the workings of the mind?

Not that Evans seems very interested in the panoply of diverse languages as an index to the range of possibilities open to the human mind. At one point he discusses Jerry Fodor's 1975 book *The Language of Thought*, which claimed that all the languages of the world comprise alternative encodings of the same universal set of fundamental concepts. Evans sees this idea as "brilliant" (though he ultimately disagrees with it). To me, Fodor's thesis was absurd, one that could be taken seriously only by people with little knowledge of languages other than their own. And one telling pointer to that absurdity was that Fodor's 200-page book, though it claimed to be about language universals, only once mentioned one small piece of any language other than English: halfway through the book Fodor cited the French word for "dog"…and got it wrong, spelling it *le chein*. Almost unbelievably, Evans while discussing Fodor makes an independent but precisely equivalent error. At one of the handful of places in Evans's book where he mentions a language other than English, he offers the

German for "cat"...and gets it wrong, spelling it *Kätze*. The German for "cat" is *Katze*, without umlaut. (The pronunciations are quite different. If *Kätze* were a word, it would sound to a German more like "heretic" – *Ketzer* – than like "cat".)

Little misprints creep in to the most responsible scholarly writing, of course, and in themselves they are fairly trivial (though adding a foreign diacritic to a word which has none is an odd kind of "misprint"). But these errors point towards a much more serious problem. Fodor, and Evans, write about language as a general human phenomenon while recognizing no need to think seriously about whether their guesses based on their own native language have general validity, or not. It is understood that "language" essentially means English; references to any other languages are hasty optional extras. Fodor, and Evans, are intellectually reckless. And in this respect they are all too typical of a large number of present-day linguistics theorists.

It is as if writers like these are telling us "Sure, we can't be bothered to look seriously at languages other than our own or to get elementary facts right; but you have to agree with what we tell you about the general nature of human language, because we are university professors". And in the academic world as it has evolved in the decades around the millennium, this attitude is not entirely absurd. A high proportion of readers of books like Fodor's or Evans's are students, who find such books listed as course homework by their teachers, and know that to get the marks they need for their degrees they must learn to reproduce what the books say in their essays and exam scripts. (When I was a young lecturer, we prayed for students who would challenge orthodox academic views intelligently in their written work. In the 21st century, it is not unusual for students who do that to be marked down or even given fail marks.[1])

The general style of work I have criticized here is all too common in theoretical linguistics, and Fodor and Evans are probably not much more blameworthy than many others. Departments of linguistics contain plenty of academics doing solid work on the description of particular languages and language-families. But much of what is published under the heading of general "linguistic theory" scarcely counts as scholarship in

1. Having retired from teaching several years ago, I wondered as I drafted this passage whether I was painting too black a picture of current practice in higher education. By a remarkable coincidence, later that same week I received an e-mail from a correspondent previously unknown to me, who is a mature undergraduate in a leading British linguistics department and who complained of suffering in just this way (getting a fail mark for work which offered a reasoned challenge to current orthodoxy).

the traditional sense at all. It might be better seen as an academic branch of show business, where the aim is not to get things right but to be famous and admired. It is hard to see such work as entitled to more respect than we accord to film stars' or pop singers' pronouncements (which are often reported as significant by the media) about political or current-affairs issues.

Another kind of intellectual recklessness consists of ignoring the work of one's predecessors, and this folly too is widespread within the discipline of linguistics. Even more telling than Evans's mistake about *Katze* is a passage on the same page where he describes Jerry Fodor's 1975 book as "[a]n early proposal" about how meaning in language works. The implication of "early" is that people were not thinking seriously about the semantic aspect of human language much before 1975. Linguisticians sometimes write as if the topic were virtually inaugurated by the article "The structure of a semantic theory", published in 1963 by Jerrold Katz and Jerry Fodor; and if that were so then 1975 could still be seen as early days. But of course it was not so. What about Book III of John Locke's *Essay Concerning Human Understanding*, for instance, published in 1690? Closer to the present, but still well before the 1960s, what about the discussions by Willard Quine, Ludwig Wittgenstein, and a number of others about the crucial issue of the analytic/synthetic distinction? (For "analytic" versus "synthetic", see chapter 7 below.) Hilary Putnam's discussion of the division of labour within a speech-community with respect to maintenance of the semantic structure of its language came after the Katz and Fodor article, but even Putnam's discussion (Putnam 1973) preceded Fodor's *Language of Thought*.

The only possible reason for describing Fodor's book as "early" would be that modern universities are divided into departments, and the writings I mentioned are usually studied in departments of philosophy, rather than departments of linguistics. But these administrative boundaries are entirely artificial. The philosophers have been treating the same subject which the linguisticians have begun trying to treat, although the linguisticians rarely read the philosophers. And, because the linguisticians have largely ignored those who came before them, they misunderstand the subject in a way that philosophers of language do not. People who discuss meaning from within departments of linguistics persistently assume that the task of defining the semantics of a language is about specifying how examples of the language can be translated into entities of some kind that are not part of the language. Katz and Fodor discussed translating English words and sentences into things called "semantic markers" and "distinguishers".

Vyvyan Evans, in common with many other linguisticians, writes about relating words and other linguistic forms to "concepts". Yet it is never made clear why a set of "markers" or "concepts" would tell us more about the meaning of a language example than the example itself tells us.

In reality, the bulk of the job of defining semantics is not about linking bits of language to anything outside language: it is about language-internal relationships. Defining the semantics of English would largely consist of specifying how English-speakers are apt to infer particular English statements as implications of other statements. At the edges of the web of inferential relationships there are observation statements, which relate directly to sense-data; but most sentences, in English or any other human language, relate only very indirectly to sense-data, while any declarative sentence is directly linked to other sentences which can be inferred from it or from which it can be inferred.

I said that specifying these inferential relationships is what a definition of language semantics "would" comprise, but I put it in the conditional because, if philosophers like Quine and Wittgenstein are right to deny the existence of a definite analytic/synthetic distinction, the task is impossible in principle. Evans writes that "for much of the twentieth century the scientific study of language swept the study of meaning under the carpet – out of sight is out of mind", as though linguisticians of that period were behaving like lazy housemaids. But leaving semantics out of scientific linguistics is probably the right thing to do. Much more clearly than in the case of the grammatical aspect of language, the semantics of a human language is not a topic that can be the subject of a successful scientific theory. (Cf. Sampson 2001: 180–207.)

These are issues that philosophers have been thinking about intensively for decades and centuries, but most present-day linguisticians appear blithely unaware of that body of discourse. Evans does use Wittgenstein quotations as epigraphs introducing some of the sections of his book, but they seem to be included chiefly for cosmetic purposes; Wittgenstein, Quine, and Putnam are never discussed in the body of the book. (Locke is fleetingly mentioned once, because his name appears in a quotation from another book by Jerry Fodor.)

The effect of this blindness to intellectual history on the part of the discipline of linguistics is rather as if a group of present-day academics were to set themselves up as, say, "thingologists", and announce that they had discovered deep truths about the nature of physical things, which when stated explicitly turned out to amount to naïve and amateurish ideas, perhaps akin to the mediaeval doctrine that different materials reflect different mixtures of earth, air, fire, and water. Provided the thingologists were able to convince university managers that they could attract students, they might succeed in establishing university Departments of Thingology, and busy themselves with training undergraduates to qualify for thingology degrees and with assessing one another's thingological research proposals. If anyone mentioned atoms, molecules, or valency bonds, they would say "Oh, that's chemistry – we don't bother with that stuff round here. If you want to know about things, obviously you need to ask thingologists." Faced with confident ranks of tenured Professors of Thingology, what laymen would dare to prick the bubble?

So far as insights about the actual workings of English or other languages are concerned, once cognitive linguistics has offered its ideas about "embodiment" it seems to have shot its bolt. I find no other novel theory or descriptive apparatus in Evans's book (and I have dealt adequately with "embodiment" above). But Evans does put a great deal of effort into making the distinctive cognitive-linguistic view of human language appear to be more than a vague waving of hands, via repeated claims that new psychological and neurological research demonstrates its correctness. For instance, he writes:

> Over the past couple of decades, a revolution has taken place in our understanding of the way in which language and the mind co-conspire to create meaning. Scientists now know that language reflects key features of mind design.

Parts of the book are studded with references to recent scientific research findings. This literature is not familiar to me, and I cannot claim to have followed up most of these citations. When I did try doing so, I seemed to find a large gap between what the scientists actually say and the grandiose statements which Evans claims to base on their findings. Thus Evans writes that:

> The psychologist Lawrence Barsalou has suggested that the function of language is to provide an executive control function, operating over body-based concepts in the conceptual system. And this view seems to be on the right lines.

The first source cited in a footnote is Barsalou (2005), though there are also references to a book-chapter co-authored by Barsalou, and to Evans's own 2014 book (without a specific page reference). Evans's allusion to "body-based concepts" clearly chimes with the "embodiment" idea, but can anyone really have argued that "executive control" is the entire function of human language? That sounds as naive as B. F. Skinner's account of language as portrayed and criticized by Noam Chomsky. I read Barsalou (2005) to check. It is a fairly slight piece of less than three pages, the content of which does not sound strikingly original to me, and I cannot see that Barsalou offers anything in it to justify Evans's alleged summary. Barsalou tells us that human cognition seems to differ from that of other species, with non-human cognitive systems perhaps serving mainly to process "current situations" and thus motivate behavioural responses to them, while human language may control "the simulation system as it represents non-present situations", linked indirectly, if at all, to executive control of behaviour. I find nothing at all in Barsalou's article that connects human language to "body-based concepts".

If this is a fair sample of the relationship between the scientific literature cited by Evans, and his own ideas, then the suspicion must arise that these literature citations serve mainly to create an impression that Evans is writing with a science-based authority which, in reality, he lacks. Television commercials for women's cosmetics and hair-care products standardly include a "science bit", a reference to some exotic chemical, or some obscure aspect of the microstructure of skin or hair, which not one viewer in thousands will understand, but which creates a favourable atmosphere for reception of the selling message in the rest of the commercial. Citations of Barsalou and others seem to be Evans's "science bits" – but, proportionately, they occupy much more of the book than one finds in a Laboratoires Garnier advert.

In some cases Evans's usurpation of spurious authority seems blatant. At one point he displays an ambiguous Figure which can be seen either as two faces looking at each other, or as a vase with an ornate stem. His source credit runs "after Tyler and Evans 2003". The word "after" in such a context is normally used to acknowledge the originator of a valuable graphic item. But this Figure was not original in a book co-authored by Evans in the last decade; it was invented a hundred years ago by the Danish psychologist Edgar Rubin. (It is well known among psychologists, though doubtless less so among linguisticians.)

Another scientific domain on which the book draws heavily is palaeontology. A chapter on the origin of language gives us a good deal of information on recent findings about the evolutionary ancestry of our species, together with speculation about which point, in the "family tree" having *Homo sapiens sapiens* at the tip of one of its branches, saw language first arise. This material is certainly interesting in its own right, but it is not clear how it can offer any support to the thesis of Evans's book. What difference could it make, for our understanding of how language functions in modern Man, whether it began among *H. sapiens* some 50,000 years back or among *H. heidelbergensis* perhaps ten times longer ago? The palaeontology material is just another of Evans's "science bits".

Incidentally, apart from the fact that some of the scientific literature cited by Evans seems to have little relevance to his thesis, there are cases where Evans clearly misunderstands the science. He links Mankind's possession of language with a claim that we are unusual in the extent to which members of our species co-operate with one another; for instance, he concludes a discussion of ethology by writing that "In the final analysis, our species is uniquely cooperative in the way that no other species is". Human beings are more co-operative than other apes, the creatures Evans has been discussing in the preceding passage, but it would be hard to argue that we are more co-operative than the so-called eusocial species, including various Hymenoptera, termites, and certain rodents. (Yet eusocial species have no languages.)

Cambridge University Press claims to be the oldest publishing house in the world (Black 1992: 1). Probably most academic presses are intended among other things to contribute towards the financial viability of their parent universities, but, particularly in the case of famous and old-established institutions, we expect their publishing decisions also to be influenced by considerations of intellectual soundness. I have noticed before that, compared with the publishing arms of some other venerable universities, Cambridge University Press appears surprisingly willing to produce books that will sell without seeming to worry too much about the reliability of their content.[2] The aegis of Cambridge University Press, together with his engaging prose style, are no doubt giving Vyvyan Evans a wide readership. But his book reassures me with respect to my ignorance of the details of cognitive linguistics. There are plenty of other reasons why I would be unequal to the task of updating my *Schools of Linguistics* book, but I have no ambition to compete with Laboratoires Garnier or L'Oréal.

2. For instance, see <www.grsampson.net/CIthaca.pdf> for a very different field of enquiry which has been distorted by a theory that would never have been taken very seriously, if Cambridge University Press had not chosen to disseminate it via the vehicle of a glossy, beautifully illustrated coffee-table volume.

Chapter 7

One Man's Norm Is Another's Metaphor

The idea that one can draw a fixed boundary around the "grammatical" word-sequences of a language was a mistake, but an understandable one. When linguisticians began putting the idea forward, about sixty years ago, they faced no particular opposition: no-one was arguing that such boundaries cannot be drawn. The question had scarcely arisen before. In those circumstances it was easy for the new idea to seem plausible. I certainly supposed for many years that it was right, until experience convinced me otherwise.

The situation was different when it came to the semantic aspect of language. Here, the linguisticians were venturing onto territory which had for some time been cultivated by another breed of academic, who were mostly members of philosophy departments. And the philosophers were pretty well united in concluding that scientific theories of meaning in a human language are an impossibility. Language just is not that kind of thing.

The way philosophers put it was that there is no distinction between "analytic" and "synthetic" statements. I used these terms in chapter 6 without explaining them; I shall do so now.

Consider two sentences written by me: *My mother was female*, and *My father was short*. Both statements are in fact true, but the nature of their truth seems different in the two cases. Simply by virtue of understanding the word *mother* and the word *female*, it seems, an English-speaker would have known that the first statement was true before I said so. On the other hand no amount of cogitation about the meanings of *father* or *short* (or about the little words) will tell anyone that the second statement is true. To know that, one needs to look at the particular facts – perhaps examine old photographs or Army records. The "mother" sentence is said to be analytic, the "father" sentence synthetic.

One way of explaining what it would be to produce a scientific theory of meaning in a language is to say that it would be a system that predicts, for each of the countless possible declarative statements in the language, which ones are analytic and which synthetic. (In principle this is an oversimplification – for a fuller explanation see e.g. Sampson 2001: 182–3 – but it is the kind of simplification which makes discussion clearer without distorting the essential point at issue.)

However, according to writers such as Morton White (1950), Willard Quine (1951), or Ludwig Wittgenstein (1953), delineating a boundary between analytic and synthetic statements is impossible, because in the real-life use of a language the boundary is vague and shifts unpredictably. "What today counts as an observed concomitant of a phenomenon will to-morrow be used to define it" (Wittgenstein 1953: §79). As human cultures and human knowledge change and grow, word-meanings fluctuate in unpredictable ways. For instance, the word *atom* was originally coined in order to stand for the supposed smallest, indivisible units of matter – it derives from Greek roots meaning "no cut", indivisibility was the essence of the word's meaning. But in due course people found out more about the fine structure of matter, and the things previously called atoms went on being called atoms even after it turned out that they were made up of smaller particles – by the twentieth century it was commonplace to speak of "splitting the atom", making it obvious that the implicit definition of *atom* must have changed. According to the philosophers I have named, this is not a specialized fact applying just to technical terms like *atom*, but applies across the board to vocabulary in general. (Wittgenstein's main example was the everyday word *game*.)

It might seem that the analytic status of *My mother was female* is unassailable. Certainly, for much of my lifetime and before, the great majority of English-speakers saw a person's sex as a fixed either–or alternative, male or female, with mothers by definition female. Yet we all know that nowadays many young people are insisting on their sexual fluidity, and physical sex-changes (the first known case of which in Britain was publicized in 1961 and recognized legally in 2004) have become, if not commonplace, at any rate a reality that everyone is aware of. So it is no longer clear that all "mothers" are necessarily "female". Someone who undergoes a sex-change after having given birth as a woman might count as both a mother and a man. I am not sure whether that is how English would be used in practice – perhaps people would rather say that this person's child had acquired a second father (in which case *My mother was female* might continue to be analytic but the statement *I had only one father* would have flipped from analytic to synthetic). But this uncertainty on my part is what I mean by saying that usage is unpredictable. I have been an English native speaker since the 1940s, but I do not by virtue of my native-speaker status know how the language would be used in this novel situation.

Agreed, the *mother/female* case is one where word-meanings are close to being fixed and definable, and for that reason linguisticians' discussions of semantics tend to focus heavily on words like these. But my point is that even these words turn out to be rather less well-defined than one might first suppose, and the idea that one could produce watertight definitions for the whole run of vocabulary in a human language is really not reasonable. Most words are ones in which we have far less emotional investment than we have in *man* and *woman*, and which are much less technical than *atom*, and for such words the defining criteria are often quite vague and labile.

Linguisticians (those who discuss semantics, at least) regularly underestimate the extent to which the world we live in is surprising and full of novelty. Scientists – good scientists – tend to know better. As Imre Lakatos put it (1976: 93), "Science teaches us not to respect any given conceptual–linguistic framework lest it should turn into a conceptual prison – language analysts have a vested interest in at least slowing down this process".

In the 1950s and early 1960s, on the eve of the linguistics "explosion", the lack of a definite boundary between analytic and synthetic statements was not just a truism among philosophers, but (at least in the English-speaking world) was possibly the single most-discussed topic within that discipline, the thing that any undergraduate philosophy student was sure to be taught about. So it seemed weird that, when linguisticians began discussing semantics, they just ignored this existing body of discourse and blandly asserted that there is a clearcut analytic/synthetic distinction (and that they were on the way to developing scientific theories which would predict where the dividing line ran). Jerrold Katz and Jerry Fodor's 1963 article "The Structure of a Semantic Theory" defined word-senses in terms of primitive units of meaning (e.g. *mother* might be defined as [+parent], [–male]), and the patterns of such units for the various words of a declarative sentence would reveal whether its predicate contained only units already present in its subject (making it analytic), or also contained other units (making it synthetic).

But of course any system like that can be taken seriously as a scientific theory only if its predictions match our independent judgements about the status of various sentences, and I have already explained that those who had thought hardest about this had concluded that the predicted distinction is unreal. Katz and Fodor gave us no reason to reconsider that conclusion. Katz and Fodor are both closely identified with the unempirical generative school of linguistics, but this blindness towards philosophical considerations is by no means confined to that school.

Charles Fillmore, for instance, is a very different breed of linguistician, but his concept of "Frame Semantics" (e.g. Fillmore and Baker 2015) seems equally incompatible with the views of philosophers such as White and Quine. On the rare occasions when linguisticians have noticed the philosophers' writings, their responses were too naïve to take seriously – cf. Sampson 1980a: 67–74.

(It is another unfortunate consequence of the change in academic "terms of trade" which I discussed in chapter 1 that even humanities academics have tended to become as specialized in their intellectual outlook as science dons have had to be for a century or more. When an academic's continued employment and promotions depend on publishing a stream of papers in learned journals, it does not pay him to spend time reading outside his narrow special subject. And hence practitioners of one discipline can get away with simply ignoring the fact that one of their assumptions contradicts a position which is axiomatic in the next-door department.)

Within linguistics, there were some who queried the notion of scientific theories of word-meaning. What was missing from the debate for many years was any contribution from the profession whose job it is to analyse and describe word-meanings in real life: namely, lexicographers. Katz and Fodor's 1963 paper had cited definitions they found in a dictionary, but it was a concise dictionary giving brief definitions, which were treated in their paper as gospel truths. It seemed unlikely that those who compile dictionaries would see their own work that way. Surely, in practice a dictionary definition (and particularly a definition in a small dictionary) is a fallible attempt at capturing a word's meaning, rather than a complete and final account?

Consequently it was good news when in 2013 there appeared a new book about this issue, *Lexical Analysis*, written by a professional lexicographer, Patrick Hanks.

Patrick Hanks was for much of his career on the staff of dictionary publishers (mainly Collins and Oxford University Press – until 2000 he was Chief Editor of Current English Dictionaries for OUP), before moving more recently into university teaching and research. His book *Lexical Analysis* offers an account of language, and particularly of the nature of word meanings, which is heavily coloured by the practical experience of taking responsibility for compiling dictionary entries using the hard evidence found in large corpora. (Both at Collins and at Oxford, lexicography in recent decades has made extensive use of corpus data.)

Perhaps the first remarkable thing about Hanks's book is that it was published by the MIT Press, which has for many years been the very *fons et origo* of linguistic theorizing in the aprioristic, unempirical, intuition-based style. To this, Hanks is outspokenly opposed. He writes:

> Relying on introspection as a source of data and appealing to intuitions for judgments about idiomaticity is common practice to this day among theoretical linguists and indeed has been vigorously defended by some. It is even used by some corpus linguists, who should know better... [I]t is indefensible, no matter how sound the theory and how well-tuned the linguist's intuitions may be. (Hanks 2013: 358)

That's most previous MIT linguistics authors told, then. Hanks even goes to the lengths, when he quotes an invented example in order to illustrate a point (as is occasionally unavoidable), of printing it in italics to ensure that no reader mistakes it for a genuine example of observed naturalistic usage.

Hanks knows, of course, that all science makes use of intuition, and that theories will never emerge mechanically from any amount of empirical observations. His position on this is subtler than that of some linguisticians who have discussed methodological issues:

> There is a huge difference between consulting one's intuitions to explain data and consulting one's intuitions to invent data. Every scientist engages in introspection to explain data. No reputable scientist (outside linguistics) invents data in order to explain it. It used to be thought that linguistics is special – that an exception could be made in the case of linguistics – but comparing the examples invented by linguists with the actual usage found in corpora shows that this is not justifiable. (Hanks 2013: 20)

A belief that linguistics is special is not just something which "used" to obtain: many theoretical linguisticians still hold it, and will no doubt object to Hanks's view. On the other hand, representatives of any other scientific enterprise would see his remark as a banal truism. Linguistics might have been "special" because, unlike the topics studied by many sciences, it deals with an aspect of our own intellectual behaviour, which could have meant that we have privileged, veridical introspective awareness of the properties of our language (whereas no-one would imagine that a marine biologist, say, could possibly have veridical intuitions about the properties of sea creatures). But the idea that our intuitions about our own speech-patterns are veridical has been tested to destruction. It turns out that they are often quite wrong.

(It must be said, though, that Hanks does not always heed his own lessons. Quite often he makes pronouncements about English that appear to be based on nothing more than his own intuitions, and these are as fallible as anyone else's. At one point, for instance, he asserts that the sentence *Prince Charles is now a husband*, found in an English Language Teaching textbook, is unnatural because "English requires that you say *whose* husband Prince Charles is or *what* sort of husband he is". Does it? My personal website has for years past told the world that *I am a husband, father, and grandfather*. Possibly that makes me an incompetent user of English, but I should like to see hard evidence for that. Linguisticians ought perhaps to do as Hanks says, not necessarily as he does.)

Because of their "indefensible" reliance on introspection as a data source, Hanks sees the generative school of linguistics as holding a grossly misleading model of language, in which all aspects of language structure, including the senses of lexical items, are formalizable in terms of clearcut rules, features drawn from a universal set of semantic primitives, or the like. Perhaps not many linguisticians today would accept the detailed technical mechanisms put forward in Katz and Fodor's 1963 paper, but the general spirit of their approach, with its exact, quasi-mathematical formal apparatus, is still very much alive. Indeed, writers such as Anna Wierzbicka (e.g. 1996), discussed at length by Hanks, have been pressing this style of theorizing further than Katz and Fodor in what Hanks sees as the wrong direction. For Hanks, any analysis in this tradition is sure seriously to misrepresent the essential messiness (my word) of real-life usage, which may not have been salient for linguisticians in the days before widespread access to large electronic corpora, but today is impossible to overlook (provided one is willing to examine the empirical data).

However, Hanks is not simply saying that the generative approach to word meaning is wrong and the opposite point of view is correct. His position is more interesting than that. He believes that the truth lies between two extremes. One extreme, the generative approach, is represented by authors such as Katz and Fodor. The opposite, "creative" point of view is represented for Hanks chiefly by the present writer (though Hanks does also refer to Wittgenstein). According to Hanks (citing chapter 11 of Sampson 2001):

> Sampson is right in that strict, quasi-mathematical symbolization of meaning is pointless, but wrong to stop there. The statistical methods that Sampson advocates for other kinds of linguistic analysis must be extended to the

> semantics of human languages. This is not as futile as chasing a rainbow… Word meaning is dynamic, but that does not mean that it cannot be measured. (Hanks 2013: 3)

As a counter to both these misguided extremes, Hanks promulgates a Theory of Norms and Exploitations, often represented by an acronym, "TNE". The main purpose of his book is to urge that words do have clearcut and relatively fixed senses, which emerge fairly unmistakably when KWIC concordancing is applied to large corpora,[1] but that speakers also have a propensity to "exploit" a word's "normal" sense by extending or modifying it in diverse directions. (By exploitations, Hanks means much the same as what some would call figurative or metaphorical usage.) Not only academic linguisticians, but practical dictionary-compilers also, get into difficulties by failing to make the distinction between established norms and creative exploitations. Dictionaries often struggle to list, as separate word-senses, long series of more or less one-off exploitations that some language user has produced. But the distinction is there to be recognized, and clarity about word meaning depends on recognizing it. Dictionaries ought to describe the norms but should not attempt to list possible exploitations.

If Hanks's distinction between norms and exploitations meant simply that much of the time speakers use a given word in ways that have abundant precedents, but sometimes their usage is less predictable, then probably few would want to disagree but he might not have said very much. Clearly, a capital-letter Theory implies something more challenging. And Hanks is explicit about the fact that he sees his Theory of Norms and Exploitations as a full-blown scientific theory of language (or at least of important aspects of language), a rival alternative to generative theory, "cognitive linguistics", Michael Halliday's "systemic linguistics", and others of the kind. "TNE…would not be a runner at all if I…did not believe that it could be entered in the Language Theory Stakes as a potential winner" (Hanks 2013: 426).

The crucial point which seems to make TNE a substantial theory, rather than a mere truism about some usage instances being more predictable than others, is Hanks's contention that the norm/exploitation contrast is sharp rather than a continuous gradient. He writes:

1. A "concordance" is a listing of all the places in a corpus where a word or phrase of interest occurs. In a Keyword in Context (KWIC) concordance, successive lines display the various instances of the word or phrase in question, surrounded by some given number of characters of preceding and following context.

> one finding of corpus linguistics is that the regularities of language in use are much more regular than predicted by speculative linguistic theories that talk about "creativity", while some of the irregularities are much more irregular than anything predicted by those same theories. (Hanks 2013: 18)

Instead of the range of grassland tracks of all degrees of width and distinctiveness which I discussed on pp. 36–7 above, Hanks is saying, as it were, that in reality we observe something much more like the route pattern in a modern society: on the one hand a network of well-defined metalled roads, and on the other hand all kinds of minor ad-hoc pathways which a cartographer (or in the linguistic case a dictionary-maker) can and should ignore. Exploitations are rare, and "Rare exploitations should not be presented as regular elements of the lexicon" (Hanks 2013: 194).

> If language in use were less patterned – that is, if it were as "creative" as some theoretical linguists have predicted, it would not be possible to tease out prototypical patterns of meaning and use from a concordance. (Hanks 2013: 81)

> The creative potential of language is undeniable, but the concordances to a corpus remind us forcibly that in most of our utterances we are creatures of habit, immensely predictable, rehearsing the same old platitudes and the same old clichés in almost everything we say. (Hanks 2013: 141)

It seems, then, that much hangs on the question whether Hanks provides convincing evidence for this bimodal model of usage – frequently repeated "normal" uses, occasional one-off or nearly one-off abnormal "exploitations", and little or nothing in between. In the case of syntax, I offered quantitative evidence against that model in chapter 3, showing that construction frequencies range quite smoothly from very common to extremely rare and every possibility in between, with no discontinuity that might be equated with a distinction between "competent behaviour" and "performance errors" or the like. My surmise is that a similar continuous model applies in the case of word meanings, though I have not myself studied that issue quantitatively. Has Hanks assembled evidence that tends to refute my surmise?

Well, one would have to say that he has not, in this book, given us quantitative evidence. Hanks writes on the basis of extensive experience of using concordances for lexicography, and he shows us a few examples of KWIC concordances for interesting words (e.g. sixty-odd concordance lines for the word *condescending*, illustrating a contrast between an earlier positive sense and the familiar present-day pejorative sense of the word).

But we get no numerical analysis that might demonstrate that the bimodal model is more than an impressionistic response by Hanks to his data (and, if it were only that, the bimodality could have originated in the prior assumptions Hanks brought to his material, rather than in the data themselves).

Indeed, there are even passages where Hanks calls the division between norms and exploitations "arbitrar[y]" (2013: 173) and says that "A problem facing the analyst of norms and exploitations is that there is not a sharp dividing line between the two phenomena. They represent opposite ends of a cline" (2013: 249). If this were Hanks's position throughout the book, then I am not clear how much of a theory he would be left with; but I take these to be odd deviations from the position he maintains elsewhere.

Another way of approaching the issue is to look at how Hanks decides that some particular usage which a reader might take as debatable in terms of norm/exploitation status is in fact one or the other. The most clearcut example of this that I found occurs in the course of a critique of work by Beth Levin, whom Hanks sees as a linguistician who goes wrong about word sense through treating introspections as reliable data. Hanks quotes two of Levin's examples (italicized because invented):

(1) *The horse jumped over the fence.*

(2) *Sylvia jumped her horse over the fence.*

Hanks calls (1) an "inchoative" and (2) a causative use of *jump*. (Hanks appears to use "inchoative" simply as a synonym for intransitive – so far as I can see, his use of this word as a grammatical category has nothing to do with its etymological sense of inceptive and rudimentary.) But then Hanks asks us to consider the following corpus example:

(3) My sister jumped me and started pounding my head.

Hanks writes:

> The default meaning [of (3)] is that my sister attacked me or leaped on me. It is unfortunate that some dictionaries imply that it might also mean that she caused me to jump. It would be really unusual for it to have this meaning… Only if I am a horse would it be normal [for (3)] to activate a causative meaning of induced action.

> In TNE, an inchoative meaning for *jump* is classed as abnormal – that is, an exploitation. The point is worth belaboring [*sic*, for "labouring"] because not only Levin's book but also other texts, including dictionaries aimed at native speakers, record innumerable senses and alternatives such as this, which are theoretically possible (and may even have been attested once or twice) but abnormal. (Hanks 2013: 193)

In the first line of the second quoted paragraph, Hanks surely intended to say that it is the *causative* (not the "inchoative") sense of *jump* – the sense found in example (2) – which is an exploitation. That is presumably just a slip. But more importantly, although I am sure that Hanks is correct to say that *jump* is used much more often intransitively than causatively, I do not follow what entitles him to call one of these uses an "exploitation", rather than seeing them as alternative norms that differ in frequency. Indeed, as we see, he says that the causative use *is* normal if the object is a horse. The fact that it would be very unusual to find *jump* used in a causative sense when object as well as subject is human is easily explained. It is not physically possible for one human being to ride on another's back and for the latter to jump: the weight precludes it. (Perhaps a little child could ride on an adult's shoulders and the adult could jump at an agreed signal; but in connexion with a game like that, (3), said by a big brother about his tiny sister, would surely be normal enough?)

We do not need a doctrine of norms versus exploitations, or any other linguistic apparatus, to explain why assertions of manifest impossibilities are rarely expressed. I have little doubt that a sentence pattern [*Subject*] *kicked a cloud* has a very low frequency, but that is not because *kick* is being used in a sense that is an "exploitation". It is because creatures with feet do not commonly find themselves standing next to clouds, and even if one should do so, a cloud would not be solid enough to be kickable. I should have thought it was quite appropriate for a dictionary to list both uses of *jump*, and while for practical purposes it might be helpful to point out that the causative sense is associated with horses (not every dictionary user will be familiar with this style of equestrianism), in principle it will be redundant to do that, because it is self-evident that riders will normally be said to make only those steeds jump which are capable of jumping under the weight of a rider.

I sympathize with the problem that dictionaries which attempt to be comprehensive find themselves recording more and more senses whose frequencies in use are lower and lower, but that is because comprehensiveness in this domain is an unattainable goal. The narrower the grassland tracks you try to record, the more you will find, and there will be no end to that process.

One might think that the difference between Hanks's position and mine is chiefly a matter of timescale. Cartographers see the outlines of the world's land-masses as fixed, mappable in detail with precise latitude and longitude figures and names for each little promontory or bay. Contrast that with the clumps of froth or bubbles that form on the surface of a boiling liquid; at any moment they have particular shapes which could be recorded in a photograph, but it would be absurd to name and record the positions of individual "capes" or "bays", because they vanish as fast as they appear in the constant roiling. Yet the theory of continental drift implies that, if there were some creature for which a million years was as brief an interval as a second is for us, to that creature the geography of Earth would be an ever-changing scene like the boiling saucepan. Analogously, one might think that the difference between Hanks's belief in identifiable norms and my belief in the creativity of usage is not a real disagreement about the nature of language, but only a difference of perspective on the passage of time, with a year or a decade perceived as a long interval, within which little changes, by Hanks, and as one of a series of short intervals, between which many things change, by me.

To this I would respond in the first place that even if there is some truth in it, I do believe that Hanks underestimates the speed at which significant language changes emerge. At one point he makes specific suggestions about the rate at which new words belonging to various parts of speech are coined. New prepositions, Hanks says, scarcely ever arise: "perhaps, one new preposition every thousand years or so" (2013: 32).

Really? I tried checking this by thinking of prepositions which felt as if they might be newish, and looking up their histories in the *Oxford English Dictionary*. The first two that occurred to me were *alongside* and *via*, and in both cases the dictionary supported my scepticism. *Alongside* is first recorded from 1781 (as a preposition – the adverbial use appears in 1707). For *via* the *OED* records four examples at dates ranging from 1779 to 1882 – though in each case the word was italicized in the original quotation, and in two cases it was given an accent to mark it as a Latin ablative, suggesting that throughout the period it was not yet thoroughly naturalized into English. (By now it surely is a fully English word – my personal experience suggests that it has been such at least since the middle of the twentieth century.)

Thus we seem to have at least two new prepositions in less than 250 years; and I have not systematically searched an electronic dictionary, merely looked up in a printed edition a couple of words which occurred to me.

In the same passage, Hanks makes even larger (though vaguer) claims that the only classes of lexical item whose numbers increase "significantly" over historical time are proper and common nouns; new verbs, he feels, are exceptional. I should have thought that novel verbs are coined fairly frequently. Thinking of verbs in *-ize* beginning with early letters of the alphabet, I quickly found (from the sixty years preceding first publication of the relevant *OED* sections): *alphabetize* first recorded 1867, *anthemize* 1837, *atomize* 1845,[2] *bowdlerize* 1836, and *caramelize* 1842. None of these are technical scientific terms, which Hanks concedes as exceptions to his generalization, and I have little doubt that a systematic electronic search would yield far more examples.

Furthermore, the findings above relate to new vocabulary items, but the "norms" with which Hanks is centrally concerned are senses of words. Most people, surely, would suppose that the rate at which existing words develop new senses or modify their senses is more rapid than the rate at which new words are coined (although the former is much harder to quantify).

It seems reasonable to conclude that, on a human timescale, the relevant aspects of language are more distant from cartography and closer to the boiling saucepan than Hanks's theory suggests, even if many would argue that the most faithful picture will lie somewhere between these extremes.

But in any case my analogy is too simple. The froth on the boiling pan does form objectively determinate shapes if one takes a short enough time-interval, as revealed by photography. In the case of language, reducing the interval does not really help, because the structure of a language has no objective existence apart from the many individual speakers of the language. Each speaker seeks to conform his usage to the system he infers as underlying the usage of others, but each of those others is likewise working on the basis of fallible hypotheses about current usage, and new speakers – children – are constantly joining the community and developing their own models of the surrounding language from scratch. Nowhere is there a well-defined standard, by reference to which a given individual's language-model might be judged fully correct, or incorrect only in specific, limited respects.

Taking this into account, I suggest that the creative picture of language behaviour really does become more plausible than the picture of language as governed by clearcut "norms".

2. As a transitive verb; an intransitive verb meaning "believe in the atomic theory", really a separate word, is recorded once from 1678.

One strategy Hanks uses, in order to reconcile his belief in rule-governedness with the manifest fact that literal meanings of natural-language forms are less cut-and-dried than linguisticians have supposed, is to suggest that rule-governedness is to be sought at another level, not the level of individual lexical items.

For instance, at many points throughout his book Hanks appeals to Paul Grice's theory of conversational co-operation, which Hanks discusses in detail and treats as authoritative truth. Indeed, Hanks's closing peroration characterizes his own Theory of Norms and Exploitations as an attempt to make Grice's ideas more fully explicit.

According to Grice (1975), conversational communication works because participants in conversation co-operate by conforming their utterances to certain "maxims", shared knowledge of which enables hearers to reconstruct the communicative intent lying behind the superficial logical sense of speakers' words. What seem *prima facie* to be difficult-to-define variations in the sense of a word in different contexts are in reality produced by interaction between the fixed literal meaning of an utterance and the Gricean maxims – recognizing this simplifies the task of defining word-senses. Hanks lists Grice's maxims: they include, for instance, "Do not make your contribution to the conversation more informative than required", and "Do not say that for which you lack adequate evidence" (Grice 1975: 45–6). For Hanks, some such co-operative mechanism is virtually a logical necessity:

> when people speak to each other, they are trying to cooperate in an activity in which they have a mutual interest. This, at any rate, is what every utterer who is not a solipsist must assume. (2013: 89)

Hanks states as a truism that "human linguistic behavior is cooperative social behavior" (2013: 345).

My first problem with Grice is that his maxims seem clearly wrong as a description of many conversations. Did Grice have no garrulous acquaintances who routinely rambled on about topics entirely irrelevant to the nominal point of a conversation, and who frequently made dogmatic assertions that far outran the available evidence? (Is there anyone who does not know someone like that?) These and others of Grice's maxims seem so breathtakingly out of line with much real-life conversation that I have sometimes wondered whether I was misunderstanding him, and whether garrulity of this kind somehow did not contradict the correct interpretation of his maxims. In fact, though, I believe Grice meant just what he seemed to say, in which case he was seriously mistaken.

But Grice also made a deeper mistake with his assumption that the essence of conversation is an attempt to co-operate to achieve a common good. There will be some examples of conversation for which that is true, but if it were *generally* true then conversation would be a very unusual kind of social behaviour. The social sciences more widely have understood since Adam Smith's *The Wealth of Nations* of 1776 that social interactions are normally about *exchange* rather than about shared goals. As Smith ([1776] 1976: vol. 1, 26–7) famously put it, "It is not from the benevolence of the butcher, the brewer, or the baker, that we expect our dinner, but from their regard to their own interest." In conversation, too, we give because we want to get; there is no solipsism in denying that conversation is necessarily co-operative. An example I used at a conference on Grice's theory (Sampson 1982) was a conversation between captured spy and interrogator: the goals of the participants are thoroughly opposed, yet they can still talk to one another and the words are not just meaningless noise.

Again, it could be that I have misunderstood, and that Grice's idea is consistent with the interrogation scenario. But I think not. At the conference in question, Grice responded to my objection with a remark about Adam Smith being one of the great writers whom he had never read; his lofty tone suggested that he saw this as a palpable hit against Sampson's quibbling (and sycophantic sniggers indicated that many of the audience agreed), though to me it was an embarrassing confession of ignorance on Grice's part. Humanities scholars of Grice's generation were a herbivorous bunch on the whole, and many linguisticians held and still hold sentimental background assumptions about talk being a domain of life where normal conflicts of interest are absent or can be ignored. But I do not believe that any Grice-like system of "maxims" or "implicatures" will help to rescue Hanks's assumptions about rule-governedness from the messy relationships we find among dictionary meanings and speakers' intentions. A particular utterance might well be shaped by its speaker partly in response to some Grice-like maxims, but the maxims will be as labile and open to innovation as the meanings of the individual words used.

Another move Hanks sometimes makes in the attempt to reconcile rule-governedness with messy usage is to appeal to the concept of probabilistic language rules. He suggests that generative linguistics in its heyday was unable to use this concept because the necessary data were inaccessible, but

> With the advent of large corpora, all this has changed; it is now possible to measure the syntagmatic and collocational preferences of words and relate these preferences to meanings. (Hanks 2013: 104)

What Hanks calls exploitations "need to be separated out and either ignored or dealt with probabilistically, as was proposed in preference semantics (Wilks 1975; Wilks, Guthrie, and Slator 1999)".

An unwary reader might perhaps imagine that, by conceding that language rules can be probabilistic rather than absolute, Hanks has taken the wind out of the sails of one who argues that language usage is unpredictably creative. We would not need the latter assumption to explain why a word or construction is not always used in a consistent way. Notice, though, that a serious "probabilistic" language description will be no less formally cut-and-dried than a traditional generative grammar. Indeed, it will contain more formal information: not just a set of absolute rules, but rules containing alternatives together with precise, numerical information about probability distributions over the alternatives, specification of the maths of how probabilities associated with separate rules interact, and so forth. If someone reacts to standard generative linguistics (as Hanks appears to do) by instinctively feeling "real-life language is not so neatly precise and well-defined as that", then it is odd if the same person would find a probabilistic grammar more congenial.

Furthermore, it is easy enough to put forward the suggestion that any seemingly messy aspect of a language might be captured by some hypothetical set of well-defined probabilistic rules, but the suggestion will not be very persuasive unless backed up at least by one or two small-scale examples – without that, why should we believe in probabilistic rules rather than in unresolvable messiness? Hanks does nothing like that. The closest he gets is in a discussion of an example taken from a 1993 issue of the *Guardian Weekly*:

> [Chester] serves not just country folk, but farming, suburban, and city folk too. You'll see Armani drifting into the Grosvenor Hotel's exclusive…Arkle Restaurant and C&A giggling out of its street-front brasserie next door. (Hanks 2013: 240)

Hanks comments:

> speech-act verbs such as *giggling* prefer a [[Human]] subject; prepositional phrases such as "out of [[Location]]" imply movement; *brasserie* is a [[Location]]. These preferences combine to induce a weak (but correct) probability that *C&A* can be coerced to the semantic type [[Human]] and *giggling* can be coerced to be a verb of movement. (Hanks 2013: 240)

"Weak probability" sounds as though Hanks has some set of explicit rules, not tailored to this specific example, but which respond to the example by yielding a probability above zero but well below 0.5 for e.g. assignment of the feature [[Movement]] to the lexical entry *giggle*. But there is no hint in Hanks's book that he or his associates have actually developed a specific structure of probabilistic rules which give that particular result in this particular instance. Yet without that, it seems equally plausible (to my mind, more plausible) to say "the only way that occurs to me to make sense of this example is to take *C&A* to refer to women who bought their clothes at (the now defunct chain) C&A, and *giggling* to mean walking while giggling – but these are extempore guesses in response to the particular example, not the outcome of general algorithms, and certainly not of algorithms with numbers attached".

(Incidentally, is "giggle" a "speech-act verb"? I thought it was a kind of laughing rather than a kind of talking, but perhaps this is just one more illustration of the variability of language.)

If there is no identifiable discontinuity between higher-frequency "normal" uses and less common "exploitations", surely it becomes implausible to suppose that speakers of a language all share a well-defined set of "normal" senses for words? Unless a speaker is given an explicit definition on first encountering a word (which happens sometimes with technical terms but rarely with ordinary words), he or she must infer a sense for the word from the features of the particular context or contexts in which it is encountered. These will differ in detail from one speaker to another, and furthermore we are given no mechanical algorithm for inferring word-senses from context. (At least, even linguisticians have never to my knowledge suggested that we have such an algorithm – it is hard to imagine how one might work.) In an open-ended situation like this, we should surely expect that different speakers' understanding of the core sense or senses of a word will overlap but not coincide perfectly, and that what is a "normal" sense for one speaker might be a figurative extension or "exploitation" for another.

Although this scenario does not agree with Hanks's theory, his detailed discussion of examples tends to confirm its accuracy. Take Hanks's list of British National Corpus concordance lines for *condescending*. If I reflect on what *condescend* "normally" means to me, I would say that it implies a certain kind of relationship between two parties, *A* and *B*, where *A* is *B*'s superior either in reality or in *A*'s own estimation. But one of Hanks's concordance lines comes from a book I know, Michael Frayn's 1967 novel *Towards the End of the Morning*. Bob is invited to dinner at the home of his work supervisor Dyson and Dyson's wife Jannie, and after dinner Bob and Jannie decide to watch an old film on television. The novel continues: *"Condescending lowbrows," said Dyson sourly.* Here it is not clear who *B* could be, unless perhaps *B* is the television or the film itself (this was a period when television was seen by the educated as a suspect medium devoted largely to entertaining the masses); and *lowbrows* seems to contradict the requirement that *A* should be superior. As I understand *condescend*, party *B* must be capable of awareness of the condescender's attitude; to condescend to an inanimate thing would be like insulting a tree. But evidently the word cannot mean for Frayn precisely what it means to me. (The novel continues with Dyson ringing the changes on *lowbrow*, *highbrow*, and *middlebrow* in a fashion that leaves me no wiser about his or Frayn's sense of *condescend*.)

That is a case where an example which, for Hanks, apparently exemplifies a norm would have to count for me as an exploitation. Contrast that with Hanks's discussion of the verb *climb*, which he considers at some length, developing points made about this word by Charles Fillmore, Ray Jackendoff, and Anna Wierzbicka. The first concordance line Hanks quotes under a heading "Examples of exploitations, metaphors, and uncertainties" runs *How good are the beetles at climbing cereal plants and locating aphid…* (Hanks 2013: 107). It is not quite clear why Hanks treats this as an abnormal usage, but one of his Appendices seems to imply that, for him, the "normal" subject of transitive *climb* has to be either human or a vehicle – "any use of the English verb *climb* not accounted for by this prototype is either an exploitation (literary trope, metaphor, etc.) or a mistake" (2013: 102). And there are constraints even in the case of vehicles as subjects. Hanks quotes, apparently with approval, an assertion by Wierzbicka (1990) that "if a train went quickly up a hill it couldn't be described as 'climbing' "; Hanks asks "Is using *climb* to denote a train going uphill a performance error?" (2013: 101).

Here, Hanks seems to see abnormality or metaphor (or mistake) in usage which strikes me as perfectly normal. I would think of a central sense of *climb* as being something like "go up with effort". To me it feels irrelevant whether the subject is human or beetle. (Agreed, there will be many more concordance lines for human subjects, but that is merely because humanity spends more time talking about itself than talking about beetles.) And (to me) it feels absolutely normal for a train to be said to *climb* a gradient. Most of us know Auden's poem *Night Mail*, about a mail train making the journey from London over the hills of northern England and southern Scotland to Glasgow, and containing the lines *Pulling up Beattock, a steady climb*, and *Dawn freshens, the climb is done*. Admittedly, poetry is specially given to figurative usage; to me these phrases do not feel like examples of that, but if someone disagrees (or objects that Auden is using *climb* as noun rather than verb), then let me offer another passage which I came across by chance the day after reading this part of Hanks's book, in a prosy popular book of local lore. It referred to

> two railwaymen, Thomas Scaife and Joseph Rutherford, who were killed when their steam locomotive blew up while climbing the nearby Lickey Incline, the steepest gradient on the British main line network. (Winn 2005: 256)

(The relevance of "quickly" in Wierzbicka's assertion is unclear to me. Speed is relative; obviously a railway train can never move as fast on an adverse gradient as it can on the level, but even in the days of steam I believe I am correct in saying that a train climbing Beattock Summit would have outpaced the fastest human athlete.)

These are no more than suggestive examples, but I hope they suffice to lend at least *prima facie* plausibility to the idea that one speaker's "exploitation" will often be another's "norm", and *vice versa.* (For a rather fuller discussion of this point of view, see Sampson 1980a.)

I am particularly sceptical about Hanks's idea that usage deviating from the norms recognized by his theory might be, not even "exploitations", but plain mistakes. Clearly, language-users do make slips of the tongue or pen, but I wonder whether these have much real relevance to the messiness of word senses in real-life usage. When Hanks asserts that "Users of a language, including highly skilled users, regularly make mistakes", his main example is a spelling error (*sow* for *sew*). Spelling mistakes have very little to do with the indefiniteness of word senses. But even if a slip of the tongue involves using a word in a sense to which, for the speaker, the word does not quite apply, how could a hearer know that? (The hearer might know it if the speaker corrects himself, but in that case the momentary error is neither here nor there.) To the hearer, the "mistaken" utterance will just be one more datum to use in inferring what the society around him means by the word in question. If similar errors are repeatedly made with a given word, presumably the "normal" meaning of the word will eventually change accordingly.

In connexion with grammar, Hanks writes "A mistake, even if repeated many times, is still a mistake". Coming from a member of the discipline of linguistics, that is an extraordinarily Platonic concept of language as an ideal system. It was a mistake when someone, perhaps a child, first regularized the past participle of *help* by saying **helped* rather than the correct *holpen.* But we have been repeating that mistake for quite a while now: would Hanks really not concede that the erroneous form is now the correct form? I feel sure he would concede it, and anyone who concedes the point for grammar must surely concede it far more readily for the less codifiable domain of word sense.

In fact Hanks does appear to accept this when he writes that "Mistakes are not infrequently the source of new norms", offering as an example a shift in the sense of *refute* from "demonstrate by logical argument the error of a proposition" to "strongly deny". In this particular case I believe Hanks is mistaken about the history of the word (both senses have ancient historical precedents), but he is surely correct about the general point that today's mistake is tomorrow's standard usage.

This seeming contradiction is characteristic of Hanks's book. More than once, an apparently strong, falsifiable theoretical claim about the nature of human language is advanced, but then in the small print (as it were) the claim turns out to be undercut by some statement which sounds much more reasonable, but which contradicts the theory. Hanks brings to linguistics a deep knowledge of the issues that arise in practice in high-quality lexicographic research, and this is something which the discipline has sorely needed. His stance as a scholar aiming to locate truth in the reasonable middle ground between two extremes is an attractive and likeable one. But in the end I find nothing here to convince me that it is an error to see language as an activity in which creativity is one essential component. Creativity, in any area of human life including language, is not something that can be predicted or reduced to a matter of statistics or probabilities. People are not machines. Their semantic behaviour cannot be captured in scientific theories.

II

Writing Systems

One consequence of the scientism which pervades linguistics has been that the subject for many decades more or less wholly ignored written language. Spoken language is a possession of all human communities everywhere in the world, and has been so as far back as our knowledge extends (and undoubtedly much, much further); so it seems at least possible on the face of it that spoken language, and the ability to learn it, could be governed by genetic mechanisms available to study by the scientific methods of biology. Writing, on the other hand, is obviously a fairly recent development. Even the earliest scripts date back just a few thousand years, not tens or hundreds of thousands. And although by the 21st century probably almost every living language has been equipped with a script, only one or two hundred years ago there were plenty of less-advanced societies whose languages were entirely unwritten. Plenty of adult individuals are illiterate today. So it is obvious that writing is a feature of human cultures, rather than of human biology.

That does not mean that the written mode of language is unimportant relative to the spoken mode. Far from it. Every child begins with speech, but in advanced societies of the kind which readers of this book inhabit, writing is quite crucial to innumerable areas of life. Without it, our societies would surely break down. Yet, because writing as a cultural phenomenon does not lend itself to scientific theorizing, linguistics ignored it. Fernand de Saussure (who as we have seen is regarded as the founder of linguistics as an independent discipline) said that linguistics "is not [about] both the written and the spoken forms of words; the spoken forms alone constitute the object" (Saussure [1916] 1966: 23–4). Jacques Derrida (1976: 44) called writing "the wandering outcast of linguistics".

From the point of view represented in this book, there is no logic here. Other than the anatomy of our vocal organs, all aspects of language are cultural developments, so why ignore written language just because it developed relatively recently? Yet I believe I can say that it was only after a book of mine on the linguistics of writing systems appeared in 1985 (second edition 2015) that discussion of writing systems began to enter mainstream linguistic discourse. And even now, though the situation is much better than it used to be, this is still in practice a minority special interest within the discipline as a whole. The "big swinging dicks" of linguistic theory would not want to be found taking an interest in writing systems.

In Section II, I redress the balance a little, with chapters illustrating the fact that there are worthwhile studies to be done on the nature and structure of scripts, just as there are in the case of the spoken form of language. It was only unreasoning scientism that excluded the "outcast" for so long.

Chapter 8

From Phonemic Spelling to Distinctive Spelling

An obvious way to approach the study of writing systems is through typology: analysis of the different kinds of script used to record various spoken languages in permanent visible form. One would not need to know much about Chinese writing, for instance, to recognize that it is a very different sort of system from the alphabetic systems used to write European languages, whereas within Europe the Roman, Greek, and Cyrillic alphabets, while different from one another in detail, are systems of much the same type as one another. I began my *Writing Systems* textbook with a detailed classification of script-types (Sampson 2015a: 20–39).

Yet, perhaps surprisingly, in this area the whole concept of typology is controversial, because there are influential scholars who believe that all the world's scripts are essentially of the same type. There has been a long though not particularly honourable tradition of discussing all writing systems as if they were more successful or less successful attempts to approximate the Roman alphabet, seen as the only possible ideal from which any other kind of script could only be viewed as a falling-off. In 1960, for instance, the distinguished anthropologist Sir Jack Goody and the literary critic Ian Watt co-authored a widely read paper (Goody and Watt 1963) which used the term "literate societies" explicitly to mean societies using an alphabetic script, as opposed to societies like China which for over three millennia has (as Goody and Watt saw it) been struggling with a system of writing too crude to confer the benefits of literacy on the society which uses it. They even held (Goody and Watt 1963: 314–15, 337–8) that the non-alphabetic nature of Chinese script makes it incapable of expressing socially or ideologically unorthodox ideas, or even logical argument (to me, these statements are just laughable). Michael and Jennifer Cole (2006: 305) note that Goody and Watt's paper, and subsequent related writings of Goody's such as Goody (1977), "have had an especially influential and continuing impact on a wide range of different disciplines... Goody's work on this topic continues to be used by anthropologists and historians, psychologists and sociologists."

This case of playing down differences among languages does not derive from a belief in genetically controlled structural universals of language, as linguisticians' belief in Universal Grammar does. The ideas certainly harmonize with one another, but the assumption that all scripts are "trying to be alphabets" is older than generative linguistics and seems best regarded as resulting from simple Eurocentrism. It is another case of scientism in linguistics: it predicts (admittedly rather vaguely) that one will not be able to find scripts that are fully adequate to their purpose and which depart too far from the alphabetic "ideal". But one can find such scripts, and indeed I shall argue that "trying to be alphabetic" is almost the reverse of the true situation.

Scholars within the tradition described have often been prepared to recognize a difference in type between alphabetic scripts (the elements of which stand for segmental phonemes), and syllabic scripts (which divide speech into whole syllables). Both of these types of script have been used in Europe and adjacent regions. But alphabetic v. syllabic is a relatively minor distinction, set against the contrast between logographic scripts, which assign distinct marks to meaningful units of a language, i.e. words or morphemes, and phonographic scripts which represent phonological units of one size or another. And even the syllabic v. alphabetic distinction was often blurred, for instance by lumping together, as "syllabic", scripts in which the symbols for distinct syllables are graphically unrelated with scripts where series of syllables such as *ka ke ki* and *ba be bi* are written with constant outlines for /k/ or /b/ respectively, modified in consistent ways to show the particular following vowel. Furthermore, syllabic scripts tended to be described as if they were little more than temporary way-stations towards the ultimate ideal of alphabetic writing. The idea that a logographic script might be a fully fledged, entirely satisfactory mode of written communication scarcely entered the purview of these scholars.

Up to a generation or two ago, such absurd views on the part of Western scholars could perhaps be explained as proceeding from widespread ignorance, even among professional linguisticians, about the details of how non-alphabetic scripts really work. But in 1989 John DeFrancis published a book subtitled *The Diverse Oneness of Writing Systems*, the central theme of which was that all scripts are indeed of a single, phonographic type. A few years earlier he had written that Chinese script "should be considered to be basically a phonetic system" (DeFrancis 1984: 125).

If true, this would rank as a falsifiable scientific theory: we can imagine scripts based on other principles, but the theory asserts that none of those will be found as the script of a real human language. DeFrancis certainly could not be dismissed as writing out of ignorance: the Chinese language was his special subject.

I have no hesitation, nevertheless, in saying that DeFrancis was quite wrong to suggest that all scripts are phonographic. I have refuted DeFrancis at length elsewhere (Sampson 1994; 2015a: 21, 184–5), and I shall not repeat all my detailed arguments here. The essence of DeFrancis's mistake lay in failing to distinguish synchronic from diachronic modes of language description. It is reasonable to suggest that all scripts used as the normal written communication medium of a society were initially created as at least partly phonographic systems – I believe that is probably true (though it certainly is not true that early scripts were wholly phonographic). But it does not follow that all present-day scripts are phonographic, because a script, and the spoken language(s) it is used to represent, both change over time, and the result may be that the phonographic relationship is eventually lost. In the case of Chinese script that is exactly what happened. Chinese script used to write the modern Chinese language can only reasonably be described as a basically logographic script, even though from its long history the script does inherit features which often give limited and unreliable hints about present-day pronunciations.

DeFrancis makes much of those features of Chinese script, but it is easy to demonstrate that a writing system need not be phonetically based even to that limited extent. Chinese is not the only spoken language which is written using Chinese script. Japanese is written in a complex script, all elements of which ultimately derive from Chinese writing, and in particular the large share of the Japanese vocabulary which is native rather than borrowed and consists of lexical rather than grammatical morphemes is written with Chinese graphs for translation-equivalents or near-equivalents. Since the two languages are genetically unrelated, there is no relationship whatever between the pronunciation of a native Japanese root and that of its Chinese translation-equivalent. Consequently, even when a Chinese graph does offer a good clue about its pronunciation *in Chinese*, it tells us nothing at all about its Japanese pronunciation.

For instance, the Chinese word for "taste", *wèi*, is written by adding the graph for "mouth", 口, to that for "not yet", 未, giving 味; and in this particular case the "not yet" element gives an excellent clue to the pronunciation of the compound graph, because in modern Mandarin "not yet" is also *wèi*, a perfect homophone of "taste". (This is an instance where the phonetic element may have become more rather than less appropriate over the millennia since the graphs were coined: Schuessler 2007: 512 shows the two words as having been only near-homophones with slightly different vowels in the Middle Chinese period.) But, in Japanese, "taste" is *aji* while "not yet" is *mada* – the words are written with the same two Chinese graphs, but their pronunciations are unrelated, so there is no phonetic basis at all for the structure of the "taste" graph. That graph is purely a logogram, and this is the normal situation with respect to the writing of native Japanese vocabulary. Scripts really can be of different types (though, just as in the case of spoken-language typology, scripts commonly do not perfectly exemplify an ideal type).

It is ironic that there has been reluctance to recognize major typological differences between scripts, because, in reality, those differences seem to have more human significance than do typological differences among spoken languages. The contrast between an extreme case of inflecting languages, such as Greek, and an extreme isolating language, such as Vietnamese, is large in terms of the technicalities of formal language structure, but it is not usually thought to have large consequences for the functioning of the respective languages as vehicles of communication. Rightly or wrongly, the consensus appears to be that languages of different structural types carry out more or less the same tasks with similar efficiency though in somewhat different ways.

In the writing-systems domain, on the other hand, it is widely believed that differences between script types really matter to their users. For instance, there has been research on both Chinese and Japanese (summarized in Taylor and Taylor 1983: 404) suggesting that developmental dyslexia is strikingly less common for users of logographic scripts than for users of alphabetic scripts. More recently, McBride et al. (2015) do not discuss an absolute difference in frequency of incidence, but they argue that the syndromes covered by the general term "developmental dyslexia" are different in detail for users of the two types of script.

Ignatius Mattingly observed (1972: 144) that logographic scripts require a longer period to master than alphabetic scripts (because the number of distinct symbols to be learned is thousands rather than a few dozen), but mastering an alphabetic script is more intellectually challenging, because it requires the learner mentally to split up the physically continuous speech stream into phonemes. William Hannas has argued eloquently that the former of these two points implies that logographic scripts impose a serious burden on societies which use them: "Instead of using language to learn, East Asians are wasting their youth and resources learning about language" (Hannas 1997: 125); "alphabetic literacy promotes creativity" (Hannas 2003: 5) whereas logographic script, Hannas believes, tends to stifle creativity, and in consequence he has argued that Chinese hopes of achieving First-World levels of economic development are doomed.

Hannas's predictions look pretty foolish in view of the huge economic strides China has been making just in the few years since he was writing, and it would not be hard to construct an argument pointing in precisely the reverse direction. The Organization for Economic Co-operation and Development's "PISA" programme is now giving us a triennial comparison of fifteen-year-olds' educational attainments in basic subjects across seventy nations and territories, and it is striking that countries with logographic scripts have been doing particularly well. The latest results, for tests taken in 2015, were published as this book was being readied for the press (OECD 2016). The ten highest scores for science (in descending order) were for Singapore, Japan, Estonia, Taipei (capital of Taiwan), Finland, Macao, Canada, Vietnam, Hong Kong, and a group of four Chinese urban areas which were treated as a unit (I will call them Peking et al.). Six of the ten use logographic script, whereas all sixty remaining countries use phonographic script. For maths the top scorers are precisely the six "logographic territories", with the 64 phonographic territories all ranked lower. And for reading, the leaders are: Singapore; Hong Kong and Canada equal; Finland; Ireland; Estonia; Korea; Japan; Norway; and Macao, New Zealand, and Germany equal. Four logographic out of twelve is again very impressive, though in this case Taipei (24th equal with the USA) and Peking et al. (27th) did less well. Results in the previous three-yearly round of tests were broadly similar, though at that time fewer Chinese-speaking places were tested.

Measuring educational attainments across countries with different schooling systems, different spoken languages, and different cultural backgrounds involves huge problems of comparability, so I cannot claim that the implications of the PISA figures are as clearcut as they appear *prima facie*. And for that matter, I am sure that the last word has not been said about dyslexia among users of different script types, or about other issues in this area. But it is at least clear that there is room for serious, informed debate about various significant implications of script-type for users' lives and welfare. I shall argue that the history of scripts shows a trend away from simple phonemic systems towards more Chinese-like systems, and that this trend is an efficient response to social pressures.

So far as I know, the field of spoken-language typology has nothing like this. For instance, it is a cliché (in Britain, at least) that the societies of northern Europe are more economically dynamic than those of southern

Europe, but I have never heard the least hint, either by economists or by linguisticians, that this might be partly explained by the fact that southern European languages are on the whole richer in inflexions than the languages of northern Europe. The two sets of facts are taken (correctly, I would imagine) to be unrelated to one another.

It is true that linguistics has moved away from its earlier assumption that spoken-language typology is independent of the nature of the society using the respective language. In particular, Peter Trudgill (e.g. 2011) has shown that there are correlations between complexity of spoken-language structure and the "connectedness" of a society. But that does not imply that some types of spoken language do a better or worse job for their speakers, in the way that some types of script seem likely to be doing better or worse jobs for their users.[1]

So the study of writing systems is certainly not a branch of linguistics where typology has little significance. That said, there is a large problem about typological theorizing in this area. It is the same problem which creates difficulties for other approaches to the study of writing systems: namely, there are few independent examples. If general linguistics is about anything, it is about identifying general truths which apply across the board to all human languages, and separating them out from the mass of properties which happen by chance to apply to some particular languages, but do not "have" to apply. For spoken languages, this should in principle be straightforward to achieve. There are thousands of distinct spoken languages, belonging to many different families which appear to be genetically unrelated. If the linguisticians were correct to believe that there are scientific laws constraining the extent to which human languages can differ in structure, hypotheses about such laws would certainly be scientifically testable. With writing systems it is different. All fully alphabetic scripts (that is, with letters for vowels as well as for consonants) descend with only minor changes from the adaptation of some version of the Semitic alphabet, probably by a single individual Greek-speaker on a particular occasion, to write Greek. The only logographic scripts used to any serious extent in the modern world are Chinese script, and its adaptations to write the languages of countries neighbouring China. It is as if we aimed to establish general theories about spoken language in a world where the only languages spoken were the Romance languages plus Finnish and Hungarian.

1. I say nothing here about correlations between spoken-language types and the script-types used to write the respective languages, an issue I have discussed at length in Sampson 2015a.

Indeed, within living memory there were scholars who thought it likely that all the world's scripts share a *single historical origin*. True, in the 21st century it is no longer seriously possible to believe that. Apart from any other considerations, the successful decipherment of the Maya script of Central America has shown us one clear case of a sophisticated writing system which could not have shared a common ancestry with the early Middle Eastern scripts from which many modern writing systems, including our own, ultimately descend. And if we know that writing has been invented at least twice in world history, it is easy to believe that it has probably been invented more than twice. The earliest examples we have of Chinese script look like a system invented independently of the ancestry of Sumerian Cuneiform, the earliest Middle Eastern script; there could have been historical links which have vanished from the record – people did come and go from one end of Asia to the other – but the probability is that there were no such links. Nevertheless, at most we have only a few independent cultural traditions of writing, nothing like the dozens of separate spoken-language families. If we think we have detected common patterns among various scripts which share a common origin, then it is hard to be sure that the common patterns are pointing to something essential about the human activities of writing and reading, rather than just to something which happened by chance to be true of the ancestral system and has been inherited by many or all of its descendants.

The result is that it becomes difficult to distinguish between facts which stem from the nature of human reading and writing behaviour, and facts which are mere matters of historical accident.

To take a simple hypothetical example: most alphabetic scripts use a single letter for the phoneme sequence /ks/ (Greek Ξ, Roman X). It is tempting to suppose that something about the phonetics of /ks/ makes it "natural" for that sequence to be treated as a single unit in writing. In reality, there is nothing natural about it; the existence of the letters Ξ and X is probably a pure historical accident. The Greek who first learned the alphabet must have struggled to interpret the alien sounds of a Semitic language in terms of the phonology of his own language, and perhaps came up with the interpretation /ks/ for a single Semitic sound.[2] Ever since then, speakers of Greek and of most languages written with the Roman alphabet have used a single letter for that pair of phonemes.

In this case, any serious hypothesis that /ks/ is written with a single letter because it is a natural phonological unit could be refuted by the fact that not all alphabetic orthographies treat it as such. The Cyrillic alphabet

2. On the specifics of the relationship between sibilant phonemes and letter-shapes in Semitic languages and in Greek see Sampson 2015a: 109.

has no equivalent of X, and some versions of the Roman alphabet do not use X even in "international" words (the Welsh for "taxi" is *tacsi*). But, with so few unrelated scripts extant, there is no guarantee that in other, comparable cases we could find orthographies which make it clear that some apparent generalization about writing systems was spurious. A generalization which turned out to hold for each one of the thousands of spoken languages, on the other hand, could hardly be a mere coincidence. Hence it is easier in the case of spoken languages than in the case of scripts to establish that some group of properties genuinely belong together and define a natural type.

All the same, we should like to establish generalizations about writing systems – even if these are likely to be probabilistic trends rather than rigid scientific laws. The difficulties perhaps just mean that we have to be specially alert to the clues which we do find in our limited data, and to make the most of what those clues offer us.

I want to argue for one tendency which I believe may be a general property of the world's writing systems. I call it a "tendency", because I certainly do not claim it as an absolute truth which would be refuted by a single counter-example. There undoubtedly are counter-examples, but in studies of social institutions we don't find many absolute rules. Probabilistic trends are often as much as one can hope to find. But a trend can be enlightening, and I hope this one is.

The tendency I postulate is that orthographies evolve from being phonetically based when they are young, towards being lexically distinctive as they mature. I shall enlarge on what I mean by "phonetically based" shortly, but for the time being the simple gloss "one sound one symbol" will do. What I mean by "lexically distinctive" is much less obvious. I am using this phrase to stand for a conjunction of two separate properties. In the first place, I suggest that more mature scripts tend to assign a constant written shape to each lexical element – each morpheme, or at least each root (as opposed to grammatical affix morphemes) – even if that element varies its phonetic shape in different environments, as in cases like English *divine* ~ *divinity*, where adding the suffix causes the stressed vowel of the root to change from /aɪ/ to /ɪ/. But also, and perhaps more controversially, I am suggesting that the letter-sequences which maturer scripts assign to various lexical elements tend to be more distinctive in the sense of having few near neighbours. There will be relatively fewer cases where substituting just one letter for another gives you the spelling of a different lexical item.

In a lexically distinctive orthography, meaningful units tend each to have one constant written form, and that form tends to be as different as possible from the spellings of other meaningful units. These two properties are logically independent of one another. An orthography could ignore morphophonemic variation, while the spellings of its vocabulary were so densely crowded together that almost any substitution of one letter for another in a word gave another word. And conversely a language might reflect every case of morphophonemic alternation by a spelling difference, yet still have its set of spellings sparsely scattered so that very few pairs of words differed by just one letter. But although the two properties are logically independent, I suggest that in practice they go together: maturer scripts tend both to ignore morphophonemic variation and also to have sparsely scattered spellings.

What is more, I am going to suggest that not only does this tendency exist, but it is good that it exists. By evolving so as to possess a greater degree of the properties I associate with maturer scripts, a writing system is adapting to the changing needs of its user community.

In the early decades of synchronic linguistics, I think it was widely taken for granted both that (i) at early stages in the history of a script, provided the script was phonographic at all, there would normally be something close to a one-to-one relationship between letters and phonemes, and that (ii) an ideal orthography *should* be like that: the "phoneme" could almost be defined as the unit of a language which would be assigned a distinct symbol in an ideal orthography for that language. So for instance Daniel Jones wrote in connexion with (i) that "it is natural that in their early attempts at representing their languages by means of an alphabet men should write them phonemically" (Jones 1967: 253);[3] and in connexion with (ii), "It is clear that the best type of spelling is a system based on the principle of one letter for each essential sound" (Jones 1944); "*orthography*, [i.e.] what is needed for ordinary current intercourse in writing...should have the principle 'one letter per phoneme' as its basis" (Jones 1967: 226). Donald Frantz wrote (1978: 308) that "most people engaged in orthography design have accepted the principle of 'one symbol for one phoneme' as an ideal", and he pointed out that the subtitle of Kenneth Pike's standard 1947 textbook on phoneme theory was *A technique for reducing languages to writing* (Pike 1947).

3. The Appendix from which this quotation is taken, "The history and meaning of the term 'phoneme' ", was first published in 1957.

The great flourishing of phonetic science which occurred in Britain in the late nineteenth and early twentieth centuries was partly motivated by the belief that English needed to be given a reformed, phonetically rational orthography. Daniel Jones was both the man who developed and publicized the (originally Polish/Russian) concept of the phoneme as a theoretical entity, and also an active member of the Simplified Spelling Society (Ripman and Archer 1948: 4).

So far as the factual issue, point (i), is concerned, it seems to me that Jones was essentially correct: early orthographies do tend to hug the phonetic ground quite closely. The example I used in my *Writing Systems* book (Sampson 2015a: 114) is Ancient Greek, which had the world's earliest fully alphabetic script. Ancient Greek had quite a lot of predictable morphophonemic variation, so that for instance the last consonant of the root /prāg-/ "do" assimilated to suffixes, yielding forms like the following cases of the perfect passive paradigm:

1st sing.	pε-prāŋ-mai
2nd sing.	pε-prāk-sai
3rd sing.	pε-prāk-tai
2nd pl.	pε-prāk^{h}-t^{h}ε

Although this variation was automatic and lacked semantic significance, it was nevertheless reflected in Greek spelling:

πεπραγμαι
πεπραξαι
πεπρακται
πεπραχθε

This is as if the English words *optic*, *optics*, *optician*, *opticist* were to be spelled < optik, optix, optishan, optisist >.[4]

Greek seems to me to have been rather typical of early phonographic scripts in conforming to the factual point (i). But my main concern in this chapter is with the evaluative issue, point (ii), and there I shall be arguing that Daniel Jones was mistaken.

4. Greek orthography did not reflect the phonetic difference between [ŋ] in the 1st singular form of the example verb and [g] in the unmodified root (e.g. πραγος /prag-os/ "a deed"), but that was because the alphabet inherited from Semitic speakers offered no letter for [ŋ]. Since that sound never occurred in Greek other than through assimilation to a following consonant, no Greek letter was created for it.

Linguisticians have often understood that other considerations come into play which mean that a perfect one-phoneme-one-symbol correspondence is not always the ideal for a practical orthography. But the considerations that people have mainly brought forward are ones of a political or social kind, unrelated to language structure: see e.g. Cahill (2014). For instance, a Third World society whose language is being reduced to writing for the first time might not be happy with an orthography which deviates too much from the norms of whichever First World language is dominant in its region. If the language has a voiceless velar stop phoneme, any linguist would be inclined to write it as < k >. But if the language is spoken in South America, by people in contact with Spanish speakers (who hardly use the letter < k >), then it might be advisable to spell the phoneme as < qu > before front vowels and as < c > in other environments, even though this use of different symbols for the same phoneme is in phonetic terms irrational.

It is also true that from the 1960s onwards, many linguisticians ceased to believe that the phonological units represented in a linguistically ideal orthography should be *phonemes* in particular – because generative linguisticians (notably Morris Halle 1959) argued that, as a theoretical entity, the "phoneme" does not make sense. But that merely led them to propose that ideal orthographies would represent phonological units of a different kind, comparable to what earlier linguisticians had called "morphophonemes". Chomsky and Halle's influential *Sound Pattern of English* (1968) argued that, even in a language whose lexical roots are phonetically realized in a variety of ways in different linguistic contexts (e.g. English *metre* ~ *metric* ~ *telemetry*, with /i/ ~ /e/ ~ /ə/ respectively), native speakers store the roots in their minds in single "underlying" phonological forms and apply rules to derive the appropriate surface forms when the roots are uttered. An ideal orthography would spell out underlying forms, which in some cases would be very different indeed from any of the surface forms which realize them. Famously, Chomsky and Halle argued that the English word *righteous* contains an underlying velar fricative | x |, corresponding to the *gh* of the spelling, even though no English word contains an /x/ sound at the surface.

Keith Snider (2014: 27) notes that this implausible-sounding theory from almost fifty years ago continues to exert a remarkable hold over current thinking. But it is not easy to accept the psychological reality of Chomsky–Hallean "underlying forms", for one thing because they assume an awareness of etymological relationships among derived words which the average native speaker seems unlikely to possess. The classic demonstration of that flimsy assumption, to my mind, came in an article by Noam Chomsky's wife Carol (C. Chomsky 1970), where she described suggesting to a schoolgirl of about 12 that she should consider the word *signature* when deciding how to spell *sign*, only to receive the response "so what's one got to do with the other?" – and then revealed in the same article that she herself, Carol Chomsky, believed the words *prodigious* and *prodigal* to share a common Latin root. (They don't.) If an English-speaker appreciates that the noun *signature* derives from the verb *sign*, it seems more likely that this is because learning the spelling of *sign* showed him the relationship, than because the spoken form *sign* is stored in his mind with an underlying | g | and that is how he knows how to spell the word.

Snider (2014: 43–4) does not advocate reverting to the pre-Chomsky–Halle idea that the linguistically ideal orthography represents phonemes. Instead, he suggests that it should represent a level intermediate between Chomsky–Hallean underlying phonology and the phonemic level, defined in terms of a modern phonological theory called Stratal Optimality Theory which I must confess I do not understand. What is common to all these different points of view, it seems to me – the early idea that an orthography should ideally be phonemic, the Chomsky–Halle idea that it should represent "underlying phonology", and Keith Snider's compromise position – is that they all assume that (apart from political or social considerations having nothing to do with the structure of a language) the only issues determining what makes for a good orthography are purely phonological considerations. I want to say that, on the contrary, lexical distinctiveness is also a highly relevant structural issue.

The first of the two tendencies I identified above as jointly contributing to "lexical distinctiveness" was constancy of shape for lexical elements, even when they have varying phonetic realizations. We have plenty of cases in English: but in English it is usually impossible to tell whether the orthographic constancy results from an abstract desire to have fixed spellings for individual morphemes, or simply from conservatism. The obvious examples are the many vowel alternations produced historically by the Great Vowel Shift, such as the *divine* ~ *divinity*, *metre* ~ *metric* examples already quoted, where the vowels are spelled alike despite being pronounced quite differently in modern English. English orthography developed long before the Great Vowel Shift occurred, so the pairs of forms were naturally spelled alike originally, and the usual explanation for why the spelling has remained the same since the Shift is that English spelling habits were too conservative to adapt to the change in pronunciation. Very likely, for English, that explanation is correct.

But there are other languages and orthographies for which a similar explanation will not work. One case is Korean. This is a language with many morphophonemic alternation rules, which have the effect of creating differences among contextual forms of the same lexical root that seem large, relative to what we find in English or other European languages. A good example is the name of the Yalu River which separates Korea from China: it derives historically from *ʔab-log-gaŋ 鴨綠江 ("duck-green-river") but is actually pronounced /ʔamnoKaŋ/ (/K/ represents a tense unaspirated stop) – every consonant but the first and last is different; and in other contexts the consonants show up in the respective morphemes in their original form, for instance the /l/ of *log "green" remains an /l/ when it follows a vowel.[5]

The phonographic script used for Korean was invented as recently as the fifteenth century, by which time most or all of the relevant sound-laws had already applied to the language. When the script was new, it was used in ways that faithfully reflected the surface phonetics. I have not seen a fifteenth-century inscription of the name Yalu River, and fifteenth-century Korean orthography was less standardized than it later became, but from what I know about it it seems pretty clear that a likely spelling would have been something like < ʔam no Kaŋ >, and the spelling of the "green" morpheme would have varied depending on whether or not it followed a vowel. But the conventions changed, so that modern Korean spelling unpicks the consequences of sound-laws which have produced alternative forms for individual morphemes, and consistently spells them as if those laws had not applied. "Yalu River" is now spelled < ʔab-log-gaʔ >, so that for instance the initial consonant of "green" is written as < l > even though probably a majority of occurrences of that morpheme, including this one, have /n/ as the actually pronounced initial consonant.[6]

This certainly cannot be seen as orthographic conservatism. It is the opposite of conservatism: it was a large change in Korean spelling habits, and its only virtue was to give lexical items constant orthographic shapes despite their varying spoken forms.

5. Like much of the vocabulary of Korean, this name is a loan from Chinese. The English name Yalu is a transliteration of the Mandarin Chinese pronunciation of the first two morphemes, which have undergone many sound-changes within Chinese since they were borrowed into Korean.

6. In modern Korean script, the originally distinct letters < ʔ > and < ŋ > have come to be written identically (and are both represented as < ʔ > here); this creates no ambiguity, because the two sounds are in complementary distribution.

To me it makes good sense that when a society first embarks on the enterprise of recording speech in a phonographic script, and the whole activity is novel and therefore difficult, the instinct would be to hug the phonetic ground closely. "Writing" would seem to *mean* making marks which give as precise as possible a record of the sounds coming out of speakers' mouths. But when reading and writing came to be a familiar, routine component of social life, skilled readers would "read for meaning", and the most efficient way for them to extract an author's meaning from a text would be for the meaningful units of the language to have a constant orthographic form, whether or not their pronunciation was subject to contextual variation. People commonly seem to imagine that if spellings are not *phonetically* rational, the only possible explanation is mindless conservatism (the quotations from Daniel Jones, earlier, suggested that he may have held this point of view). But that is not so. The desire to have constant forms for meaningful units is another kind of rationality, which may sometimes pull in the same direction as simple conservatism, but sometimes pulls in other directions.

The other property contributing to what I call lexical distinctiveness is whether or not words (or other meaningful units of a language) have many close orthographic neighbours – other words which differ by only one letter, or by few letters in a long sequence.

Commonly, linguisticians who think about distinctive spellings are concerned with perfect homophones. Linguisticians frequently suggest that even though it is phonetically irrational that the English /i/ vowel is spelled < ee > in some words and < ea > in others, this does have the advantage of providing distinct written forms such as *meet* and *meat*, or *seem* and *seam*. But the spelling of a word can be distinctive or non-distinctive even if the word has no homophones. Thus, the English syllables /ʃɑk/ and /wɔf/ are alike in representing only one morpheme each, *shark* and *wharf* – there are no homophones of either word. But the spelling *shark* is only one letter away from a number of other English words: *stark*, *spark*, *shirk*, *shank*, *share*, *sharp*, perhaps more; but so far as I can think, it is not possible to turn *wharf* into any other word by changing just one letter. The spelling *wharf* is very distinctive, the spelling *shark* is not very distinctive.

Common sense would suggest that a skilled reader's task of extracting meaning efficiently and rapidly from a written text will be easier, if meaningful elements tend to be written distinctively. And there has been quite a lot of psycholinguistic research showing that that is so. It is harder to read words if they have more orthographic neighbours, particularly when the neighbours are common words. As Manuel Perea and Eva Rosa (2000: 331) put it, "the number of higher frequency neighbors inhibit[s] lexical access in normal reading... [T]his inhibition...could be conceptualized as a competition process among lexical entries".

Note that this effect applies to *normal reading*. In the artificial experimental task of lexical decision, where the subject is presented with a letter-string and has to decide whether or not it is a word of his language – and particularly when the subject is a child – distinctiveness of spelling has the opposite effect: decisions are made more efficiently when words have many orthographic neighbours (e.g. Andoni and Vidal-Abarca 2008). The psycholinguists' findings are complicated, but one plausible way of making sense of them would be to say that, for less-skilled readers, being able to make analogies with the spellings of other words helps them to work out what word a given letter-string might represent, whereas skilled readers well know which words correspond to what letter-strings, and merely need to avoid momentary confusion with similar-looking strings.

Even linguisticians who concede that unphonemic spellings could be advantageous if they allow diversely pronounced allomorphs to appear in a constant visual shape normally see no virtue in a spelling like *foreign*. This English lexical item has no allomorphs, it is always pronounced /fɒrən/ both as an independent word and in derived forms (*foreigner*, *foreignness*), and the < -eign > spelling obviously makes no phonological sense at all. The consensus view is that the spelling was originally just a mistake, which has been preserved because of the dogged reluctance of English-speaking society to rationalize its orthography.[7] But in terms of lexical distinctiveness, *foreign* is a good spelling. It certainly looks very different from any other English word – more distinctive than it would look if it were spelled *foran* or *forain*, in line with its true etymology. The spelling may have originated through a mistaken etymology, but the fact that it has been retained is not necessarily irrational.

I am arguing that orthographies tend to begin phonetically based and move towards lexical distinctiveness. It is easy to find further examples of "beginning phonetically based". Just to quote one example from my recent reading, Joachim Yeshaya (2014: 530) mentions changing spelling conventions in the tradition among Arabic-speaking Jews of writing their native Arabic language in Hebrew letters. Initially, "words were transcribed

7. The history in brief is that *foreign* was so spelled because someone erroneously took it to be related to the word *reign*, which has a < g > because it derives from Latin *rēgnum* (in Latin of course the < g > was pronounced). *Foreign* actually derives via Norman French from Latin *forāneus*, which never had a /g/.

on the basis of phonetic principles, free from the influence of Classical Arabic orthography", though in the course of the tenth century of our era this developed into a system which reflected Classical Arabic spelling conventions.

Unfortunately Yeshaya gives no examples of these conventions, and I do not know enough about Arabic to guess whether the changes he refers to led to greater lexical distinctiveness. As an example of "moving towards lexical distinctiveness" I tentatively offer the changing English spelling of the spoken abbreviation /maɪk/ for *microphone*. For most of the twentieth century this had a well-established spelling *mike*, predictable from the spoken form. But recently I have often encountered the phrase *open mic*, which puzzled me when I first saw it because one would expect < mic > to represent spoken /mɪk/. However, the < mic > spelling improves lexical distinctiveness: it resembles the full form of the word, and it has far fewer orthographic neighbours than < mike > (the only two which occur to me are *mac* and *tic*).

I admit to being hesitant about this example, because I am not sure I am aware of all the facts. (Is there some special reason why *mic* seems to occur only in a phrase following *open*?[8]) And in general it is harder to produce indisputable examples of "moving towards lexical distinctiveness" than of "beginning phonetically based", because it is so often difficult to distinguish distinctiveness-increasing developments from simple conservatism. Korean is unusual in having a phonographic script that was created from scratch in rather recent times, so when spellings were changed to "undo" the effects of morphophonemic variation we can be sure that the motive was not conservatism in any sense. Nevertheless, while many cases are open to alternative interpretations, I believe linguisticians are often too quick to assume that conservatism is the best interpretation.

Nobody suggests – certainly I do not suggest – that a drive towards greater lexical distinctiveness is the *only* factor moulding the evolution of scripts. They are influenced by a mass of factors, many of which are pure historical accidents having no structural rationale of any kind. (Consider for instance the point mentioned in note 4, that early Greek spelling had no special letter for the [ŋ] sound which existed in the language, because the Semitic languages from which the Greeks borrowed the alphabet happened to lack that sound.) But a trend towards greater lexical distinctiveness is one significant factor, I believe, which linguisticians have often overlooked.

8. Since drafting the above, I have encountered one instance of *mic* used other than following *open*.

At this point, sceptical readers may suspect that I am verging on a *reductio ad absurdum*. If the best orthography is one with high lexical distinctiveness, then presumably one could produce a great improvement on traditional English spelling by assigning completely random letter-strings to our vocabulary items. We might spell *cat* as < pfg > and *dog* as < wxxq >. We could certainly reduce the number of near orthographic neighbours for an average word quite substantially that way. And of course we could still ensure that a root like *divin-* was always spelled the same way, whether in context it was pronounced /dɪvaɪn/ as an isolated word or /dɪvɪn/ before *-ity*: we might spell both forms alike as < hpzu >, say. If that would be such a wonderful orthography, how come we never find orthographies like that in real life?

Well, in a way we do. The logographic Chinese script can be seen as approximating a system which assigns to each element of the vocabulary a random distinctive visual form; and it works very well. Chinese graphs, other than the simplest, are not unanalysable Gestalts: most of them are assemblages of simpler components, each of which occurs as part of many other graphs. But that is like the fact that my suggested spelling < pfg > for *cat* is an assemblage of letters drawn from a limited alphabet. The point relevant here is that one cannot normally *predict*, from a knowledge of the sound and meaning of a Chinese word, what its written form will be – just as, in my hypothetical new English orthography, one could not predict that *cat* would be spelled < pfg >.

Consider, for instance, the word /tʃ^{h}yan^2/ "authority", which is written as in Figure 3. Each of the five graphic components is very familiar to literate Chinese, since each occurs in many other graphs. But why the word "authority" should involve that particular array of components is entirely opaque.

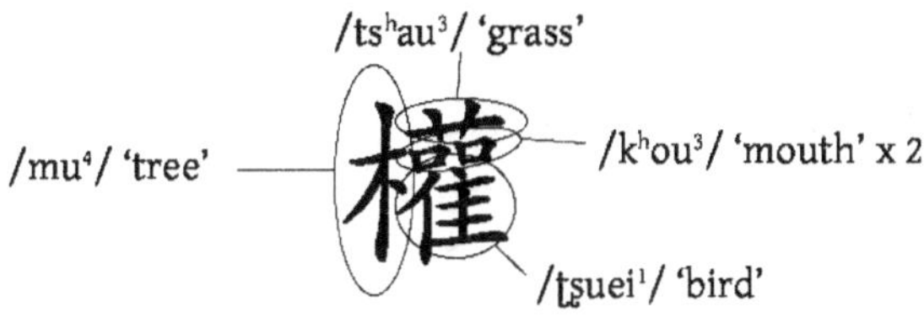

Figure 3

It is true that there was a clear logic in the way that Chinese writing was originally developed (see chapter 9), and as a result most present-day Chinese graphs can be divided into two parts, one of which was originally chosen as an approximation to the pronunciation of the target word while the other part was chosen to reflect the general semantic field within which the meaning of that word was located. Linguisticians such as John DeFrancis who want to believe that no respectable writing system can fundamentally be too different from alphabetic European writing have suggested that this structure makes it unreasonable to think of the Chinese script as assigning arbitrary written forms to words. But the script was developed more than three thousand years ago, and Chinese words have changed both their pronunciations and, in many cases, their meanings a great deal since then, while the script has remained largely stable. Consequently graphs whose structure was logical when they were invented have often lost that logic long ago. The "authority" graph is a good example. The sense "authority" began as a metaphorical extension of a (now long-obsolete) concrete sense referring to the weight on a steelyard; the weight was made of wood, hence the "tree" component was appropriate. The remainder of the graph without that component (all the right-hand side) stood for a word /kuan^4/ "heron" and was originally a picture of a heron, though as the script lost its pictorial character this single graphic unit was resolved into four simpler shapes. When the script was developed, the "heron" graph was phonetically appropriate to write "weight on steelyard", because the pronunciations of the respective words were closer than the present-day pronunciations /kuan^4/, /tʃ^{h}yan^2/ – but for a 21st-century Chinese that issue is irrelevant, since the "heron" word is obsolete (the modern name for the heron is an unrelated word).

This loss of transparency tends to be particularly applicable to higher-frequency words. According to Shu and Wu (2006: 113), of the graphs occurring in school textbooks which began as phonetic/semantic compound graphs, only about seventeen per cent now have a pronunciation matching their "phonetic" element.[9] (I know of no comparable figure for the extent to which semantic elements of compound graphs remain appropriate – the percentage is probably higher, but it is certainly easy to think of graphs whose "semantic" element is wildly at odds with current word-sense.[10]) An additional loss of logical transparency has

9. I surmise that this figure refers to graph-tokens rather than types, though Shu and Wu are not explicit about that.

10. Peng and Jiang (2006: 346) quote research which claimed that the figure for appropriate semantic elements is *lower* than for appropriate phonetic elements. But

occurred since the 1950s within the People's Republic of China, as a result of the replacement of many visually complex graphs by visually simpler alternatives, e.g. /tʃ^{h}yan^{2}/ "authority" is now written 权. The right-hand side of the simplified graph is a word pronounced /jou^{4}/ and meaning "also" – even historically it never had any phonetic or semantic connexion with /tʃ^{h}yan^{2}/ "authority", it is merely a simple shape arbitrarily used as a substitute for various complex graph-components.

As in the case of alphabetic writing, it seems that with Chinese writing transparent graph structure is something that matters to young children, but for skilled readers what matters is distinctiveness of overall graph shape. Zhao et al. (2012) experimented with schoolchildren of different ages identifying graphs having many or few orthographic neighbours, in the sense of shared graph-components, and they found that high neighbourhood density is a positive factor for young children but an inhibiting factor for older children, with the crossover coming about age 11–12 years.

So I do not believe that my hypothetical orthography which spells *cat* as < pfg >, *dog* as < wxxq >, and so forth is a *reductio ad absurdum*. For sure, no real-life language is ever going to adopt an orthography like that, but that is because complex cultural institutions are things that evolve gradually – we just don't throw central aspects of our culture overboard in favour of artificial replacements dreamed up by scientists who assure us that for abstract reasons, hard for most people to understand, they will be more efficient than what we have now. But if, *per impossibile*, the English-speaking world were to abandon our traditional orthography for a *pfg/wxxq*-type spelling system, with higher lexical distinctiveness than current spelling, then the evidence does suggest that for those who became skilled users of the new orthography, it might be more efficient than our familiar system. It just so happens that gradual cultural evolution in China has given them an orthography which is much closer to the *pfg/wxxq* type than any alphabetic script will ever be.

I have the impression that many Western linguisticians feel that it is irrelevant to introduce allusions to Chinese script into discussions of ideal alphabetic orthographies, because they imagine that the Chinese type of script is unreasonably cumbersome and is retained mainly for reasons unrelated to reading and writing efficiency, such as national pride, the need for a unified script in a country with mutually unintelligible regional

both of the figures given by Peng and Jiang are so high that it seems the research must have used some specialized and very lax criterion of appropriateness. (I have not seen the material cited by Peng and Jiang, which was published in China.)

dialects, and so forth. As I see it, that is no more than an ignorant reaction to the unfamiliarity of the Chinese system. (Consider the PISA data quoted on p. 113 above.)

Uncontroversially, moving away from phonetically transparent orthography does have disadvantages. Notably, it makes life harder for learners. There does not seem much doubt that if the script a child is faced with is alphabetic at all, then the learning task is easier if there is a regular, predictable relationship between pronunciations and spellings, with few or no irregularities, as we find with languages such as Spanish or Finnish.

But what is good for literacy-acquiring children is probably not what is good for mature, skilled readers. Discussions of ideal orthographies have given far too much weight to the interests of the child learner, as opposed to those of the skilled reader. That is understandable: we can see the visible struggles our children go through in the process of learning to read, so of course anything that promises to ease those struggles looks attractive. We are not in the same way directly aware of efficiency differentials in the process of skilled reading of diverse orthographies. If such differentials do exist, they can only be inferred indirectly and abstractly, so we take little account of them.

Furthermore, both sets of interests are valid, so an "ideal orthography" ought to represent some kind of trade-off between them, and I cannot imagine any way of calculating what the optimal trade-off would be. Reverting for a moment to my hypothetical *pfg/wxxq* orthography for English: if it were possible to bring about a situation in which this was the standard English orthography, then its additional lexical distinctiveness might make word-recognition and hence the activity of reading a bit more efficient – but surely the gain could only be marginal. On the other hand, it is easy to believe that the additional challenge for young children in learning an entirely arbitrary mapping from vocabulary into letter-strings would be much more than marginal. Learning to read might take significantly longer, consume more teaching resources, and many more children might fall by the wayside than is the case today. If so, on balance society would have lost rather than gained.

But although it seems impossible to know precisely where the ideal balance would fall, what we can say is which direction it has been moving in. When a society is newly literate, almost everyone is a learner, and written documents play only a limited role in the life of the society: making the learner's task easy is worthwhile, while the precise degree of efficiency of the activity of fluent reading is a minor consideration. In advanced modern societies, on the other hand, almost everyone learns to read in early childhood, so that most individuals spend the bulk of their lives as relatively skilled readers, and the role of written material in such societies is much greater than before – so the overall balance of advantage must have shifted towards somewhat greater weight for the skilled reader's interests. Furthermore life expectancy has shot up, so that although it may take as long as it ever did to learn to read, the time spent acquiring literacy has become much shorter as a fraction of the average individual's lifetime. Again this suggests that the skilled reader's interests are now more significant, and the child learner's less so, than in earlier states of society. Lexical distinctiveness matters more than it did; phonetic transparency less.

So we might expect that in an ideal world, orthographies which historically began as perfectly phonemic or nearly so, might have gradually evolved to increase lexical distinctiveness, by spelling roots in constant forms despite sound-laws which create contextual variation in their pronunciations, and by adopting idiosyncratic spellings which might be phonetically illogical, but which have the effect of making words less visually similar than they would be in a perfectly phonemic spelling.

In other words, we might expect the history of an ideal orthography to look rather like the history of English spelling. The many oddities of modern English spelling may well have come about because of factors such as conservative reluctance to adapt to changing pronunciation, or the economics of early-modern printing which paid compositors by the line (and hence gave them an incentive to spell words with extra letters), or various other "irrational" considerations. But those who over the centuries shaped the English spelling system were working better than they could have known. The fact that we have retained this odd system, despite advocacy by such as Bernard Shaw and the Simplified Spelling Society for a more regular orthography, may be a wise response (though not a consciously planned response) to modern social conditions.

The topic of this chapter concerns an issue – literacy – of considerable practical social significance, and it seems that longstanding assumptions in this area may be wrong. Investigations of this kind are very much, surely, what society should expect from scholars interested in the nature of language. Yet the scientism of linguistics has systematically diverted most linguisticians' attention away from them.

Chapter 9

The Reality of Compound Ideographs*

Scientism is about asserting that precise laws constrain diversity among phenomena which, in reality, are not governed by laws. An odd example of this is found in Western linguisticians' ideas about the origins of the complex Chinese script.

If one asks about the process through which Chinese script emerged from simple beginnings, we currently face a surprising situation: the nature of the answer received is likely to depend on where the question is put. A Chinese scholar will usually frame his answer broadly in line with the classification of graph-formation principles into "six writings" in the preface to the dictionary *Shuo Wen Jie Zi* 說文解字 (compiled by Xu Shen 許慎 about AD 100). A 21st-century Western academic with a general interest in writing systems but no special knowledge of Chinese epigraphy is more likely to cite the account by William Boltz (1994). These sources are in an important respect contradictory. Our aim here is to argue that, although Xu Shen certainly got some things wrong (which is in part explained by his lack of access to data that first came to light in the past hundred years), with respect to the contradiction just mentioned the Chinese tradition stemming from his dictionary is essentially correct, and Boltz essentially mistaken.

The contradiction relates to the extent to which the creators of Chinese script relied on phonetic principles when they went beyond drawing simple pictures to represent "picturable" words by combining two or more simple graphs into compound graphs for less readily picturable words.

For Xu Shen, *xing sheng* 形聲 graphs – literally, "form–sound"; we shall call them phonetic–semantic compounds – in which one part represents a homophone or near-homophone of the target word while the other part gives a clue to its meaning, were one very important category of

* This chapter is co-authored with Chen Zhiqun 陳志群 of Monash University.

compound graph, but not the only category. There were also *hui yi* 會意 graphs – "compound ideographs" – which indicate the meaning of a word by linking simpler graphs, each of which relates to the target word semantically rather than phonetically.

For Boltz there are essentially no such things as "compound ideographs"; all Chinese graphs which are not simple pictographs are phonetic–semantic compounds. In saying this, Boltz associates himself with the Eurocentric tradition of maximizing the role of a phonetic principle in all writing systems. Sometimes, Boltz claims, the phonetic–semantic status of a graph is concealed from us by the fact that a simple graph originally had alternative readings (i.e. the same graph was used to write different words), and the reading which motivated its role as the phonetic half of a phonetic–semantic compound happened to become obsolete. Thus for instance the word 安 *ān* "peace" is explained by Xu Shen as a compound ideograph: "woman" below "roof" suggests "tranquil, peaceful". Perhaps the connexion of ideas may strike us as a little tenuous, but *prima facie* there seems no alternative possibility of explaining 安 as a phonetic–semantic compound: neither in modern Mandarin nor in their reconstructed Old Chinese pronunciations does 女, "woman", as a simple graph sound anything like 安 (and the same is true of the "roof" element 宀, though this in any case has scarcely existed in historical times as an independent word). However, Boltz says that alongside the usual reading *nǚ* for 女 "we can speculate that it had a second reading that must have been approximately **ʔ(r)an*, in which it functioned as a phonetic in [安 and three other graphs all containing the 女 element]" (Boltz 1994: 108).[1]

Boltz summarizes his position by saying (1994: 149):

> the evolution of the Chinese writing system does not, in our view, allow for compound characters that do not have a phonophoric element within their graphic structure… We may not be able to identify it, but that is a limitation of our own knowledge…not a sign that our phonetic principle is invalid.

1. In this chapter asterisks are used to mark postulated reconstructions of forms from an ancestor-language. (That was the original use of the symbol in linguistics, before it was used for "impossible forms".) There are many uncertainties about the phonology of Old Chinese, and different scholars reconstruct wordforms in different ways; but what matters here is that no-one supposes that *ān* "peace" and *nǚ* "woman" ever sounded similar. In the system of Baxter (1992), these words had the Old Chinese forms **ʔan*, **nrjaʔ* respectively. (Boltz offers a more idiosyncratic reconstruction for the Old Chinese reflex of *nǚ*, details of which are not relevant here.) Except where otherwise stated, reconstructed forms will be shown in Baxter's (1992) system.

Boltz sees it as a law that the creation of compound graphs must involve a phonetic principle.

In arguing this way, Boltz is reviving one side of a controversy of the 1930s about the nature of Chinese script between the Western scholars H. G. Creel and Peter Boodberg (Creel 1936; Boodberg 1937; Creel 1939; Boodberg 1940). Creel argued that the script was purely "ideographic"; indeed he seems to have believed that, as used in the Classical period, it did not represent utterances of a spoken language at all (Creel 1936: 125). Boodberg by contrast held that all complex Chinese graphs were phonetically motivated. Boltz arguably takes Boodberg's point of view even further by suggesting (e.g. 1994: 14) that the script was in some sense "trying" to develop into a "normal", phonetically based script (the words in scare quotes are ours rather than Boltz's), but that this evolution was regrettably arrested before it proceeded to completion.

Both of these accounts of Chinese writing seem misguided. In Creel's case it is not necessary to argue this at length, because probably no knowledgeable scholar would support his account today. Suffice it to say that we do believe that written Chinese was created as a system for recording utterances of the contemporary spoken Chinese language. It is uncontroversial that, as the grammar and vocabulary of Chinese evolved towards those of modern *bai hua* 白話 (colloquial speech), the written language for many centuries failed to keep pace, so that the *wen yan* 文言 (literary language) of modern times has lost touch with the spoken language and is not even comprehensible if read aloud. But to say that written and spoken languages gradually diverged after the creation of the former is very different from saying that the written language was not originally based on the spoken language.

Boodberg's general point of view, on the other hand, is very much alive among Western scholars today. Boltz (1994: vii) is explicit about his intellectual debt to Boodberg. We saw in chapter 8 that other scholars, including John DeFrancis and Sir Jack Goody, have independently expressed extreme claims about the necessity of a central role for a phonetic principle in any writing system sophisticated enough to merit the name. And Boltz's version of what we might call "script phonocentrism" has been widely received among Western readers. Boltz's book was published in 1994, and reprinted only nine years later – for a book on a relatively arcane topic this represents considerable success. Other writers quote Boltz's view, often as though it constitutes established fact rather than a controversial hypothesis (see for instance Keightley 1989: 190–1; DeFrancis 1989: 100, both quoting Boltz 1986). Boltz was selected to contribute the chapter on "Language and writing" to the standard reference work on early Chinese history, Loewe and Shaughnessy (1998). Some contributors to Houston (2004) are more cautious about Boltz's script phonocentrism; but all in all it would be very easy at the beginning of the 21st century for a non-specialist reader of the Western literature to take Boltz's view as a solidly established consensus position. We know of no-one before ourselves who has explicitly spelled out the fallacies in Boltz's argument.

It is perhaps natural for Western scholars, whose native languages are all written alphabetically, to assume that a script adequate for comprehensively recording the utterances of a spoken language must necessarily be based on a phonetic principle. However, the necessity here is not logical (one can certainly *imagine* a script devised without any reference to pronunciations, as on p. 125 above, though such a script might well not be practical to learn); and, in the extreme form in which Boodberg and Boltz express it, we do not believe that the assumption is true of Chinese script. This script did make heavy use of a phonetic principle in creating written forms for words, but alternative principles were also at work: "compound ideographs" were devised independently of phonetics. Although Keightley, citing Boltz, writes (loc. cit.) that "recent research" has called the "compound ideograph" category into question, we shall see that Boltz's rejection of the category has very little to do with empirical research. It is based mainly on aprioristic assumptions about what "must" necessarily be the case, and we find those assumptions unpersuasive. The evolution of scripts is not a law-governed process.

Our own understanding of the early history of Chinese script runs as follows. Initially, a number of words were assigned simple pictographs, ranging from concrete depictions of physical objects, e.g. (now written 鳥) for *niǎo* "bird", to more abstract indications of non-physical concepts, e.g.  (now 下) for *xià* "below". Then other words were given graphs in various ways.

Simple graphs were used not just for the word for which they had been invented, but also for homophones or near-homophones having unrelated meanings. The resulting high degree of ambiguity was in due course alleviated, in many but not all cases, by adding semantic determiners to distinguish (near-)homophones written with the same basic graph. Thus we find e.g. (now 眉) used for *méi* "eyebrow"; with the addition of 氵 "water", 湄 represented a homophone *méi* "brink of a stream"; with the addition of 女 "woman", 媚 represented *mèi* "attractive, seductive"; and so on; but the basic graph 眉 without semantic determiner was used for *wěi* "indefatigable" (which in Old Chinese began with *mw-*) as well as for *méi* "eyebrow", the word which originally motivated the graph shape.

At the same time, other words were assigned compound graphs in which each element was chosen for its meaning rather than its sound. For instance *wǔ* "military" was written as 武 (now 武), a combination of the elements now written 戈 *gē*, an archaic weapon commonly called in English "dagger-axe", and 止 *zhǐ* "foot, walk". Graphs like 武 are the *hui yi* or compound ideographs. Note that 武 was never a single, complex picture of a soldier marching with a weapon: the soldier was not depicted, rather the graph consisted of two separate pictures, representing a word whose meaning has to do with weapons and also has to do with marching.

Xu Shen's account of the "six writings" is certainly open to criticisms of detail. It would be remarkable if he did not get some things wrong, considering that the earliest form of Chinese script of which he made extensive use was the "small seal" script of the Late Zhou–Qin period (mid- to late first millennium BC), which was already a highly evolved system. Examples of the much older "oracle bone" script only began to come to light about a hundred years ago, and the stylization and simplification of graphic elements that occurred between oracle bone and seal style scripts was quite enough to obscure many aspects of the logic of individual graphs. Nevertheless, Xu Shen offered a classification of graph-formation principles which corresponds reasonably well to our account above. Two of Xu Shen's categories, *xiang xing* 象形 "iconic form" and *zhi shi* 指事 "conceptual indication", covered the simple pictographs, with the former standing for concrete pictures and the latter for more abstract forms such as 丅 for "below". We might object that concrete v. abstract is a cline rather than a sharp two-way distinction; Xu Shen does not seem to have recognized the possibility of clines, but his two categories function to indicate the two ends of a spectrum along which simple pictographs can be placed. Xu Shen's *jia jie* 假借 "borrowing" category covers graphs used for (near-)homophones of the words which motivated the graph shape, where no semantic determiner was later added (e.g. 肙 used for *wěi* "indefatigable"); and his *xing sheng* "form–sound" category covers the many cases where a semantic determiner was added, yielding a phonetic–semantic compound. Xu Shen's category *hui yi*, "compound ideograph", as we have seen, covered compound graphs such as 武 "military" in which the elements were semantic + semantic rather than phonetic + semantic.[2]

2. The graph 武 "military" is our example of an S + S compound, not an example Xu Shen uses in his preface to define this category. In the body of his dictionary, Xu Shen explains the graph 武 by quoting an implausible "folk etymology" attributed to a past king of the state of Chu; we are not obliged to take that seriously.

Xu Shen did have one further category, *zhuan zhu* 轉注 ("expressing by reciprocation"), which would have been better omitted from his list: he seems to have supposed that words for near-synonyms were sometimes created by making small arbitrary changes to a simple graph shape. But he offered only one pair of examples, 老 *lǎo* and 考 *kǎo*, both of which originally meant "old".[3] Even now that we have access to the oracle-bone forms of these graphs, the logic of their shapes is not apparent, so there can be little reason to claim that one was formed by making a change to the other (rather than the two graphs having been devised independently). Xu Shen never uses the term "expressing by reciprocation" in the body of his dictionary, after the preface where it is defined (whereas he often describes graphs as phonetic–semantic compounds or as compound ideographs). It appears that the only reason why Xu Shen's preface discussed graph-formation in terms of "six writings" rather than "five writings" (excluding *zhuan zhu*, "expressing by reciprocation") was out of undue deference to Liu Xin 劉歆 (died AD 23), editor of the classic work *Zhou Li* 周禮, who glossed the term "six writings" as it appears in that work via a list (without examples) of six categories including *zhuan zhu*. (In context it is not clear that the original author of the *Zhou Li* was referring to methods of constructing graphs at all.)

Apart from the redundant "expressing by reciprocation" category, one can pick holes in a number of the specific examples Xu Shen chose to illustrate his other categories. For instance, one of the examples for "compound ideograph" in Xu Shen's preface is 信 *xìn* "to believe, trust": apparently Xu Shen thought that the logic of combining the graphs 人 for "man" with 言 for "speech" was that what a man says ought to be trustworthy. This is obviously far-fetched, and in fact the graph is probably a phonetic–semantic compound. One could not guess that from the present-day pronunciation of the relevant words, and perhaps not from the pronunciations of Xu Shen's day; but Baxter (1992) reconstructs *xìn* as reflecting an Old Chinese **snjins*, making 人 *rén* < **njin* "man" a reasonable phonetic match.

This last case, then, is a case where what was taken to be a compound ideograph should probably, in the light of current knowledge, be recategorized as a phonetic–semantic compound. If *all* apparent compound ideographs were subject to similar recategorization, of course, Boltz's account of Chinese script would be correct. But the fact that Xu Shen,

3. The sense "examine" for *kǎo*, the usual sense of the word in modern Chinese, seems to have begun as a *jia jie* use of the graph for a homophone of *kǎo* "old".

through lack of adequate data, made a mistake about one such graph (and, unfortunately, chose it as one of his two illustrations of the compound-ideograph category in his preface) does not imply that other apparent compound ideographs are not genuine semantic + semantic compounds.

In the case of 武 *wŭ* "military", for instance, we have no reason to doubt that the logic of its construction is as described above; and there are other reasonably clear cases. For instance, 鮮 *xiān* "fresh (as of food)" was and is a clear combination of 魚 *yú* "fish" with 羊 *yáng* "sheep": fish and mutton are two kinds of food that need to be eaten fresh. (Karlgren 1957: 72 cites passages from early texts where the word referred specifically to fresh meat or fish.) The graph 𨑃 (now 農) *nóng* "agriculture" originally consisted of 田 *tián* "field" and a picture of a plough (now 辰 *chén*, and now used exclusively, presumably as a result of *jia jie* borrowing, as one of the cyclical graphs used to identify days, years, etc. in the Chinese calendar). The field is shown *above* the plough, so this cannot be seen as a single picture of a field being ploughed – it is a complex graph for a word whose meaning has to do with fields and also has to do with ploughs.[4]

Note that, in all these cases, 武, 鮮, 農, there seems to be no phonetic resemblance (either now or in reconstructed Old Chinese pronunciations) between the words represented by the complete graphs, and those represented by their constituent parts. (Of course, a "speculation" that e.g. 魚 "fish", normally *yú* < **ng(r)ja*, once had some alternative reading similar to *xiān* < **sjen* would be unrefutable.)

The number of clear compound-ideograph cases is not huge, and has often been exaggerated. Some writers tend to apply the compound-ideograph category to any graph containing separate elements not related in a phonetic–semantic fashion, so e.g. 東 *dōng* "east", if (as commonly supposed) it shows 日 the sun behind 木 a tree, might be called a compound ideograph. Xu Shen himself did this; e.g. he calls 圂 *huàn* "pigsty" a compound ideograph, because 豕 "pig" and 囗 "enclosure" exist as separate graphs. We would prefer to see graphs like 東 or 圂 as single pictures each comprising two elements. Assuming that 東 did originate as a combination of the graphs 日 and 木, its meaning is not "something to do with the sun and also something to do with trees", it is the direction (or at any rate one of the two directions) in which one can

4. An alternative form for *nóng*, attested earlier, had two tree or plant symbols in place of "field"; this might also be counted as a compound-ideograph combination, but our point here is that the variant which gave rise to the later standard graph certainly was one.

see the sun behind trees.[5] Likewise, 圂 is a single picture of an enclosure containing a pig.

On the other hand, there are so many uncertainties about early Chinese graph-forms that the compound-ideograph principle could well have applied to more cases than can now be recognized confidently. Often, even when a word is written by what appears to be a simple pictograph, despite knowing the meaning of the word we cannot recognize the picture; so quite naturally when a word is written by a set of elements we are often unclear about the logic behind the grouping. The graph 罰 *fá* "punish" in both modern and early forms shows "net" + "speak" + "knife"; it might be tempting to speculate that criminals when caught were held in nets and that after a verdict was spoken they were typically punished by mutilation with a knife – but that is pure guesswork, so the graph may or may not be an example of a compound ideograph.

In the case of phonetic–semantic compounds, the pronunciation of the phonetic half is usually known and the semantic half is almost always drawn from a smallish set of standard semantic determiners, so that the status of the combination as an example of the phonetic–semantic category is obvious. If we count graphs belonging to Xu Shen's various categories, we are not likely to miss many cases of phonetic–semantic compounds, whereas we might easily miss cases of compound ideographs. Nevertheless, there are sufficiently many compound-ideograph cases whose logic remains relatively clear today to establish the reality of this category.

Indeed, although the P + S structure eventually became by far the most fertile mechanism for coining graphs, so that a large majority of all present-day Chinese graphs are of this type, there is some evidence that in the early stages of script evolution the compound ideograph principle played proportionally a greater role than it did later. Li Xiaoding 李孝定 (1986) claimed that the proportion of compound ideographs in the then-deciphered oracle-bone inscriptions was as high as one in three, while the corresponding proportion in the *Shuo Wen* was only one in eight or nine. (We do not press this point, because it is not clear that the respective counts were carried out in a manner guaranteeing comparability with one

5. It may be that 東 did not originate as a combination of 日 and 木. Oracle-bone forms of 日 standardly show the central bar short, separated by space at either end from the enclosing circle, while forms of 東 consistently show the corresponding bar as extending fully from side to side. Our point here, though, is that even if the origin of the graph were as usually supposed, it ought not to be counted as an example of a compound ideograph.

another or with our understanding of the "compound ideograph" concept.) Bottéro (2004: 253) states that the very earliest extant inscriptions contain compound ideographs but no phonetic–semantic compounds at all.

For Boltz's mentor Boodberg, it seemed that the main reason to disbelieve in compound ideographs was that for some reason he found the concept simply too absurd to take seriously. Discussing the graph 明 *míng* "bright", which in its modern form displays sun 日 and moon 月 side by side and to non-experts looks like one of the most obvious examples of a compound ideograph, Boodberg (1940: 270–1) suggested that people who believe in compound ideographs

> imagine the composition of the character…somewhat as follows: "The Chinese creators of the script said to themselves: 'How shall we write "bright"? Now the sun is "bright" and the moon is "bright". We shall put the pictures of the moon and the sun together, and that shall represent the "idea" of "bright". Henceforth we should endeavour not to "call" this "ideogram" *sun*, or *moon*, or *sun-moon*, but "bright".' "
>
> The obvious questions that immediately occur to anyone with linguistic sense [include]:…would not the "ideogram" be confused with a picture of the conjunction of the sun and moon?…lost in the contemplation of his little icon representing the "idea" of "brightness", [the believer in compound ideographs] only shrugs his shoulders at the irreverent questioner.

Now in this particular case it may well be that 明 did not in fact originate via a *hui yi* linking of the concept "bright" with the concepts "sun" and "moon", because (as Boodberg knew) the word has an alternative form 朙, and the usual modern form 明 including a "sun" element probably arose as a graphic simplification of that form.[6] But in the passage quoted, Boodberg is claiming that even if the original form had consisted of sun + moon, it would be ridiculous to suppose that the graph for *míng* "bright" could have been invented by linking the meanings of "sun" and "moon" to that of "bright".

We see nothing ridiculous here. Boodberg's objection that the graph might be seen not as the word for "bright" but as "a picture of the

6. This would not necessarily mean that the graph did not have a compound-ideograph origin. The left-hand side of 朙 did not survive as an independent graph into later Chinese, but it is claimed to have been a pictograph for "window", with a pronunciation beginning with *k*- ; so it would not have been a suitable phonetic for *míng* "bright", whereas "window + moon" is perhaps almost as plausible as "sun + moon" to hint at the meaning "bright".

conjunction of the sun and moon" is a non-issue: someone who reads a written document is looking to translate its elements into words, not into pictures of the natural world (and as a matter of fact, in Nature one never does see sun and moon adjacent in the sky). In any case, since for centuries many people have indeed believed that the graph 明 was motivated by the semantic relationship between "bright", "sun", and "moon", how can that belief be *self-evidently* false? If it is in fact false, that would need to be demonstrated by empirical argument, not mere mockery.[7]

Boodberg's other "obvious questions", omitted from the displayed quotation above, related to possible etymological links between spoken Chinese words for "bright", "sun", and "moon", which might explain the graph 明 without appeal to the semantic relationships. He argued (pp. 272–3) that the graph 日 "sun", in Mandarin *rì* reflecting an Old Chinese form **njit*, may have had an alternative reading **bdang*, and in that reading may have functioned as phonetic element in 明 as a phonetic–semantic compound graph. We do not attempt to reproduce the steps of this argument (which we find quite obscure); we do not in any case understand why a hypothetical pronunciation **bdang* would have made 日 a suitable phonetic for a word which has always begun with an *m* sound – Boodberg offered nothing at all to bridge this gap in his argument. We wonder whether this aspect of Boodberg's discussion has ever been accorded much weight: it appears to us that the force of his exposition derived much more from his scornful rejection of the "compound ideograph" concept as untenable *a priori*. But, as already said, despite the vigour of its expression we find that aspect of Boodberg's discussion entirely unpersuasive.

Boltz's more recent attempts to reduce apparent compound ideographs to phonetic–semantic compounds do not, at least at first sight, share the *ad hoc* quality of Boodberg's discussion of 明 *míng*. We saw that, alongside the normal reading *nǚ* for 女 "woman", Boltz postulated a second, obsolete and previously unknown Old Chinese reading **ʔ(r)an* to explain how the graph could serve as phonetic element within 安 *ān* "peace" as a phonetic–semantic compound. (Boltz explains "roof" as the semantic determiner by claiming that the early sense of *ān* was something like "settled", a point which for the sake of argument we shall not challenge.) But for Boltz this

7. It has been pointed out (e.g. Tranter 2001: 194) that, whether or not the compound-ideograph system was used in the development of Chinese script, it certainly was used in the development of some other scripts, e.g. the Sumerian.

hypothetical reading is not linked just to the single graph 安. He cites a series of graphs all containing the 女 “woman” element and having similar pronunciations (Boltz 1994: 107):[8]

安 *ān* < *ʔan, “settled”
妟 *yàn* < *ʔrans, “tranquil”
奻 *nàn* < *nrans, also read *nuán* < *nruan, “to quarrel”
姦 *jiān* < *kran, “licentious”

Now in principle this could be a good argument for interpreting these graphs as phonetic–semantic compounds. Where a series of complex graphs both share some particular graphic component, and resemble one another in pronunciation, unless we are prepared to treat these common features as chance coincidences the obvious explanation will be that the graphs form a phonetic series, comparable to the many series listed in Bernhard Karlgren’s *Grammata Serica Recensa*. The common graphic component will be the phonetic element, and the varying remainders will be contrasting semantic determiners.

However, this particular set of graphs would be a very strange phonetic series.

In the first place, the Old Chinese pronunciations as Boltz reconstructs them are not all that similar. Is there any non-controversial phonetic series in which some words begin with glottal stop, other(s) with *n*-, and other(s) again with *k*- ?[9]

But also: the graph 妟 is very rare – the twentieth-century dictionary–encyclopaedia *Ci Hai* 辭海 quotes a single occurrence in (some editions of) the *Book of Odes*, which we have not succeeded in locating in the editions available to us. Karlgren (1957) has a graph-series (no. 253) in which 妟 acts as phonetic, but from what *Ci Hai* says about this graph we

8. We replace Boltz’s Wade–Giles transcriptions of modern pronunciations with their *pinyin* equivalents; otherwise the information here is as given by Boltz, with Boltz’s Old Chinese forms.

9. At one point (1994: 93) Boltz claims that we know so little about Old Chinese initial consonants and consonant-clusters that we can never be justified in rejecting a proposed phonetic series because the initials are too dissimilar. In saying this he sets himself against all the leading authorities on Old Chinese phonology; Bernhard Karlgren, Li Fang-Kuei 李方桂, William Baxter, Axel Schuessler, and others routinely use apparent phonetic–semantic graph-series to offer reconstructions of Old Chinese initials, and their systems, while differing in some details, are sufficiently similar and linguistically plausible to have been broadly accepted by the research community. If Boltz’s claim were correct, this research would be worthless.

take it to have originated as an occasional reduced variant of the standard graph 晏 *yàn* "clear sky, peaceful". (Boltz quotes the latter graph on his p. 95 with the same modern and Old Chinese pronunciations as he gives on p. 107 for 旻.) If 旻 is a reduced form of 晏, then its phonetic similarity to 安 is no argument for 女 functioning with a non-standard pronunciation as phonetic element in both graphs: 安 as a whole would be the phonetic element within (the original form of) 旻.

The other two graphs in Boltz's list, 奻 and 姦, would be peculiar phonetic-semantic compounds even if we accepted that 女 could function as a phonetic pronounced **ʔ(r)an*, because the remaining parts of the graphs are respectively one and two copies of that same simple graph 女. (Incidentally, the graph 奻 seems to be purely a "dictionary word", listed in Xu Shen's dictionary but never having been sufficiently current for inclusion in the *Ci Hai*; we accept for the sake of argument that the word did exist.) Normally, a graph with a P + S structure represents a word which sounds like the word P, and has a meaning related to that of the word S. If P and S were identical, the word indicated by the whole should logically be the same word which functioned as both P and S, so that there would be no point in using the complex graph. Certainly we know of no uncontroversial phonetic–semantic compound graphs where phonetic and semantic elements are identical.

It seems much easier to understand a graph comprising many "woman" elements as indicating, by virtue of the meaning "woman", independently of pronunciation, a target sense such as "womanizing, adulterous, licentious".[10] And, if there was a word *nàn* or *nuán* meaning "quarrel", we do not find it difficult to believe that politically incorrect inhabitants of a polygamous society might have seen two "woman" symbols as a suitable way to suggest that sense; again this is more reasonable than treating one "woman" as phonetic and the other as semantic determiner (which would in any case imply a recognized link between the concepts "woman" and "quarrel").

To sum up: although Boltz tries to establish the plausibility of his reanalysis of 安 *ān* "peace", as a phonetic–semantic compound which used an obsolete reading of 女 as phonetic, by offering a series of other graphs in which the same 女 element allegedly functions in the same way,

10. Whether the graph, interpreted this way, should be categorized as a compound ideograph or as an abstract "conceptual indication" graph would be a matter of definition; the boundary between these two categories also seems blurry, though we have seen that Xu Shen did not deal in blurry distinctions. Our point here is that we see no temptation to categorize the graph as a phonetic–semantic compound.

when that series is examined the plausibility melts away. And, if 安 *ān* is considered in isolation, the hypothesis of a hitherto-unknown reading in *-an* for 女 can be seen to be purely *ad hoc*, invented to shore up the claim that apparent compound ideographs are really phonetic–semantic compounds, and having no independent justification.

We shall not go through the various other novel "phonetic series" which Boltz (1994) proposes in the attempt to explain away apparent *hui yi* combinations, but we do not find them more persuasive than the series he constructs to explain 安.

One can make any scientific theory seem to work, if one is willing to make sufficiently many special assumptions. If someone believes that the Earth is flat, it is easy to refute him by pointing to the mast and then the hull of an approaching ship gradually emerging over the horizon. But a believer in a flat Earth might respond by postulating some novel physical force which gradually deflects light rays towards the Earth's surface: that would create the same appearance for an observer. If there were good independent reasons for recognizing the reality of this force, then we might have to take the flat-Earth theory seriously. But if the flat-Earth defender says "There must be such a force, because otherwise the Earth could not be flat", we recognize that the novel force is just an *ad hoc* device postulated in order to try to rescue a doomed theory.

The many novel readings for familiar graphs, such as **bdang* for 日 or **ʔ(r)an* for 女, postulated by Boodberg and Boltz in order to reinterpret apparent compound ideographs as phonetic–semantic compounds are like the alleged force which deflects light. Chinese graphs do sometimes have multiple readings, and if the readings postulated by Boodberg and by Boltz were independently justified, their arguments might have weight. But in reality these novel readings are motivated only by the wish to rescue the claim that there are no compound ideographs in Chinese script.

We should accept that, as Xu Shen told us two millennia ago, diverse principles were at work in the evolution of Chinese writing. The principle which ended by accounting for the largest share of the modern dictionary was, certainly, a phonetic principle. But there were other mechanisms, having no parallel in European writing systems, which also played an important part. There is no universal law according to which all scripts must originally be based on phonetic principles.

III

Language Complexity

For much of the twentieth century, linguistics was strongly attached to a principle of invariance of language complexity *as one of its bedrock beliefs – and not just the kind of belief that lurks as a tacit assumption in the background, so that researchers are barely conscious of it, but a claim that linguisticians were very given to insisting on explicitly. The first thing to say about this is that, if the claim were true, it certainly would go a considerable way to establish the scientific status of linguistics. A statement "For any human language, its total complexity is always such-and-such" – or even the slightly weaker but more plausible version, "…its total complexity is always within this-or-that per cent of such-and-such" – draws a clear boundary round a range of possibilities and asserts that nothing outside that range will be observed. No language will be found to deviate (or deviate by more than the stated percentage) from the value specified. Any such statement would raise an obvious question about how complexity is measured (an issue to be discussed in chapter 11), but if that question could be answered and the claim survived testing, it would be a discovery akin to that of the constants known to physicists.*

On the other hand, linguisticians never seemed to offer much justification for their claim. They appeared to believe it because they wanted to believe it, much more than because they had reasons for believing it.

Then, quite suddenly at the beginning of the new century, a range of researchers began challenging the assumption. I mentioned in chapter 1 the workshop I initiated at Leipzig in 2007, which led to the book Sampson, Gil, and Trudgill (2009). Another important book, which beat ours into print (though at Leipzig I was not yet aware of it), was Miestamo et al. (2008), which emerged from a workshop in Helsinki. Initially almost all questioning of the equal-complexity axiom had come from Europeans, but soon the same ideas were taken up in North America. And suddenly rejecting that axiom, a move which for decades had ranked as heresy, was accepted as a perfectly reasonable thing to do. Another workshop on the topic was held in Seattle in 2012, and the editors of the book which emanated from Seattle commented that "linguists of all stripes are increasingly willing to entertain the idea that one language might indeed be simpler or more complex than another" (Newmeyer and Preston 2014: 7).

Linguisticians and non-linguisticians alike agree in seeing human language as the clearest mirror we have of the activities of the human mind, and as a specially important component of human culture, because it underpins most of the other components. Thus, if there is serious disagreement about whether language complexity is a universal constant or an evolving variable, that is surely a question which merits careful scrutiny. In chapter 10 I scrutinize the equal-complexity issue via a version of the keynote talk I gave at Leipzig, and in chapter 11 I deal with an interesting objection to my point of view.

Chapter 10

A LINGUISTIC AXIOM CHALLENGED

When I first studied linguistics, in the early 1960s, the mainstream subject as my fellow undergraduates and I encountered it was the "descriptivist" tradition that had been inaugurated early in the twentieth century by Franz Boas and Leonard Bloomfield. It was exemplified by the papers collected in Martin Joos's anthology *Readings in Linguistics*, which contained Joos's often-quoted summary of that tradition as holding "that languages can differ from each other without limit and in unpredictable ways" (Joos 1957: 96).

Many fundamental assumptions about language changed completely as between the descriptive linguistics of the first two-thirds of the twentieth century, and the generative linguistics which became influential from the mid-1960s onwards. For the descriptivists, languages were part of human cultures; for the generativists, language is part of human biology. The descriptivists thought that languages could differ from one another in any and every way, as Martin Joos said; the generativists see human beings as all speaking essentially the same language (p. 57). But the invariance of language complexity is an exception: this assumption is common to both descriptivists and generativists.

The clearest statement that I have found is the passage from Charles Hockett's influential 1958 textbook *A Course in Modern Linguistics* which I quoted briefly in chapter 1:

> ...impressionistically it would seem that the total grammatical complexity of any language, counting both morphology and syntax, is about the same as that of any other. This is not surprising, since all languages have about equally complex jobs to do, and what is not done morphologically has to be done syntactically. Fox, with a more complex morphology than English, thus ought to have a somewhat simpler syntax; and this is the case. (Hockett 1958: 180–1)

Although Hockett used the word "impressionistically" to avoid seeming to claim that he could pin precise figures on the language features he was quantifying, notice how strong his claim is. Like Joos, Hockett believed that languages could differ extensively with respect to particular subsystems: e.g. Fox (an American Indian language) has complex morphology, English has simple morphology. But when one adds together the complexity derived from the separate subsystems, and if one can find some way to replace "impressions" with concrete numbers, Hockett's claim is that the overall total will always come out about the same.

Hockett justified his claim by saying that "languages have about equally complex jobs to do", but it is very difficult to define the job which grammar does in a way that is specific enough to imply any particular prediction about grammatical complexity. Hockett's remark seems to assume that the job done by a human language is in some sense definable without reference to the properties of the language, which is surely at least questionable – one might alternatively feel that a language defines the range of tasks it is capable of executing, and that many of those tasks could not be identified independently of linguistic structure. And a one-line comparison between just two languages is clearly very thin evidence indeed on which to establish a profound axiom about relationships among all the world's languages. It is vulnerable to any pair of languages in which morphological and syntactic complexity differences pull in the same direction rather than balancing each other. A Hungarian linguistician, Ilona Koutny, commented in a discussion of this topic that her native language has more complex morphology than English and a syntax which is at least no simpler than that of English. That brief observation is already enough to counterbalance Hockett's claim, and I believe similar remarks could be made about very many language-pairs. John McWhorter (2001) has argued that creole languages as a class possess "the world's simplest grammars". One can debate that, as a number of linguisticians have done, but McWhorter's generalization was at least backed up with a great deal more concrete evidence than Hockett gave in his comparison of Fox and English.

If it really were so that languages varied greatly in the complexity of subsystem *X*, varied greatly in the complexity of subsystem *Y*, and so on, yet for all languages the totals from the separate subsystems added together could be shown to come out the same, then I would not agree with Hockett in finding this unsurprising. To me it would feel almost like magic. It would certainly lend considerable substance to the claim of general linguistics to be a science, if it were true. But is it true?

At an intuitive level it is hard to accept that the totals do always come out roughly the same. Consider for instance Archi, spoken by a thousand people in one village 7500 feet above sea level in the Caucasus. According to Aleksandr Kibrik (1998), an Archi verb can inflect into any of about 1.5 million contrasting forms. English is said to be simple morphologically but more complex syntactically than some languages; but how much syntactic complexity would it take to balance the morphology of Archi? – and does English truly have that complex a syntax? Relative to some languages I know, English syntax as well as English morphology seems to be on the simple side.

Or consider the Latin of classical poetry, which is presumably a variety of language as valid for linguisticians' consideration as any other. Not only did classical Latin in general have a far richer morphology than any modern Western European language – but, in poetry, one had the extraordinary situation whereby metrical requirements can be satisfied by permuting the words of a sentence almost randomly out of their logical hierarchy, so that Horace (*Odes* Book I, XXII) could write a verse such as:

> *namque me silva lupus in Sabina,*
> *dum meam canto Lalagen et ultra*
> *terminum curis vagor expeditis,*
> *fugit inermem*

which means something like:

> for a wolf flees from me while, unarmed, I sing about my Lalage and wander, cares banished, in the Sabine woods beyond my boundary

but expresses it in the sequence:

> for me woods a wolf in the Sabine while my I sing about Lalage and beyond my boundary cares wander banished flees from unarmed

where correspondences between words criss-cross as in Figure 4 (see overleaf).

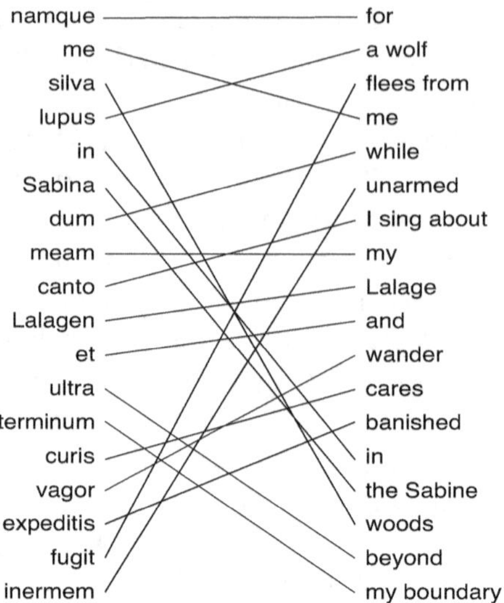

Figure 4

We know, of course, that languages with extensive case marking, such as Latin, tend to be free word order languages. But it seems to me that what linguisticians normally mean by "free word order" is really free constituent order – the constituents of a logical unit at any level can appear in any order, when case-endings show their respective roles within the higher-level unit, but the expectation is that (with limited exceptions) the logical units will be kept together as physical units. In Latin poetry that expectation is comprehensively flouted, creating highly complex relationships between the physical text and the sense-structure it encodes.[1]

For the descriptivist school, I believe the assumption of invariance of total language complexity as between different languages was motivated largely by ideological considerations. The reason why linguistics was worth studying, for many descriptivists, was that it helped to demonstrate that "all men are brothers" – Mankind is not divided into a group of civilized nations or races who think and speak in subtle and complex ways, and another group of primitive societies with crudely

1. In the example, the logical constituency of the Latin original can be inferred straightforwardly from that of my English translation, except that *inermem*, "unarmed", belongs in the original to the main rather than the subordinate clause – a more literal translation would run "...flees from unarmed me...".

simple languages. Edward Sapir wrote that "the delicate provision for the formal expression of all manner of relations…meets us rigidly perfected and systematized in every language known to us" ([1921] 1963: 22). The descriptivists assumed that more complex languages would be more admirable languages, and they wanted to urge that the unwritten languages of the Third World were fully as complex as the well-known European languages, indeed the Third-World languages often contained subtleties of expression having no parallel in European languages.

One point worth making about this is that it is not obvious that "more complex" should be equated with "more admirable". We all know the acronym KISS, "Keep it simple, stupid", implying that the best systems are often the simplest rather than the most complex ones. Whoever invented that acronym probably was not thinking about language structure, but arguably the principle should apply as much to that domain as to any other. We English-speakers do not seem to spend much time yearning to use languages more like Archi or poetic Latin.

Still, it is certainly true that the popular layman's idea of language diversity was that primitive Third-World tribes had crude, simple languages, whereas the languages of Europe were precision instruments. The descriptivists were anxious to urge that this equation just does not hold – unwritten Third-World grammars often contain highly sophisticated structural features. And they were surely correct in making that point.

It is worth adding that the founders of the descriptivist school seem often to have been subtler about this than those who came after them, such as Hockett. Edward Sapir, for instance, did not say that all languages were equally complex – he did not believe they were, but he believed that there was no correlation between language complexity and level of civilization:

> Both simple and complex types of language…may be found spoken at any desired level of cultural advance. When it comes to linguistic form, Plato walks with the Macedonian swineherd, Confucius with the head-hunting savages of Assam. (Sapir [1921] 1963: 219)

Franz Boas was more knowledgeable about detailed interrelationships between language, race, and culture than later descriptivist linguisticians, who tended to focus on language alone in a more specialized way, and Boas was responsible for the classic discussion of how Third-World languages sometimes enforced precision about intellectual categories that European languages leave vague:

> In [the American Indian language] Kwakiutl this sentence [*the man is sick*] would have to be rendered by an expression which would mean, in the vaguest possible form that could be given to it, *definite man near him invisible sick near him invisible*... [I]n case the speaker had not seen the sick person himself, he would have to express whether he knows it by hearsay or by evidence that the person is sick, or whether he has dreamed it. (Boas 1966 [1911]: 39)

But Boas did not claim, as later linguisticians often have done, that there was no overall difference in the intellectual nature of the ideas expressed in the languages of culturally primitive and culturally advanced societies. Boas believed that there *were* important differences, notably that the languages of primitive cultures tended to lack expressions for abstract ideas and to focus almost exclusively on concrete things, but he wanted to say that this was because life in a primitive society gave people little practical need to think about abstractions, and whenever the need did arise, languages would quickly be adapted accordingly:

> Primitive man...is not in the habit of discussing abstract ideas. His interests center around the occupations of his daily life... (1966 [1911]: 60)

> ...the language alone would not prevent a people from advancing to more generalized forms of thinking if the general state of their culture should require expression of such thought; ...the language would be moulded rather by the cultural state. (1966 [1911]: 63)

If we come forward to the last fifty years, we find that most linguisticians have lost interest in discussing whether language structure reflects a society's cultural level, because they do not see language structure as an aspect of human culture. Except for minor details, they believe it is determined by human biology, and in consequence there is no question of some languages being structurally more complex than other languages – in essence they are all structurally identical to one another. Of course there are some parameters which are set differently in different languages: adjectives precede nouns in English but follow nouns in French. But choice of parameter settings is a matter of detail that specifies how an individual language expresses a universal range of logical distinctions – it does not allow for languages to differ from one another with respect to the overall complexity of the set of distinctions expressed, and it does not admit any historical evolution with respect to that complexity. According to Ray Jackendoff (1993: 32), "the earliest written documents already display the full expressive variety and grammatical complexity of modern languages".

I have good reason to know that linguisticians are attached to that assumption, after experiencing the reception that was given to my 1997 book *Educating Eve*, written as an answer to Steven Pinker's *The Language Instinct*.[2] Pinker deployed many different arguments to persuade his readers of the reality of a biologically inbuilt "language instinct", and my book set out to refute each argument separately. I thought my book might be somewhat controversial – I intended it to be controversial; but I had not foreseen the extent to which the controversy would focus on one particular point, which was not specially central either in my book or in Pinker's. I argued against Ray Jackendoff's claim just quoted by referring to Walter Ong's (1982) discussion of the way that Biblical Hebrew made strikingly little use of subordinate clauses, and also to Eduard Hermann's belief (Hermann 1895) that Proto-Indo-European probably contained no clause subordination at all.

On the electronic Linguist List, this led to a furore. From the tone of some of what was written, it was clear that some present-day linguisticians did not just factually disagree with Ong and Hermann, but passionately rejected any possibility that their ideas might be worth considering.

This did not seem to be explainable in terms of politically correct ideology – people who use words like "imperialism" or "racism" to condemn any suggestion that some present-day human societies may be less sophisticated than others are hardly likely to feel a need to defend the Jews of almost 3000 years ago, and still less the mysterious Indo-Europeans even further back in the past: those peoples cannot now be touched by 21st-century neo-imperialism. So it seemed that the generative doctrine of innate knowledge of language had created an intellectual outlook within which it became just unthinkable that overall complexity could vary significantly between language and language, or from period to period of the historical record. The innate cognitive machinery which is central to the generative concept of language competence was taken to be too comprehensive to leave room for significant differences with respect to complexity. Linguisticians still think this way. For instance, Ioannis Fykias and Christina Katsikadeli write (2015: 37) that Hermann's idea about Proto-Indo-European grammar simply "cannot be seriously maintained… since this would be tantamount to rejecting the idea that all languages at all times reflect the same basic U[niversal]G[rammar]".

2. The most recent edition of my book was published in 2005 as *The "Language Instinct" Debate*.

Summing up, the idea that languages are similar in degree of complexity has been common ground between linguisticians of very different theoretical persuasions. In 1981 Richard Hudson made a well-known attempt to identify things that linguisticians all agreed about, and his list turned out to be sufficiently uncontentious that the updated version of it is nowadays promulgated as "Some issues on which linguists can agree" on the website of the UK Higher Education Academy, as mentioned on p. 9 above.[3] Item 2.2d on the list runs:

> There is no evidence that normal human languages differ greatly in the complexity of their rules, or that there are any languages that are "primitive" in the size of their vocabulary (or any other part of their language [*sic*]), however "primitive" their speakers may be from a cultural point of view. (The term "normal human language" is meant to exclude on the one hand artificial languages such as Esperanto or computer languages, and on the other hand languages which are not used as the primary means of communication within any community, notably pidgin languages. Such languages may be simpler than normal human languages, though this is not necessarily so.)

Echoing Hockett's comparison of English with Fox, Hudson's item 3.4b states that "Although English has little inflectional morphology, it has a complex syntax …"

This axiom became so well established within linguistics that scholars in other fields have treated it as a reliable premiss. For instance, discussing the relationship between language and thought, the philosopher Stephen Laurence wrote:

> there seems to be good evidence that language *isn't* just [*sic*] a cultural artefact or human "invention". For example, there is no known correlation between the existence or complexity of language with cultural development, though we would expect there would be if language were a cultural artefact. (Laurence 1998: 211)

– Laurence cites Steven Pinker as his authority.[4]

3. See <www.llas.ac.uk/resources/gpg/135.html>, accessed 20 March 2017.
4. The word "just" in the Laurence quotation seems to imply that products of cultural evolution will be simpler than biological structures. This may well be a tacit assumption among proponents of the "language instinct" concept more generally, but if so it is a baseless one. The English legal system, for instance, with its common-law foundation overlain by massive corpora of statute and case law, its hierarchy of courts, its rules of evidence, arrangements for legal education, dress codes, and so forth is

So far I have discussed the existence or non-existence of complexity differences between different languages: linguisticians either believed that no sizeable differences exist, or that what differences do exist do not correlate with other cultural features of the respective societies. That is not the only sense in which linguisticians have believed in complexity invariance, though. One can also hold that an individual's language remains constant in complexity during his or her lifetime.

If the period considered were to include early childhood, that would be an absurd position: everyone knows that small children have to move through stages of single-word utterances and then brief phrases before they begin to use their mother tongue in the complex ways characteristic of adults. But the generative school believe that the language-acquisition period of an individual's life is sharply separate from the period when the individual has become a mature speaker, and that in that mature period the speaker remains in a linguistic "steady state". According to Chomsky:

> children proceed through a series of cognitive states…[terminating in] a "steady state" attained fairly early in life and not changing in significant respects from that point on… Attainment of a steady state at some not-too-delayed stage of intellectual development is presumably characteristic of "learning" within the range of cognitive capacity. (Chomsky 1976: 119)

Chomsky's word "presumably" seems to imply that he was adopting the steady-state hypothesis because he saw it as self-evidently plausible. Yet surely, in the sphere of day-to-day common-sense social discussion, we are all familiar with the opposite point of view: people say "you never stop learning, do you" as a truism.[5]

And this is a case where the generative position on complexity invariance goes well beyond what was believed by their descriptivist predecessors. Leonard Bloomfield, for instance, held a view which matched the common-sense idea rather than Chomsky's steady-state idea:

> there is no hour or day when we can say that a person has finished learning to speak, but, rather, to the end of his life, the speaker keeps on doing the very things which make up infantile language-learning. (Bloomfield 1933: 46)

certainly a product of cultural rather than biological evolution, but no-one would describe it as simple. Analogies between language and law will be discussed further in chapter 11.

5. Although the steady-state idea was treated as axiomatic by generative linguisticians for decades, it has recently been called into question by Joan Bybee and Clay Beckner (2015: 976).

There is a third sense in which language complexity might or might not be invariant. Just as one can compare complexity between the languages of separate societies, and between the languages of different stages of an individual's life, one can also compare complexity as between the idiolects spoken by different members of a single speech-community. I am not sure that the descriptivists discussed this issue much, but the generativists have sometimes explicitly treated complexity invariance as axiomatic at this level also:

> [Grammar acquisition] is essentially independent of intelligence… We know that the grammars that are in fact constructed vary only slightly among speakers of the same language, despite wide variations not only in intelligence but also in the conditions under which language is acquired. (Chomsky 1968: 68–9)

Chomsky goes on to say that speakers may differ in "ability to use language", that is, their "performance" levels may differ, but he holds that their underlying "competence" is essentially uniform. Later, he wrote:

> [Unlike school subjects such as physics] Grammar and common sense are acquired by virtually everyone, effortlessly, rapidly, in a uniform manner… To a very good first approximation, individuals are indistinguishable (apart from gross deficits and abnormalities) in their ability to acquire grammar… Individuals of a given community each acquire a cognitive structure that is…essentially the same as the systems acquired by others. Knowledge of physics, on the other hand, is acquired selectively… It is not quickly and uniformly attained as a steady state… (Chomsky 1976: 144)

In most areas of human culture, we take for granted that some individual members of society will acquire deeper and richer patterns of ability than others, whether because of differences in native capacity, different learning opportunities, different tastes and interests, or all of these. Language, though, is taken to be different: unless we suffer from some gross disability such as profound deafness, then (according to Chomsky and other linguisticians) irrespective of degrees of native wit and particular tastes and formative backgrounds we grow up essentially indistinguishable with respect to linguistic competence.

Admittedly, on at least one occasion Chomsky retreated fairly dramatically from this assumption of uniformity between individuals. Pressed on the point by the polymath Seymour Papert at a 1975 conference, Chomsky made remarks which seemed flatly to contradict the quotation given above (Piattelli-Palmarini 1980: 175–6). But the consensus among generative linguisticians has been for linguistic uniformity between individuals, and few generativists have noticed or given any weight to what Chomsky said to Papert on a single occasion in 1975. When Ngoni Chipere decided to work on native-speaker variations in syntactic competence for his MA thesis, he tells us that his supervisor warned him that it was a bad career move if he hoped to get published, and he found that "a strong mixture of ideology and theoretical objections has created a powerful taboo on the subject of individual differences", so that "experimental evidence of such differences has been effectively ignored for the last forty years" (Chipere 2003: xv, 5).

Now let us consider some of the ways in which the consensus has recently been challenged. I shall not attempt a comprehensive survey, but it is worth listing some of the publications which first showed that the constant-complexity axiom was no longer axiomatic, in order to demonstrate that it is not just one facet of this consensus that is now being questioned or contradicted: every facet is being challenged simultaneously.

For me, as it happened, the first item that showed me that my private doubts about complexity invariance were not just an eccentric personal heresy but a topic open to serious, painstaking scholarly research was Guy Deutscher's year-2000 book *Syntactic Change in Akkadian*. Akkadian is one of the earliest languages to have been reduced to writing, and Deutscher claims that if one looks at the earliest recorded stages of Akkadian one finds a complete absence of finite complement clauses. What's more, this is not just a matter of the surviving records happening not to include examples of recursive structures that existed in speech; Deutscher shows that if we inspect the 2000-year history of Akkadian, we see complement clauses gradually developing out of simpler, non-recursive structures which did exist in the early records. And Deutscher argues that this development was visibly a response to new communicative needs arising in Babylonian society.

That is as direct a refutation as there could be of Ray Jackendoff's statement that "the earliest written documents already display the full expressive variety and grammatical complexity of modern languages". I do not know what evidence Jackendoff thought he had for his claim; he quoted none. It seemed to me that we had an aprioristic ideological position from Jackendoff being contradicted by a position based on hard, detailed evidence from Deutscher.

This was particularly striking to me because of the Linguist List controversy I had found myself embroiled with. I had quoted other writers on Biblical Hebrew and Proto-Indo-European, and I was not qualified to pursue the controversy from my own knowledge, because I had not got the necessary expertise in those languages. One man who knew Biblical Hebrew well told me that Walter Ong, and therefore I also, had exaggerated the extent to which that language lacked clause subordination. But I have not encountered anyone querying the solidity of Deutscher's analysis of Akkadian.

If the complexity invariance axiom is understood as absolutely as Stephen Laurence expressed it in the passage I quoted on p. 152, it was never tenable in the first place. For instance, even the mainstream generative linguisticians Brent Berlin and Paul Kay, in their well-known cross-linguistic study of colour vocabularies, recognized that "languages add basic color terms as the peoples who speak them become technologically and culturally more complex" (Berlin and Kay 1969: 150), in other words there is a correlation between this aspect of language complexity and cultural development. But vocabulary size was not seen by linguisticians as an ideologically charged aspect of language complexity. Grammatical structure was, so that Deutscher was contradicting a significant article of faith.

The way that linguisticians were muddling evidence with ideology was underlined by a book that appeared in English just before the turn of the century: Louis-Jean Calvet's *Language Wars and Linguistic Politics* (a 1997 translation of a French original published in 1987). You could not find a doughtier enemy of "linguistic imperialism" than Calvet; but, coming from a separate national background, his conception of what anti-imperialism requires us to believe about language structure turned out to differ from the consensus among English-speaking linguisticians. One passage (chapter 9) in his book, based on a 1983 doctoral dissertation by Elisabeth Michenot, discusses the South American language Quechua, and how it is being deformed through the influence of Spanish. According to Calvet, the Quechua of rural areas, free from Spanish contamination, has very little clause subordination; the "official" Quechua of the towns has adopted a richly recursive system of clause subordination similar to Spanish or English.

Many American or British linguisticians might take Calvet's statement about rural Quechua as a shocking suggestion that this peasant society uses a crudely simple language; they would want to insist that rural Quechua-speakers have recursive structures at their disposal even if they rarely choose to use them. For Calvet, the scenario was a case of domineering European culture deforming the structural properties which can still be observed in Quechua where it is free from imperialist contamination. I do not doubt the sincerity of any of these linguisticians' ideological commitments, but surely it is clear that we need to establish the *facts* about variation in structural complexity, before it is reasonable to move on to debating their ideological implications?

I have already mentioned Ngoni Chipere's 2003 book *Understanding Complex Sentences*. Chipere sets out from a finding by the scholar who was his MA supervisor, Ewa Dąbrowska (1997), that adult members of a speech community differ in their ability to deal with syntactic complexity. Chipere quotes the English example:

> The doctor knows that the fact that taking care of himself is necessary surprises Tom.

The grammatical structure here is moderately complicated, but any generative grammarian would unquestionably agree that it is a well-formed example of English. Indeed, the grammar is less tangled than plenty of prose which is in everyday use in written English. But Dąbrowska found that native speakers' ability to understand examples like this varied fairly dramatically.

> When she asked participants in her experiment to answer simple comprehension questions…she found that university lecturers performed better than undergraduates, who, in turn, performed better than cleaners and porters, most of whom completely failed to answer the questions correctly. (Chipere 2003: 2)

What is more, when Chipere carried out similar experiments, he

> found, unexpectedly, that post-graduate students who were *not* native speakers of English performed better than native English cleaners and porters and, in some respects, even performed better than native English post-graduates. Presumably this was because non-native speakers actually learn the grammatical rules of English, whereas explicit grammatical instruction has not been considered necessary for native speakers… (Chipere 2003: 3)

If our mother tongue is simply part of our culture, which we learn using the same general ability to learn complicated things that we use to learn to play chess or keep accounts or program computers, then it is utterly unsurprising that brighter individuals learn their mother tongue rather better than individuals who are less intelligent, and even that people who go through explicit language training may learn a language better than individuals who are born into the relevant speech community and just pick their mother tongue up as they go along.

The linguistic consensus has been that mother-tongue acquisition is a separate issue. According to the generativists, "we do not really learn language", using general learning abilities; "rather, grammar grows in the mind". Descriptivist linguisticians did not believe that, but they did see native-speaker mastery as the definitive measure of language ability. For many twentieth-century linguisticians, descriptivist or generativist, I believe it would simply not have made sense to suggest that a non-native-speaker might be better at a language than a native speaker. Native-speaker ability was the standard; to say that someone knew a language better than its native speakers would be like saying that one had a ruler which was more precisely one metre long than the standard metre, in the days when that was an actual metal bar held in a town in France.

However, in connection with syntactic complexity there are quite natural ways to quantify language ability independently of the particular level of ability possessed by particular native speakers, and in those terms it is evidently not axiomatic that mother-tongue speakers are better at their own languages than everyone else.

The minor contribution I made myself to this process of challenging the linguistic consensus related to the idea of complexity invariance over individuals' lifetimes. It concerned what some have called *structural complexity* as opposed to *system complexity*: complexity not in the sense of richness of the set of rules defining a speaker's language, but in the sense of how many cycles of recursion speakers produce when the rules they use are recursive.

The British National Corpus contains transcriptions of spontaneous speech by a cross-section of the British population; I took a subset and looked at how the average complexity of utterances, in terms of the incidence of clause subordination, related to the kinds of people the speakers were (Sampson 2001: 57–73). It is well known that Basil Bernstein (1971) claimed to find a correlation between structural complexity and social class, though by present-day standards his evidence seems quite weak.

I did not find a correlation of that sort (the BNC data on social class are in any case not very reliable); but what I did find, to my considerable surprise, was a correlation with age.

We would expect that small children use simpler grammar than adults, and in the BNC data they did. But I had not expected to find that structural complexity goes on growing, long after the generativists' putative steady state has set in. Forty-year-olds use, on average, more complex structures than thirty-year-olds. People over sixty use more complex structures than people in their forties and fifties. Before I looked at the data, I would confidently have predicted that we would not find anything like that.

Meanwhile, John McWhorter moved the issue about some languages being simpler than others in an interesting new direction, by arguing that not only are new languages simpler than old ones, but big languages tend to be simpler than small ones.

Everybody agrees that pidgins are simpler than established, mother-tongue languages; but the consensus has been that once a pidgin acquires native speakers it turns into something different in kind, a creole, and creoles are said to be similar to any other languages in their inherent properties. Only their past history is "special". McWhorter (2001) proposed a metric for measuring language complexity, and he claimed that, in terms of his metric, creoles are commonly simpler than "old" languages. He came in for a lot of flak (e.g. DeGraff 2001) from people who objected to the suggestion that politically powerless groups might speak languages which in some sense lack the full sophistication of European languages.

But, perhaps even more interestingly, McWhorter has also argued (e.g. 2002) that English, and other languages of large and successful civilizations, tend to be simpler than languages used by small communities and rarely learned by outsiders. Indeed, similar ideas were already being expressed by Peter Trudgill well before the turn of the century (e.g. Trudgill 1989). It possibly requires the insularity of a remote, impoverished village community to evolve and maintain the more baroque language structures that linguisticians have encountered. Perhaps Archi not only is a language of the high Caucasus but could only be a language of a place like that.[6]

6. One particularly striking and well-publicized claim about a small tribal language being simpler than well-known European languages has been Dan Everett's description of the Pirahã language of the southern Amazon basin (Everett 2005). Early Akkadian, according to Guy Deutscher, lacked complement clauses, but it did have some clause subordination. Pirahã in our own time, as Everett describes it, has no clause subordination at all, indeed it has no grammatical embedding of any kind, and in other ways too it sounds astonishingly crude as an intellectual medium. For instance, according to Everett Pirahã has no quantifier words, comparable to *all*, *some*, or *most* in English; and it has no number words at all – even "one, two, many" is a stage of mathematical sophistication outside the ken of the Pirahã. However, I do not press the Pirahã example: Everett's data and analyses have been heavily criticized by others (Nevins et al. 2009), and I do not know where the truth lies in this controversy.

Finally, David Gil documents a point about isomorphism between exotic and European languages. Where non-Indo-European languages of distant cultures in our own time do seem to be structurally more or less isomorphic with European languages, this is not necessarily evidence for biological mechanisms which cause all human languages to conform to a common pattern. It may instead merely show that the "official" versions of languages in all parts of the world have nowadays been heavily remodelled under European influence.

Gil has published a series of comparisons (e.g. Gil 2005) between the indigenous Indonesian dialect of the island of Riau and the formal Indonesian language used for written communication, which outsiders who study Indonesian are encouraged to see as the standard language of that country. Formal Indonesian does share many features of European languages which generative theory sees as necessary properties of any human language. But colloquial Riau Indonesian does not: it fails to conform to various characteristics that linguisticians describe as universal requirements. And Gil argues (if I interpret him correctly) that part of the explanation is that official, formal Indonesian is to some extent an artificial construct, created in order to mirror the logical properties of European languages.

Because the formal language has prestige, when a foreigner asks a Riau speaker how he expresses something, the answer is likely to be an example of formal Indonesian. But when the same speaker talks spontaneously, he will use the very different structural patterns of Riau Indonesian.

At the Seattle workshop, Gil (2014) argued, as he has frequently done elsewhere, that languages which fail to encode logical distinctions that are basic to English and other European languages must often be seen not as "ambiguous" but as just "vague" with respect to those distinctions. If a young American child produces the utterance *Mommy sock*, this could be interpreted into adult English either as "Mommy's sock" or as "Mommy is putting a sock on me", i.e. as a case of attribution or of predication. Gil suggests that we may be wrong to suppose that the distinction is meaningful in the child's mind; and whether or not that is so he argues, alluding to extensive evidence from Riau Indonesian and other languages, that there are languages spoken by adults in which such a contrast is meaningless. Gil believes that linguisticians often fail to notice this because of mental blinkers imposed on us by the dominance of European-derived cultures and languages in the modern world.

Ray Jackendoff and Eva Wittenberg's chapter in the Seattle volume (Jackendoff and Wittenberg 2014) was intended as an answer to Gil, but they began by writing "We assume that…people across the planet…think the same thoughts, no matter what kind of grammatical system they use". Surely, one cannot refute an empirically based claim by simply "assuming" its converse? Gil was saying that members of different cultures *don't* think all the same thoughts, and to my mind he was right. Languages spoken far from centres of power, or before the period of European cultural dominance, often lack or lacked logical distinctions that are crucial to European languages, and contain(ed) other distinctions which European languages do not make; and the language structures are the best guide we have to the nature of the speakers' thought-patterns. (Cf. Sampson and Babarczy 2014.)

What is more, even as a believer in Universal Grammar, Lisa Matthewson (2014) demonstrated at Seattle, using evidence from a native language spoken in British Columbia and Washington State, that languages are *not* "equally capable of expressing any idea" and that Universal Grammar "does not plausibly contain a list of meanings which all languages must be able to express". I do not understand how Jackendoff and Wittenberg could hope to refute arguments like Gil's and Matthewson's via what the former described in their opening line as a "thought experiment".

In modern political circumstances Gil's argument is very plausible. Consider the opening sentence of the United Nations Charter, which begins: *We the peoples of the United Nations determined to save succeeding generations from the scourge of war, which twice in our lifetime has brought untold sorrow to mankind, and to reaffirm…* In English the full sentence contains 177 words, consisting of one main clause with three clauses at one degree of subordination, eight clauses at two degrees of subordination, four clauses at three degrees of subordination, and one clause at four degrees of subordination. Although the sentence was composed by speakers of modern European or European-derived languages (specifically, Afrikaans and American English), it would translate readily enough into the Latin of 2000-odd years ago – which is no surprise, since formal usage in modern European languages has historically been heavily influenced by Latin models.

On the other hand, the early non-European language I know best is Old Chinese; so far as I can see, it would be quite impossible to come close to an equivalent of this sentence in that language (cf. Sampson and Babarczy 2014). Old Chinese did have some clause-subordination mechanisms, but they were extremely restricted by comparison with English (Pulleyblank 1995: e.g. 37, 148–62). However, if the community of Old Chinese speakers were living in the 21st century, their leaders would find that it would not do to say "You can say that in your language, but you can't say it in our language". In order to survive as a society in the modern world they would have to change Old Chinese into a very different kind of language, in which translations were available for the UN Charter and for a great deal of other Western officialese.

And then, once this new language had been invented, linguisticians would come along and point to it as yet further corroboration of the idea that human beings share innate cognitive machinery which imposes a common structure on all natural languages. A large cultural shift, carried out in order to maintain a society's position vis-à-vis more powerful Western societies, would be cited as proof that a central aspect of the society's culture never was more than trivially different from Western models, and that it is biologically impossible for any human society to be more than trivially different with respect to cognitive structure. Obviously this scenario is purely hypothetical in the case of Old Chinese of three thousand years ago. But essentially that process has been happening a lot with Third-World languages in modern times.

That turns the belief that all languages are similar in structural complexity into something like a self-fulfilling prophecy. What European or North American linguisticians count as the "real language" of a distant part of the world will be the version of its language which has been remodelled in order to be similar to European languages. Because of the immense dominance nowadays of European-derived cultures, most or all countries will have that kind of version of their language available, and for a Western linguistician who arrives at the airport and has to spend considerable time dealing with officialdom, that will be the version most accessible to study. It takes a lot of extra effort to penetrate to places like Riau, where language varieties are spoken that test the axiom of constant language complexity more robustly.

If we are concerned about the moral duty to respect alien cultures, what implies real lack of respect is this insistence on interpreting exotic cognitive systems as minor variations on a European theme (cf. Sampson 2007) – not the recognition that languages can differ in many ways, including their degree of complexity.

The traditional consensus on linguistic complexity was accepted as wholly authoritative for much of the past century – more than a century, if one reckons from Henry Sweet to the Helsinki and Leipzig workshops. And it did have the effect of making linguistics sound "scientific". Yet, as soon as it was challenged, it melted away faster than snow in springtime.

Chapter 11

Complexity in Language and in Law

In chapter 10 I urged that the many linguisticians who have told us that all human languages are equal in complexity have never given us any real reasons to believe this. I suggested that, on the contrary, languages like other products of human culture probably differ in level of complexity.

There are two ways in which one might challenge that suggestion. First, one might claim that, as a matter of observation, languages are in fact about equal in complexity. But alternatively, one could argue that languages are incommensurable in complexity, so that it is meaningless to assert either that their overall complexity varies or that it does not vary. I shall call these objection (i) and objection (ii) respectively.

It is objection (i) which seems to correspond to what many linguisticians of the past hundred years saw as axiomatic. That, surely, is what Benjamin Fortson was asserting when he wrote that "A central finding of linguistics has been that all languages…are equally complex in their structure" (quoted on p. 8 above). But this position is not easy to take seriously. Fortson wrote as if there were some well-known body of "finding[s]" which establish the point, but I know of nothing of that kind in the literature of linguistics (and Fortson gives no reference).

More interesting and weightier, to my mind, is objection (ii), that comparing languages with respect to their complexity is meaningless. That objection was never voiced in the days when almost all linguisticians believed in equal complexity. But now that a number of people are asserting that languages differ in complexity, the incommensurability objection has been powerfully argued against that assertion, by Guy Deutscher (2009). (If one says that languages cannot be compared in terms of complexity, this of course contradicts both the traditional axiom of equal complexity and the new suggestion that there are complexity differences.) To claim that languages may vary in complexity seems to imply that we have some kind of unit or metric in terms of which we can assign a numerical value to the overall complexity of a language, so that we might be able to say "language *A* is 1.07 times (or 5.8 times, or…) as complex as language *B*". It might seem unrealistic to think of reducing systems as nebulous and abstract as human languages to numbers in that way. Certainly the linguisticians who treated equal complexity as axiomatic never, to my knowledge, suggested that they had a way of quantifying the invariant complexity which they postulated.

In fact some of the scholars who are now arguing for complexity differences do propose ways of quantifying complexity. For instance, Johanna Nichols (2009) defines a measure of what she calls "grammatical complexity" (but using "grammatical" to cover phonology and lexis as well as syntax and morphology) which she applies to a sample of 68 languages from different language-families and continents. A few of her figures, including the lowest and highest, are:

Basque	13.0
Mandarin	14.6
Japanese	16.0
Egyptian Arabic	21.7
Ingush[1]	27.9

Similarly, Theresa Biberauer et al. (2014) describe a measure of "average grammatical complexity" of a language (using "grammatical" in a narrower sense), which gives the following scores for a sample of five languages (for their measure, higher percentages mean lower complexity, in other words English is deemed to be by far the most complex language in the Biberauer et al. sample):

Japanese	0.391%
Mohawk	0.195%
Mandarin	0.098%
Basque	0.098%
English	0.003%

But proposals like these are surely at best very provisional, and highly debatable. Any human language is a structure of such endless detail that one might well question whether such numerical measures can respond to more than some tiny fraction of all the considerations which might be felt to contribute to the complexity of a language. (Indeed, it is noticeable that the three languages which appear in both Johanna Nichols's and Theresa Biberauer et al.'s samples, namely Japanese, Mandarin, and Basque, are assigned quite different complexity-ordering by the respective proposals.

1. Ingush is a language of the Caucasian family, the best-known member of which is Georgian. The Archi language discussed on p. 147 above is another member of this family.

I do not know how far this might be explained by the different definitions of "grammar" on which the two metrics are based, but it must raise questions about the solidity of one or both proposals.)

For myself, I have no commitment to belief in any particular quantitative measure of language complexity. I am sure many will feel that no metric of that sort could possibly be realistic or adequate, and for the sake of argument I am happy to concede that that might well be true (I do not know whether it is true or not).[2] My aim in the present chapter is to argue that, even if it is true, it would not follow that human languages cannot be said to differ in overall complexity.

In order to show that this does not follow, I shall draw an analogy between language and another aspect of human culture with which language has much in common (though one which is not often discussed by linguisticians), namely law. The evolution of law offers a clear example of a process which yields a system that is indisputably much more complex at later periods than it was when it was young, but where nobody claims to be able to put figures on that difference and it is quite unlikely that anyone ever could.

As is well known, the legal systems of various Western countries fall into two families: many Continental European nations have so-called Civil Law systems, which trace their ancestry to Roman law, whereas England, the USA, and many other English-speaking countries have Common Law systems, which have evolved ultimately out of the customs of the Germanic tribes who immigrated into southern Britain over the centuries immediately preceding and after the collapse of the Roman Empire. The highly codified nature of Civil Law makes it less relevant for our present purposes; I shall develop my analogy by reference to English Common Law (which was classically expounded by Sir William Blackstone in the eighteenth century – Blackstone 1768–9; for an up-to-date layman's introduction, see e.g. Elliott and Quinn 2008).

The "Common Law" as such was established over the period between the Norman Conquest of 1066 and about 1250, during which time the sometimes divergent legal customs of the tribes who inhabited different parts of England were merged into a single nationwide "Common" system, and the fundamental principle of *stare decisis* (follow precedents) was adopted. From the thirteenth century onwards, the body of English law

2. Several speakers at the 2012 Seattle workshop that I mentioned on pp. 143–4 held that language complexity is quantifiable in terms of a definition due to the physicist Murray Gell-Mann (1995), but to me Gell-Mann's idea makes no sense (Sampson 2015b).

grew through the accumulation of precedents set in individual cases. Human life is so complex that no finite set of rules will ever explicitly cover all the issues which fall to be resolved; when a judge confronts an open issue, he makes a decision that harmonizes as well as possible with the existing body of law, and that precedent then becomes a fixed rule binding on future cases. (This considerably simplifies the reality, of course; for instance, higher courts are entitled to overrule precedents set by lower courts. But my purpose here is to describe the general complexion of the system rather than to go into detail.)

Judges are not supposed to make new law on their own initiative. The traditional doctrine was that judges respond to novel questions by "discovering" rules which were somehow implicit in the existing body of law but had not previously been spelled out. However, this was a fiction. In reality, precedents might often have been settled differently, but, whichever way they were settled, those decisions then became part of English law.

From the thirteenth to the nineteenth century this was close to a complete description of the process of English legal development. The picture has changed over the past hundred years or so, because of an explosion of statute law. Parliament can enact a statute on any topic it pleases, which will override any common-law rules with which it conflicts; by the present day probably most issues that arise are governed by some statute (though, since no form of words is ever entirely precise, the mechanism of precedent-setting comes into play again in determining what a given statute means in practice). But the large current role of statute law is a new thing (and the impact of the rather different type of law emanating from the European Union is of course much newer still). Until the late nineteenth century, Acts of Parliament were relatively few, and tended to relate to specialized purposes that did not affect the population as a whole. (In the eighteenth century, for instance, divorces were individual Acts of Parliament.) As late as about 1910, a lawyer was able to write:

> Parliament is continually pouring forth a stream of legislation: but that legislation rarely touches the law as it affects people in their ordinary everyday life. I venture to say deliberately that the law relating to business and trade, the law as it affects the household, the family man, the shopkeeper and the merchant, the employer and the workman, the mistress and her maid, has not changed appreciably since Queen Anne died. (Anonymous ca 1910; emphases in original removed)[3]

3. The publication quoted is undated, but internal evidence shows that it was published not earlier than 1908 and not later than 1913. Lawyers' professional etiquette of the period required it to be published anonymously; on the title page it is attributed to "A Barrister-at-Law".

Another hundred years later, the same could no longer be said. To keep things simple, let us consider just the 600-year development of the legal system from the thirteenth to the nineteenth century.

My point is that, on the one hand, English law at the end of that period was a far more complex system than at the beginning. Anyone knowledgeable about legal history would, I believe, see that as too obviously true to be worth discussing. The statement just quoted that the law had not "changed" meant that the principles round which precedents accumulated had not been altered by statute, but that accumulation certainly made the overall body of law more complicated. (The paragraph following the one quoted referred to the law having been "built up by succeeding generations of judges".) The standard cliché, originally coined by the poet Tennyson (1842), describes how the law "broadens slowly down / From precedent to precedent", where we are entitled to take "broaden" as amounting to "grow more complex".[4] But on the other hand, there is no way of putting figures on that complexity difference.

One might imagine that, if nobody has attempted to define a metric in this area, that is merely because doing so is not something that would interest legal scholars. But there is more to it than that: quantification is not possible. One could not merely count precedents, for instance. Some precedents are simple, others are individually complex; but also, most legal decisions do not constitute precedents (established law is adequate to resolve the cases), and there is no algorithm for deciding which particular cases extend the law and hence count as precedents. (One might say that a case counts as a precedent if it is reported in one of the standard series of law reports, but it takes human judgement to decide whether a case merits reporting.) Furthermore, new precedents do not invariably add complexity to the existing body of law; on occasion they simplify it, for instance by treating a series of previous precedents as special cases of a more general rule, or by deciding that two apparently relevant precedents cannot be reconciled with one another in the circumstances of a new case and must be replaced by a more straightforward rule. (For how precedent-based legal evolution works in practice, see Manchester and Salter 2000.)

4. Tennyson's poem actually says that *Freedom* "broadens slowly down…", but this is poetic compression. "Precedent" is inherently a legal rather than political concept, and Tennyson's lines are regularly understood as meaning that English freedom is underpinned by a system of laws which grow increasingly complex through accumulation of precedents.

I believe that knowledgeable people would not see it as controversial to maintain both that English law in the nineteenth century was (much) more complex than English law in the thirteenth century, and also that this difference is not open to formal quantification. Thus, it can make sense to say that alternative systems in some area of human culture may vary in complexity although their respective degrees of complexity are incommensurable. In the legal example, one system was directly ancestral to the other, but if systems in an ancestor–descendant relationship can differ in complexity, systems which exist simultaneously and do not share a common ancestor must equally be able to differ in complexity. In other words, objection (ii) is not unanswerable.

Some might accept that this is true in principle, but yet argue that languages are so different in kind from legal systems that objection (ii) remains valid in practice. As we have seen, much of linguistics has been wedded to an assumption that human languages are definable in terms of clearcut sets of formal grammatical rules, akin to the Backus–Naur notation which defines the well-formed code sequences of a computer programming language.[5] If so, this would make languages very different kinds of animal from legal systems. However, that assumption looks quite threadbare, now that it is widely recognized after decades of effort that "No-one has ever successfully produced a comprehensive and accurate grammar of any language" (quoting David Graddol, from p. 32).

Human languages are not formally definable systems. Languages, like the Common Law, are systems which evolve through usage rather than in accordance with clearcut plans. In chapter 3, I likened the patterns of grammatical frequency that emerge from analysis of real-life usage to the range of paths available in a prairie inhabited by a society lacking developed systems of property rights: there will be a few broad, well-beaten tracks (corresponding to the most basic sentence structures, such as, in English, Subject–Verb–Object), and many other lesser routes, ranging smoothly down to barely detectable disturbances of the grass where only a handful of people have passed, corresponding to grammatical patterns which have been used less frequently or scarcely ever. It makes no more sense to partition the set of possible sentence patterns into a group of "grammatical" sheep and a complementary group of "ungrammatical" goats than it would to offer a comprehensive route-map of the prairie. The most one could aspire to is to map the more heavily used tracks (in the prairie case) or

5. For Backus–Naur notation see <foldoc.org/Backus-Naur>, accessed 14 November 2013, or the Wikipedia article "Backus–Naur Form".

the more usual grammatical patterns (in the case of a language), down to some cut-off which will be essentially arbitrary in either case, without pretending that these are "all and only" the available paths or grammatical patterns. This is a fair characterization of what traditional, "pedagogical" grammars of English and other languages did. Before the rise of generative linguistics in the 1960s, that was all that grammarians claimed to do, and it is the most that can be done. To try to go further and define "all and only" the valid sentences of a language really is chasing a rainbow.

Describing the current state of a human language is a task much more like specifying the current state of some area of Common Law, which is generally acknowledged as a task that cannot be done perfectly because the unavoidable vagueness and messiness of law will always escape precise definition, than like specifying what counts as well-formed code in a programming language (which is routinely done by a compiler – if code compiles, it is well-formed, and if not, not).

In sum: of the two standard objections to the idea that human languages vary in overall complexity, the first (that complexity is observably equal) has never been seriously justified and seems intuitively implausible, while the second (the idea that complexity of various languages is incommensurable) may look plausible at first sight but embodies a fallacy. In reality, there is nothing illogical in the assertion that languages differ in complexity although the differences are unquantifiable; this assertion, I believe, is true. In this respect, languages resemble many other components of human cultures.

IV

And Now for Something Completely Different...

My last two chapters are different in flavour from the chapters that preceded them. For one thing, these closing chapters are about phonology. The sound patterning of languages is an aspect of their structure with special relevance to the linguistics delusion: the idea that human languages obey scientific laws is most plausible in the case of phonology. Linguisticians often remark that commercial firms are happy to invent meaningless strings of sounds as names for new products, but these always obey the laws of phonological grammar. According to one standard linguistics textbook, "we would hardly expect a new product or company to come on the market with the name Zhleet...*an impossible word in English – [but] we do not bat an eye at [names like]* Bic,...Kodak, Glaxo, or Spam*" (Fromkin et al. 2010: 302). The lawlikeness of phonological rules is surely the reason why, until the 1960s, phonemic analysis and other aspects of phonology were the "centre of gravity" of linguistics. (Only with the arrival on the scene of Noam Chomsky did majority attention begin shifting to syntax.)*

In fact the kind of phonological norms described by Victoria Fromkin and her co-authors are not scientific laws. Speakers can be creative with phonology as they are with grammar. I once saw in an English shop window an electric blanket marketed under the name "Fnug". Any linguistician defining the phonological structure of English would say that /fn–/ is not a legal initial consonant cluster and that Fnug *is as impossible a word as* Zhleet, *but the manufacturer evidently felt that phonology rules were less important than coining a name which would be reminiscent of "snug" but fuzzier and friendlier.*

Still, phonological rules can come close to being lawlike. And, correspondingly, cross-linguistic generalizations can come close to being the kind of true universals which general linguistic theory claims to uncover. Chapter 12 discusses a case where a convincing, evidence-based argument has been put forward for such a universal truth of phonology. The trouble is, the universal statement is contradicted by the facts of Chinese – but this yields a paradox: the evidence for the universal is strong. Can it make sense for a single language to be an exception to a valid universal law? The original version of chapter 12 was published as a "target article" on which a range of scholarly specialists, Oriental and Western, were invited to comment. The comments were interesting and enlightening, but they did not dissolve the paradox. In a book which has argued at length that the concept of scientific linguistics is a delusion, it is good for one chapter to point to an open question about that judgement. Like most intellectual issues, the topic of this book is not closed to further debate.

Another way in which this section differs from what went before is that, I hope, it is more positive. In particular, chapter 13 is about a topic which, unlike most issues in academic linguistics, has real practical significance for the wider world of business. It seems surprising that the question it discusses has never, to my knowledge, been asked by linguisticians before – but it does not pretend to be a "scientific" question, so perhaps to many of them it would seem unimportant. One might think that, on the contrary, it is just the kind of topic on which academics knowledgeable about language can make a useful contribution to society.

Chapter 12

A Phonological Paradox

This chapter is about a contradiction which has emerged between, on one hand, well-established facts about the history of Chinese phonology, and on the other hand a claimed linguistic universal for which robust evidence has recently been produced.

One of the most striking properties of Chinese, to people more familiar with European languages, is its very high incidence of homophony. All languages contain some homophones, for instance English /raɪt/ can represent any of the unrelated words *right*, *write*, or *rite*. But in English and other European languages, words which coincide in pronunciation with other words are a minority, and even in such cases it is rare for more than two or three etymologically distinct words to share a spoken form. In Chinese, and particularly in the standard, Mandarin dialect, there are very few words which are not homophonous with other words, and a set of homophones may contain ten or twenty members. It is difficult to be precise about which of all the words that have been used in the long recorded history of Chinese should be counted as elements of present-day spoken Mandarin, but one linguistically sophisticated attempt to do so is Chao and Yang (1962); on average a Mandarin syllable is ambiguous between about four of the words listed there (Chinese words coincide with syllables), with a maximum of 25-way homophony for the syllable *yù*.

(This is why Chinese words quoted in romanized form in this book are always accompanied by their Chinese written form. To identify a specific Chinese etymon it is almost never enough to give its pronunciation.)

Before going further I need to draw attention to a problem about applying the term "word" to the Chinese language. Europeans take for granted that their languages are composed of "words", although they might be hard put to define the term. Chinese has not traditionally had a concept equivalent to "word". The units which are salient and universally recognized by Chinese speakers are individual roots or "morphemes" – the minimal meaningful elements of language of which the English words *faith*, *faiths*, and *unfaithful* contain respectively one, two, and three. In Chinese, with marginal exceptions all roots are complete, clearly delimited single syllables, and the elements represented as units by the script are roots – they are not grouped together as word-like sequences in writing. Roots, and the graphs used to write them, are called *zi* 字.

Furthermore, in the Literary Chinese which was the colloquial language of the classical period and remained the standard written language until the early twentieth century, roots and words were interchangeable – nothing in Literary Chinese gave a reason to think of roots as grouped into larger lexical units.[1] In the modern colloquial language, on the other hand, many lexical units consist of two-root compounds, and there have been developments in pronunciation which give some of those compounds a phonetic unity – so, for the modern language, it makes sense to identify the Western term "word" with those larger units, and Chinese linguisticians have adopted the term *ci* 詞 to refer to those units and to translate "word" and its equivalents in European languages. (That historical development is part of what the present chapter will discuss.) But *zi* remain much more "obvious", salient units of the modern language than *ci*. How to group *zi* into *ci* is often far from self-evident. The homophony I discuss is homophony among *zi* rather than among *ci*.

Studies initiated in Qing-dynasty China have shown that this high incidence of homophony results from a series of sound-changes over a long period which merged phonemes that previously contrasted, or eliminated phonemes altogether (merged them with zero). Many categories of evidence, including Tang dynasty rhyme tables, comparison among dialects, vocabulary borrowings between Chinese and other languages, and the structure of the script, make it certain that at earlier periods the phonology of Chinese was much richer than it is today. (The subject is surveyed concisely e.g. by J. Norman 1988: chapter 2; for a more detailed account of developments from Old Chinese through Middle Chinese to Mandarin, see e.g. Baxter 1992.) Scholars differ about details of reconstruction, but the large areas of consensus suggest that homophony in the Old Chinese of three thousand years ago may not have been strikingly greater than in European languages. Homophony has increased so much that, if the language had retained the largely monosyllabic vocabulary of the classical period, it would now be too ambiguous to be usable. (No-one can understand a passage of Literary Chinese read aloud without sight of the script.) Consequently a vocabulary of simple roots has been replaced

1. Even (postclassical) Literary Chinese did contain a few disyllabic loans, e.g. *luòtuó* 駱駝 "camel", *shānhú* 珊瑚 "coral", which were written with two graphs each but were undoubtedly single "words". However, that was a marginal phenomenon with no relevance to the substance of this chapter.

by one that now consists largely of compounds and derived forms of various types (cf. Li and Thompson 1987: 816–24) – a two-syllable compound is typically unambiguous even if each of its component roots is many-ways ambiguous.

In general linguistics, though, there is a longstanding belief that the historical sound-changes which occur in all languages are subject to a constraint by which they avoid creating a high degree of homophony. Contrasting phonemes merge, it is claimed, only if there are not too many pairs of words distinguished by that particular contrast. This idea can be traced back to Jules Gilliéron (1918) and became central to the linguistic theories of André Martinet (especially 1955), who used the term *rendement fonctionel* (literally "functional yield", often translated "functional load" – the term was not original with Martinet) for a quantitative measure of the work done by a particular phonemic contrast in keeping words apart, and hence of the probability that future sound-changes would eliminate that contrast. Intuitively it is very plausible that changes which create more ambiguity are less likely to happen, and many linguisticians have taken this to be an uncontroversial truism (see the Google count of quotations in Baerman 2011: 2 n. 4). Clearly, a rule linking sound-changes to a measure of functional yield would have a good claim to be a predictive scientific law.

But, intuitively plausible or not, Martinet's idea seems to be directly refuted by the Chinese facts already cited. And even with respect to European languages the idea soon proved problematic: Robert King (1967) attempted to test Martinet's theory quantitatively, using data from Germanic languages, and concluded that functional yield has little or no influence on which sound-changes occur in a language. I took it that the functional yield theory, though attractive, had to be wrong, and when I became aware recently that the theory was being revived (e.g. by Campbell 1996: 77; Blevins and Wedel 2009; Baerman 2011) I pointed out that Chinese appears to refute it (Sampson 2013).

However, the literature reviving the functional yield theory has been growing, in number of papers and in strength of evidence and argumentation, so that some recent publications cannot be dismissed as lightly as the ones quoted in my 2013 paper. Martinet (1955: 58) expressed some caution about how significant a factor functional yield is in practice in determining the course of phonological evolution, but recent writers have claimed a decisive role for it. Particularly strong evidence is discussed by Wedel, Kaplan, and Jackson (2013), who examine 41 phoneme mergers in six European languages together with Korean and Cantonese, all of which occurred recently enough to allow vocabularies to be studied statistically. Comparing phoneme mergers which have actually occurred with hypothetical mergers that are equally phonetically plausible but have not occurred, Wedel, Kaplan, and Jackson find support at a very high level of significance ($p < .001$) for the hypothesis that the likelihood of a merger correlates inversely with the number of homophones it creates.[2]

As things stand, then, we have arguments which seem quite cogent that language-change avoids creating excessive homophony; if I did not know about Chinese I would certainly find those arguments convincing. It has been rare for linguisticians to use statistical tests, as Wedel, Kaplan, and Jackson do, to establish the robustness of their theories. When they not only do this but obtain a probability of less than one chance in a thousand for their null hypothesis, we need to take the theories in question seriously. Yet at the same time we know that sound-changes in the history of Chinese have created a massive level of homophony. This is a real paradox. Both statements appear to be true, but they contradict each other. The aim of the rest of this chapter is to explore various ways in which one might hope to resolve the paradox. None of the alternatives seems to me satisfactory. But some resolution there must be.

One solution might simply be to say that homophony avoidance is a valid law of sound change but Chinese is an exception. Indeed, although he does not mention Chinese by name, Matthew Baerman implies that this is reasonable when he suggests (2011: 25) that languages may differ with respect to homophony avoidance. However, I find it scientifically unacceptable. Laws by which societies control human conduct can have "special cases": there might be a law by which all ordinary residents are subject to income tax but the monarch is exempt (this was the law in Britain until the 1990s). Scientific laws are not like that: they only count as laws if they apply across the board, so an apparent exception means that the law has been inadequately formulated.

A better approach would be to look for some special factor which might cause Chinese to behave differently from other languages with respect to sound-changes. One distinctive property of Chinese is the logographic rather than phonographic nature of the script, which means that words which fall together in pronunciation remain distinct in writing. This was the factor which enabled Literary Chinese to remain the standard

2. Other relevant publications which I had not seen when I wrote my 2013 paper include Silverman 2010; Kaplan 2011; Wedel, Jackson, and Kaplan 2013; Bouchard-Côté et al. 2013; Kaplan 2015.

written language until 1919, centuries after it ceased to be intelligible as a spoken language. It might be suggested that the true linguistic universal is not that languages avoid changes which make too many words *phonetically* indistinguishable, but rather that they avoid changes which make too many words indistinguishable *in all respects*. For a language with a perfectly phonemic script, the two versions of the law would have identical consequences. But for Chinese the latter version allows any amount of homophony, since written word-forms remain distinct.

This meets the requirement for laws to be universal, but it is empirically implausible. If there is indeed a constraint on words becoming indistinguishable, the obvious reason would be that users of a language need their communications to be understood. But until recent times the literacy rate in China was not high (UNESCO 2006: 192 n. 6); even in 1949 it was only about twenty per cent (*Economist* 2014). How could phoneme mergers in the speech of an entire population be affected by the presence of a literate minority within the population for whom the mergers did not destroy the psychological distinctiveness of words containing the phonemes? Indeed, even that minority did plenty of speaking and listening as well as reading and writing, so problems caused by homophony affected literate people too.

Linguisticians do not normally think of writing as capable of playing a large role in determining the historical evolution of spoken languages, and they are surely correct not to do so. (Yishaï Norman (2009) surveys various ways in which spoken language can be influenced by script, but it is fair to say that these are all marginal, relative to the issue of Chinese homophony.) It is difficult to see how our paradox could be resolved by reference to the nature of Chinese script.

A further possibility would be to query the timing of the shift from monosyllabic to disyllabic vocabulary. This is normally seen as having been a response to the increasing homophony among monosyllabic roots. Thus, Li and Thompson (1987: 817–18) referred to the sound-change by which final -m merged with -n in Mandarin, so that e.g. 金 "gold" and 斤 "tael" (a unit of weight), respectively *kim and *kin in Middle Chinese, have fallen together as Mandarin *jīn*, and they wrote:

> If [the word 金 *jīn*] hadn't become the disyllabic form [金子 *jīnzi*], the… words for "gold" and "tael" would have been homophonous. The threat of too many homophonous words has forced the language to increase dramatically the proportion of polysyllabic words…

Likewise Jerry Morgan (1988: 112) wrote:

> Given this progressively radical reduction in the overall number of contrasting syllables, and the consequent falling together of many words once phonologically distinct, it is not surprising that the old one-word/one-syllable pattern began to weaken, and that the use of disyllabic words began to increase.

However, if it should be that the shift from monosyllabic to disyllabic words took place *before* the contrast-eliminating sound-changes, those changes would not have created much homophony between words when they occurred, so Chinese would not be an exception to the generalization about homophony avoidance.

As it happens, Li and Thompson were ill-advised in their choice of example. Instances of the particular disyllable-creating process they cited, namely suffixing *–zi* to a noun without any diminutive connotation,[3] are known to have occurred early (Jerry Norman 1988: 114 quoted examples from the Tang dynasty), while on the other hand -m and -n still contrasted for the 14th-century rhyme-book *Zhongyuan Yinyun* 中原音韻. And many disyllable-creating innovations may well have occurred in speech before they showed up in the written record.

Nevertheless, it seems unlikely that in general the shift to disyllabic vocabulary could have preceded the loss of phonemic contrasts. One leading disyllable-creation process was a type of compounding which conjoins synonyms or near-synonyms. Li and Thompson (1987: 819) gave examples such as *pífá* 疲乏 "tired-tired = tired", *fángshǒu* 防守 "defend-defend = defend", *fàngqì* 放棄 "loosen-abandon = to give up". From what they wrote one might suppose that this process occurred mainly with verbal meanings, but there are also many examples with other grammatical functions, e.g. *péngyǒu* 朋友 "friend", *mínzú* 民族 "a race", *fénmù* 墳墓 "a grave", etc. etc. If synonym compounds of this type arose earlier than the phoneme mergers, that would imply that Chinese adopted a habit of saying the same thing twice even though saying it once would have been unambiguous. Is it realistic that any speech community would adopt such a pointlessly redundant habit of speech? I am not aware of any empirical evidence that the Chinese did so.[4]

3. The suffix *-zi* originated as a word meaning "son, child" and developed into a suffix for small concrete objects, where the etymological meaning retained some relevance. When it developed further into a general nominal suffix, as in the *jīnzi* example, it is hard to see that the suffixation had any function other than reducing ambiguity.

4. Synonym compounds are of course only one type of Chinese compound, and it may well be that they seem disproportionately salient to Western linguists because European languages contain little or nothing that is analogous. But that very fact

Daniel Silverman suggests to me (and cf. Silverman 2006: 76–8) that the two developments may have co-evolved, so that vocabulary replacement was both triggered by phoneme mergers and enabled them to proceed further. (Relevant sound-changes are likely to have been long-drawn-out affairs in which modifications to a phoneme spread gradually from word to word across the vocabulary; on Chinese evidence for this model of sound-change as against the Neogrammarian concept of abrupt across-the-board changes, see e.g. Feng and Yip 2014.) But Silverman's suggestion seems to reduce homophony avoidance to an unfalsifiable doctrine with no predictive power. In itself the co-evolution idea appears plausible, but if *prima facie* violations of homophony avoidance can readily be explained away in that fashion, then I do not understand how findings such as Wedel, Kaplan, and Jackson's could obtain.

Li and Thompson (1987: 817) note that southern dialects of Chinese, such as Cantonese, in which fewer mergers have occurred than in Mandarin, also retain a more monomorphemic vocabulary. That is as predicted, if it was the increase in homophony which triggered the Mandarin shift to bimorphemic words.

Another attempt to resolve the paradox might point to the restricted nature of the hypothesis examined in Wedel, Kaplan, and Jackson's statistical research. Their technique limited them to considering only homophones created by phoneme mergers, rather than those created when phonemes drop altogether in particular environments; they make no prediction about the latter type of sound-change. So, logically, it is possible that those Chinese sound-changes which merged phonemes did conform to their findings, and that the very high incidence of homophony in modern Mandarin was produced by other types of change. For instance, when final -m merged with -n, leaving the third final nasal -ŋ distinct, because -m was a low-frequency final consonant it is probably true, as Wedel, Kaplan, and Jackson would predict, that the change created substantially fewer homophones than would have been created by a (counterfactual but equally phonetically plausible) merger of -n and -ŋ, leaving -m distinct. On the other hand the number of homophones that were or would have been created by either of these changes might well have been dwarfed by the number that were created by the loss of all final oral stops -p -t -k, but that would not falsify Wedel, Kaplan, and Jackson's claim.

strengthens my point. I know of no language other than Chinese which uses compounding of synonyms as a word-formation technique, so there must presumably be some special reason why Chinese uses it. I cannot think of any alternative to the pressure of homophony as an explanation.

But, in the first place, although the particular statistical techniques used by Wedel, Kaplan, and Jackson restricted them to considering homophony resulting from phoneme mergers, they do not suggest that this is anything more than an unavoidable limitation of their research method. Other publications reviving the functional yield theory have argued that sound-changes in general, not just one category of sound-change, avoid creating homophones. And that is surely what we would expect. A universal tendency for languages to avoid becoming inefficient through excessive ambiguity is very natural and understandable, if it is indeed a reality, whereas a universal tendency to avoid generating homophones via one type of process while allowing any amount of homophony to be produced in other ways would be inexplicable and implausible.

In any case, some of the Chinese sound-changes to which Wedel, Kaplan, and Jackson's findings ought to apply do seem to refute them. Consider the Mandarin sound-change which produced the sounds spelled *j q x* in the *pinyin* romanization scheme by merging /k kʰ x/ with /ts tsʰ s/ respectively before close front vowels. (This sound-change is the reason why for instance the Chinese capital, traditionally spelled Peking in English, is nowadays written Beijing. The word 京 "capital" is *jīng* in standard Mandarin, but the older romanization was deliberately archaizing, representing an earlier /kīŋ/, distinct from /tsīŋ/ 菁 "luxuriant" which is now also pronounced *jīng*.) This sound-change affected about an eighth of the entire vocabulary, and created a huge number of homophones. When distinct wordforms which are each, say, three ways homophonous fall together, the result is nine new homophone-pairs: each word of one set is newly confusable with each word of the other. Many words affected by the *j q x* merger will have been more than three ways homophonous before it applied. The number of new homophone-pairs it created must have approached ten thousand. I am not quite sure what range of hypothetical mergers Wedel, Kaplan, and Jackson would count as comparable in phonetic plausibility to this one, but I would surmise that these must include mergers which would have created substantially fewer homophones.

Comparing this quantitatively with the mergers in Wedel, Kaplan, and Jackson's data is not easy, because their "online supplemental material" includes no figures and lists only mergers between individual phonemes, whereas sound-changes commonly affect classes of phonemes. For instance, the first merger they list for RP English is between /θ/ and /t/, while in reality this is one case of a sound-change which also merges /ð/ and /d/. (I believe it applies in some Irish dialects.) But, using an English dictionary which feels comparable in scope to Chao and Yang for Chinese,

I find that this sound-change yields 142 homophone-pairs.[5] In line with Wedel, Jackson, and Kaplan (2013: 410) this figure does not count inflected forms separately (e.g. *heat* ~ *heath*, *heats* ~ *heaths* count as one pair), but it does include some quite obscure pairs, e.g. *dhow* ~ *thou* or *bath* ~ *Bt.* (A dhow is a type of Arab boat; *Bt* is an abbreviation for *baronet* but can apparently be pronounced /bɑt/ as a separate word.) Whether or not this particular English merger is wholly typical, the disparity between 142 and "approaching ten thousand" for the Chinese *j q x* merger is broadly representative of the difference between homophony in Chinese and in European languages.

Abby Kaplan (2015) argues against my 2013 paper by pointing out that a claim that languages tend to prefer sound-changes which create fewer homophones over other sound-changes which would create more homophones does not imply that there is some absolute threshold level of overall homophony which languages cannot cross. She suggests that many of those linguisticians who have advocated a functional-yield theory have explicitly argued for the former but have said nothing about the latter.

I accept that the one idea does not logically entail the other, but again I would appeal to the concept of general scientific plausibility. If it were universally true that languages prefer those sound-changes which create fewer homophones, that could surely only be because an excessive level of homophony interferes with communication. And if that is so (as seems undeniable) then there must be some level of homophony which is in practice intolerable. Of course that would not be a threshold expressible as a specific number, so that N homophone-pairs in a language are all right but N+1 pairs are forbidden. But when things reach the point where a largely monomorphemic vocabulary has to be replaced by a largely bimorphemic vocabulary in order to preserve intelligibility, as happened in Chinese, it seems certain that the language as it would have been without vocabulary replacement would have exceeded any tolerable level of ambiguity.

Kaplan also points out, correctly, that those who have discussed homophony avoidance have done so in terms of statistical tendencies rather than absolute rules, and she says that the existence of one example violating a tendency cannot refute a statistical law. This might protect the functional yield theory from the Chinese counterexample, if the move

5. I used the computer-usable version of the *Oxford Advanced Learner's Dictionary*, available by ftp via <www.filewatcher.com/m/CUVOALD.tar.gz.816821-0.html>, ignoring proper names (the file includes many obscure names which would be unfamiliar to the average English-speaker, a phenomenon having no parallel in Chinese).

from low Old Chinese homophony to very high Mandarin homophony had resulted from a single sound-change. But in fact the present-day situation is the outcome of many separate sound-changes over thousands of years. Various different types of consonant cluster were reduced to single consonants between Old and Middle Chinese, almost certainly in a series of separate changes rather than just one. Since the Middle Chinese period, apart from the three changes already mentioned (loss of -p -t -k; merger of -m and -n; mergers yielding *j q x*) there was loss of voicing in obstruents (which created new homophones among non-level-tone words), and loss of initial ŋ-. (I do not discuss vowel changes, because these are harder to individuate and may not always have affected the incidence of homophony.) Various scholars have posited further, smaller-scale changes which also reduced the range of phonetic contrasts, but the changes listed above are agreed by everyone. So we are not talking about a single exception to a universal tendency. Rather, one particular language has again and again changed in ways which increased, and often massively increased, the number of homophones. That is not consistent with a universal law of homophony avoidance even if that law is statistical rather than an absolute prohibition.

I cannot find a statement in Wedel, Kaplan, and Jackson's paper of whether they believe merger probabilities relate to minimal-pair counts linearly or by some other mathematical function. If linearly, then one might think that the number of homophone pairs produced by a Chinese merger such as the *j q x* case, being orders of magnitude larger than the numbers produced by European-language mergers, ought to be associated with a probability so minuscule that one would not expect to find a single example in the few thousand languages spoken in the world.

I did not offer to provide a solution to this paradox I have discussed, and I cannot suggest a solution. A version of this chapter was originally published as the "target article" for a discussion section in the *Journal of Chinese Linguistics*. Three Chinese and four other relevant scholars commented on the paradox I presented. As I wrote in my response, "Many things said by the commentators…are very reasonable and just. But none of them, so far as I can see, removes the incompatibility with the otherwise well-confirmed functional yield theory."

The paradox is real. It ought to concern anyone who claims that the discipline of linguistics is uncovering truths about human language in general, rather than just features of English or some other individual language.

Chapter 13

How Many Possible Trade Names Are There?

Trade depends on names. Firms need distinctive names for themselves, for their brands, and for their individual products or services. Owners of trade names put considerable effort into protecting their rights in their names. We often read of cases where a firm takes legal action to try to prevent another business, perhaps in an unrelated business sector, using a name which they believe might be confused with their own name.

Fifty years ago, it may have seemed as though there would always be abundant not-yet-used names to go round. Today, in a globalized society with more liberal business régimes, there are indications that it is becoming harder to find names which are available and suitable. Company names used commonly to be formed from owners' surnames or placenames, or consisted of ordinary English words. But the days when names of those kinds were enough are behind us. Shortly after the English confectionery manufacturer Cadbury's was taken over in 2010 by an American company, the section containing it was spun off under the exotic-looking name *Mondelēz*, with a macron to encourage the pronunciation /li:z/ for the last syllable. This name was apparently derived from French *monde* and *délice*, but it seems unlikely that many English-speaking consumers will see it as more than an arbitrary orthographic sequence. *The Economist* recently ran an article discussing the many strange types of name which some firms have recently taken to using, "resorting to ever more desperate means in order to stand out from the crowd" (*Economist* 2015); the article refers to a story by Arthur C. Clarke (1953) in which an early computer is put to enumerating "all the possible names of God" – when it finishes listing all nine billion names, the world ends.

One area where the need for invented names has become specially salient is medicine. Drugs used to be given names with meaningful derivations, for instance the name *aspirin* referred to the fact that the active ingredient occurs naturally in a plant then assigned to the genus *Spiraea*. But with the huge outpouring of novel drugs in recent times, each needing a generic name and one or more proprietary names, it has become usual for these names to be meaningless and often rather outlandish-sounding.[1] A few pain-relief drugs have the following generic names, and corresponding capitalized proprietary names: *celecoxib*, *Celebrex*; *diclofenac*, *Cataflam*, *Voltaren*, *Zipsor*; *ibuprofen*, *Advil*, *Haltran*, *Motrin*, *Trendar*, etc.; *sulindac*, *Clinoril*; *meloxicam*, *Mobic*.[2] I have not researched the background of these names, but they appear for the most part to be concatenations of meaningless syllables. The *flam* of *Cataflam* was doubtless chosen because diclofenac is an anti-in*flamm*atory, and the *Clin-* of *Clinoril* was perhaps chosen to echo the word "clinical", but etymologizing seemingly cannot go much further than that. Moreover, while all the names are certainly pronounceable, some of their phonological patterns seem unusual, relative to the patterns found in ordinary non-name words. The four-syllable length of the first name, *celecoxib*, for instance, would suggest a derivation from a classical language if the word were part of the ordinary English vocabulary, but so far as I know no Greek or Latin word could give rise to an English polysyllable ending in *-ib*.

Another area rich in novel names is information-technology startups, where (unlike in the pharma industry) new products need distinctive names *before* a decision is taken about launching them on the market. For instance, among the many startup names listed as participating in the 2014 programme of one accelerator organization, MassChallenge, were: *Accel*, *Admetsys*, *Agira*, *Aldatu*, *Anfiro*, *Bubbi*, *ConsortiEX*, *Droplette*, *Eulysis*, *gameblyr*, *Jisto*, *KnipBio*, *Kuona*, *Lengio*, *Lig*, *Medlio*, *noonee*, *Oto*, *Recardo*, *Sano*, *SproutslO*, *Twiage*, *Unima*, *Varada*.

In this situation, it is of interest to ask how large the universe of potential names is. Could a time come when we exhaust the supply of possible names? From a legal point of view, debates about whether a new trade name is too close to an existing proprietary name ought to be informed by data about how much separation between names is in principle possible. This chapter can do no more than broach the issue and offer order-of-magnitude answers, but even these may be informative when the questions are new.

1. It is perhaps inappropriate to call a generic drug name a "trade name". But the issue we are concerned with is the supply of new names in general; the chapter title refers to trade names, because it is chiefly commerce which is revealing the limits to that supply.

2. The names capitalized here are believed to be registered proprietary names, and the respective owners' rights are hereby acknowledged. Later in this chapter, many examples of hypothetical trade names will be cited; so far as I know, none of these are actually in use, but I apologize in advance if, unknown to me, any of them should coincide with real proprietary names.

Of course, we can have as many different names as we want, if we do not care how long they are. But owners of trade names do care. A trade name needs to be memorable and convenient to use, so a six-syllable name might scarcely be worth considering. The question to be addressed below is how many potential names of a given length exist, and the lengths considered in detail will be reasonably short.

We shall consider this question from the viewpoint of the English language. We aim to count potential words that would be pronounceable in English, and could be given a written form which would identify that pronunciation in terms of the norms of English orthography.

When computing numbers of possible distinct English words, we have a choice between basing the computation on written wordforms (letter sequences) or on spoken forms (phoneme sequences). In a legal context the main focus would normally be on written forms (a registered trade name would standardly be defined as a letter sequence), however I assume that in order to be satisfactorily distinctive, a trade name should be unique in pronunciation as well as spelling. The owner of a hypothetical name *Meelok* might not be happy to find others using the names *Mealok* or *Meelock*, since the natural way to pronounce all three would be /mi:lQk/. How much this mattered, commercially or legally, would no doubt depend in practice on how far the firms or products in question were in competition with one another, but that consideration lies outside the purview of this chapter. For our purposes, I assume that names are required to be distinct in both sound and spelling, irrespective of what they refer to.

(Spoken wordforms will be transcribed in this chapter using the computer-oriented SAMPA system, see Gibbon et al. 1997: 699–702, which replaces the special characters of the International Phonetic Association alphabet with characters drawn from the ASCII character-set. Of the alternative SAMPA symbols for the DRESS vowel, we shall use /E/, since /e/ will be used for another purpose below; and, as an exception for the sake of ease of reading, the TRAP vowel will be transcribed as "&" rather than as SAMPA "{ ".)

In order to count possibilities, it is easiest to treat spoken forms as basic. The boundary between pronounceable and unpronounceable phoneme sequences is more determinate than the boundary between possible and impossible written letter sequences. Furthermore, while the unsystematic nature of English spelling means that correspondences between letter sequences and phoneme sequences are one-to-many in both directions, for instance, a name *Ledonac* might be read as /li:dQn&k/, /lEdQn&k/, or /lEd@Un&k/, while the first of these possibilities, /li:dQn&k/, might be spelled *Ledonac*, *Leedonac*, *Leedonack*, or *Leadonac*, there usually seem to be more alternative spellings for a given pronunciation than alternative pronunciations for a given written form. Both of these considerations suggest that a suitable strategy will be to aim initially to calculate numbers of pronounceable phoneme sequences, and to modify the results in the light of properties of English spelling, rather than to begin from spellings.

Alternative spellings for the same phoneme sequence will often yield names which differ greatly in "flavour". For instance, the sequence /r&lih&k/ could be spelled *Rallyhack*, suggesting a compound of native Germanic roots and hence a "relaxed" name appropriate for, say, the leisure sector; as a drug name the same phoneme sequence would more likely be given a Latinate spelling such as *Ralihac*, to suggest a "scientific" background. Nevertheless, for our investigation the single phoneme sequence will be counted once only.

Even the boundary between pronounceable and unpronounceable phoneme sequences is not perfectly determinate. Some sequences (for instance, those which correspond to actual words of the language) are clearly pronounceable, and some, e.g. /rbgtp/, /Ni:bE/ are clearly unpronounceable, as English words. (What sequences of sounds are pronounceable varies greatly from language to language – there are many languages in which /Ni:bE/, beginning with the velar nasal and ending with the DRESS vowel, would be a very normal-sounding word.) But there is also a penumbra of marginal possibilities. For instance, probably all English-speakers know the word *psst*, which might be glossed as something like "Over here, but keep quiet!" It is quite conceivable that *Psst!* might be adopted as a trade name, perhaps for some product associated with secrecy. Yet at the same time it is clear that the phoneme sequence /pst/ falls well outside the patterns used for words of the ordinary vocabulary. The approach adopted here will be to omit the "penumbra" and count only phoneme sequences which fit the pattern of ordinary English vocabulary.

Inevitably there are debatable cases; as said on p. 171, phonological structures are not governed by scientific laws, though they come closer to it than syntactic structures do. Thus, I have counted word-initial /sf-/ as a permissible cluster because of *sphere*, *sphincter*, but it is very rare. I have assumed that diphthongs resemble one another with respect to the range of consonant(-cluster)s which can follow them, but although /-aUT/ is certainly possible (*mouth*), and /-OIT/ *-oyth* seems utterable with ease by phonetically naive English speakers, I am not aware of any English words that contain /-OIT/. We also find words from foreign languages used as trade names in the English-speaking world, some of which contain un-English phonology; for instance, Dior markets a perfume under the name *J'adore*, beginning with a sound /Z/ that does not occur initially in English (and which my calculations exclude accordingly). There can scarcely be any hard-and-fast line drawn between foreignisms like this which English-speakers find acceptable, and other sounds or sound-combinations which seem too alien to be used in trade names.[3]

A special problem is that some phoneme sequences are common in inflected forms but never occur in uninflected words. Thus /-md/ occurs in past tenses, e.g. *seemed* /si:md/, and /-bz/ occurs in plurals, e.g. *ribs* /rIbz/, but one will not find uninflected words ending in these clusters. It is not entirely clear what is the "right" way to handle these cases for present purposes (there certainly are businesses whose names are plural nouns, though I have not encountered one whose name is a past tense). But on the whole trade names tend to be uninflected forms, so rightly or wrongly the decision was to exclude these special phoneme sequences from the calculations. On the other hand, final /-ps, -pt/ are treated as valid possibilities because of a handful of words such as *apse*, *crypt*, though the great majority of words ending in these clusters are inflected forms.

For debatable cases like these, my calculations are based on rough-and-ready common-sense decisions. Rather than taking space here to detail all these decisions, I have placed online at <www.grsampson.net/SWordGen.html> the software which I wrote for purposes of the Monte Carlo experiments to be discussed below. This contains explicit lists of the sounds and sound-combinations I deemed permissible; readers who disagree with my decisions can easily check how the results would be affected by making those decisions differently. My surmise is that, at the level of precision relevant to this enquiry, other reasonable decisions would not give vastly different results.

Looking at English phonology in more detail, another source of indeterminacy relates to reduced vowels in unstressed syllables. The successive syllables of polysyllabic words receive different degrees of stress, and syllables having least stress also have fewer contrasts between vowels than other syllables: rather than a six-way contrast between the "checked" vowels /I E & Q V U/ one finds just a two-way contrast between the "obscure" vowels /i @/, neither of which occurs in stressed syllables. For

3. This issue is only partly a matter of the intrinsic "alienness" of sounds. *J'adore* is evidently acceptable although initial /Z-/ does not occur in English. On the other hand the popular Korean car marque Hyundai (Sino-Korean 現代 /hjɤndæ/, "modern") seems invariably to be pronounced in English as three syllables, /haIVndaI/, even though /hj/ is a normal initial sequence in British English (*huge*, *humour*). Relevant factors in this case are probably that English /hj/ is not spelled using the letter *y*, and also that to English-speakers French is a much more familiar language than Korean.

our purposes there is no perfect way to incorporate this issue into calculations: English spelling does not explicitly indicate stress patterns, so one cannot expect that individuals who encounter an invented polysyllabic trade name in written rather than spoken form will agree on how to stress it. The solution I have chosen is to assume that all syllables in a trade name are given sufficient stress to contain stressed-syllable vowels rather than obscure vowels. As compared with a solution which attempts to recognize the possibility of obscure vowels, this decision will in one way reduce the calculated number of possible wordforms (two vowels which English does in reality use will be omitted from the calculated possibilities), but in another way will increase that number (in some longer words, one or more syllables would in practice have to be stressless, but our calculations will counterfactually pretend that the full range of alternative stressed-syllable vowels are available in those syllables). The consequence is that the numbers emerging from the calculations below can only be regarded as order-of-magnitude estimates rather than exact; but we shall see that order-of-magnitude figures are the best one could hope for in any case, and arguably for commercial and legal purposes it is ballpark estimates rather than precise numbers which are of most interest.

A further source of indeterminacy has to do with the English spelling conventions for vowels and diphthongs. English phonology has a contrast between checked vowels, which must be followed by a consonant, and "long" or "free" vowels, which can occur finally in a syllable or a word. (Many of the "free vowels" are diphthongs: for the purposes of this investigation, English diphthongs – and affricate consonants /tS dZ/ – are regarded as single phoneme units, and references to "vowels" below will include diphthongs.) The vowel letters are each regularly ambiguous between a checked and a free vowel; for instance, the letter *o* can stand for the checked vowel of *cot*, /kQt/, or for the diphthong of *cold*, /k@Uld/. Furthermore, the letter *u* can stand for either of the distinct checked vowels /V U/. In monosyllables these distinctions can often be made explicit in the spelling, for instance by using "silent *e*": the invented form *fot* could only be /fQt/, while *fote* is unambiguously /f@Ut/. But even for monosyllables English orthography is not systematic enough to eliminate all these ambiguities (e.g. the spelling *-ut* can represent /Ut/ as in *put*, or /Vt/ as in *gut*). And in polysyllables there will very often be no recognized way of showing which of the alternative regular phonetic values of a vowel letter is intended by a particular spelling.[4]

4. One might object that this is not entirely true, if we consider devices like the Mondelēz macron. But, apart from the fact that this orthography is a large departure from the norms of English naming, I surmise that Mondelēz would not be happy if a

Therefore, to ensure that we do not separately count wordforms which are phonologically distinct but could not reliably be distinguished in writing, our calculations will treat sets of vowels which are standardly written with the same vowel letter as if they were a single vowel – the calculations will recognize no distinction between e.g. the /Q/ of *rot* and the /@U/ of *rote*. (For monosyllables this approach would severely distort the facts, but monosyllables are such a tiny fraction of all possible words of reasonable length that for our purposes the distortion will be negligible.) My software implements this decision by using the symbols /a e i o u/ as cover-symbols for the sets of vowels regularly written with the respective letters, as follows:

a = /&/ or /eI/
e = /E/ or /i:/
i = /I/ or /aI/
o = /Q/ or /@U/
u = /V/, /U/, /u:/, or /ju:/

(In the same way – though this point will make far less difference to the eventual results – since the voiceless and voiced fricatives /T D/ of *thigh, thy* are both spelled *th*, they will be treated as if they were the same sound.) I shall identify distinct wordforms as distinct sequences of what I shall call "graphones": units which contrast phonologically and can also be reasonably reliably distinguished orthographically.[5] Thus /a e i o u/ will be graphones with the alternative phoneme values just listed, and /T/ will be a graphone with the values /T/ and /D/. The symbols /C J W Y/ will be graphones representing /tS dZ aU OI/ respectively. (The diphthongs /aU OI/ differ from the other English diphthongs in that they cannot be spelled with single letters, and their spellings are not also regularly used for simple vowels.) In all other cases graphones and phonemes will be interchangeable.

Finally, the range of pronunciation contrasts in English differs to some extent between regional accents. For practical commercial and legal purposes it will make sense to treat spoken forms as distinct only if they would contrast no matter whether they were spoken in standard British "Received Pronunciation" or in "General American English". In particular, my calculations will not separately count spoken forms differing only in

competitor named itself Mondelĕz, and pointed to the breve to establish that its name was different because pronounced with /-lEz/ rather than /li:z/. In practice, identity of letter-sequences is probably a sufficient condition for perceived identity of names.

5. The irregularity of English spelling means that perfect reliability is not achievable.

presence versus absence of postvocalic /r/, since this distinction does not occur in RP: a pair of words such as *taught* and *tort* are distinct for most American speakers but, in RP, they are homophones. On the other hand, no account is taken of more localized accents. For many speakers in the US South, words like *pin* and *pen* are homophones, but my calculations will treat /I/ and /E/ as distinct vowels in all environments.

For a first approximation, the numbers of possible names of a given length in syllables can be calculated algebraically. Let us represent the sizes of various classes of phonemes and phoneme-sequences as follows:

a	initials
z	finals
v	vowels regularly spellable by single letters
d	diphthongs not so spellable
Z	post-free finals

The terms "initial" and "final" refer to the consonants and consonant clusters which can occur respectively at the beginning and at the end of a syllable (including zero, in cases where a syllable begins or ends with a vowel). Every English consonant phoneme other than the velar nasal /N/ can occur as an initial, and every consonant other than /h j w/ can occur as a final, but there are also sequences of two or three consonants (e.g. /sp, pl, skr/) which can occur initially, and sequences (e.g. /mp, rd/) which can occur finally.[6] "Post-free finals" refers to the fact that the range of finals which can occur after a free vowel is very limited by comparison with those that occur after checked vowels. We find no English words like /li:mp/ *leemp* or /leINk/ *laink*, for instance. "Post-free finals" are the small set of finals (various dental consonants and consonant clusters) which can occur in these positions (and hence are the only finals that can follow /W Y/).

Then it seems to follow that the number of possible names having *s* syllables should be $(a \,.\, (vz + dZ))^s$. The values *v* and *d* will be 5 and 2, for the graphone-sets /a e i o u/ and /W Y/ respectively. According to my analysis (again, see the associated software), *a*, *z*, and *Z* have the values 55, 69, and 14 respectively. The formula just given thus yields the results shown in Table 3. (The notation *xey* means $x \times 10^y$.)

6. In RP English, a postvocalic /r/ is realized as modification of the quality of the preceding vowel, e.g. the sequence treated for present purposes as /kard/ *card* is pronounced [kA:d]. But our calculations will be simplified by treating postvocalic /r/ as a separate phoneme, as it is in General American English.

Table 3

syllables	*wordforms*
1	20,515
2	421 million
3	8.6e12(8.6 trillion)
4	1.8e17(180 quadrillion)

However, as it stands the formula overestimates numbers of possibilities. First, it involves some double counting. For instance, allowable syllable-finals include zero, /s/, and /sk/, while allowable initials include /skr/, /kr/, and /r/, so, medially between successive syllable nuclei, the sequence /-skr-/ could arise in three different ways. In all such cases, the single resulting sequence should be counted once only. Furthermore, not all the different graphone sequences implied by the formula will be genuinely distinct. English does not usually distinguish geminate from single consonants in speech: the surname *Hatrick* would commonly be a homophone of the word *hat-trick*. (Some speakers may distinguish them, but the distinction seems too evanescent to be a satisfactory basis for a distinctive name.) Hence graphone sequences including geminates should be discounted. Also, before /r/ followed by a consonant, or word-final /r/, the phonemes /e i u/ are neutralized (as /3:/). And, since one of the values of the graphone /u/ is /ju:/, we should not count /-u-/ and /-ju-/ as separate possibilities.

It would be difficult to allow for these issues by modifying the algebraic formula, but it is easy to take account of them experimentally. The software is set to generate wordforms of a given length randomly, to filter out all but one alternative in cases like these (for instance wordforms containing /-skr-/ between two vowels are accepted only when generated with zero final followed by /skr-/ initial), and to keep a running tally of the proportion of forms generated which pass the filter. After a few hundred iterations the tally converges on a value constant to a couple of significant figures, sufficient precision for our purposes, and this value can be multiplied into the relevant figure in Table 3 to give a corrected result.

The proportions of forms of one, two, three, and four syllables accepted by this filtering process are respectively 0.89, 0.67, 0.53, and 0.43. Thus Table 3 can be replaced by the corrected Table 4. The numbers in Table 4 are lower than those they replace, but from a practical point of view they are hardly significantly lower. Product names are often three syllables long, and we have seen that drugs can have four-syllable names. So, in view of figures like these, it may seem that there is not the slightest danger of running out of names.

Table 4

syllables	*wordforms*
1	18,300
2	280 million
3	4.6 trillion
4	76 quadrillion

However, the numbers here are upper bounds. Readers may feel less optimistic about trade-name abundance when they appreciate the nature of the bulk of wordforms making up these numbers.

As a sample, Table 5 shows the first twenty forms output when the software was set to generate disyllables and trisyllables randomly. The left-hand columns show the forms as sequences of graphones; the right-hand columns give the same forms in one of the ways in which they might be spelled in practice. (We have seen that a given phoneme sequence will typically be spellable in many different ways. Here and below, I have deliberately varied the spellings used to render given graphones orthographically, in order to draw attention to the fact that the "obvious" spellings for given phoneme sequences are not the only, or sometimes the most likely, possible spellings if that sequence is used as a name.)

Clearly, in the main these are fairly absurd "words". *Crossbone*, and perhaps one or two of the other disyllables, might be plausible names, but most of the wordforms feel Martian, or like the deliberately repulsive names of devils in C. S. Lewis's *Screwtape Letters*. They are all pronounceable: English phonology allows quite complex sequences of consonants, for instance /mpsTw/ in the name of the village Hampsthwaite near Harrogate. But in practice complex sequences are infrequent, and one certainly does not expect to find them at more than one place in a word. However, because there are far more possible consonant combinations than there are single consonants, a system like the present one which chooses among alternatives treated as equally probable is bound to make unnaturally heavy use of complex combinations. For a more realistic count of forms which would make plausible names, we need to rein in the use of consonant sequences. But any restriction of that kind will greatly reduce the numbers of possible wordforms.

Monosyllables generated randomly in the same fashion perhaps seem on the whole more plausible; see Table 6. A higher proportion of possible monosyllables coincide with actual words (e.g. *Tub*, *Hath*), and even in monosyllables that are not real words the possibilities for complex consonant sequences where one syllable meets another do not arise.

However, since (as already mentioned) the number of possible monosyllables is tiny relative to longer words, we shall not consider monosyllables further.

Different methods could be used to force the system to generate more plausible polysyllables. The approach taken here is based on the fact that, probably in all languages, the most natural pattern for polysyllabic words is alternation of single consonants and vowels: (C)VCV...(C). For each wordform generated, the system counts the number of violations of that pattern (points where a consonant is immediately followed by another consonant, or a vowel by another vowel), and filters out forms in which the number of violations exceeds a threshold. (Likewise, the computer in Arthur C. Clarke's story was made to "eliminate ridiculous combinations".) Since the set of graphones divides straightforwardly into vocalic and consonantal subsets, defining CVCV violations in a phonetic sense is straightforward. But one can also think of cases where a graphone of either subset is realized as a pair of letters as a "visual CVCV violation", so the count of violations is incremented by one for each occurrence of the graphones /S C J N T W Y/ in a wordform.[7]

The total number of possible wordforms having no more CVCV violations than a given threshold is estimated as before by applying an empirically determined "filter factor" to the relevant figure from Table 3.[8]

Tables 7, 8, and 9 give samples of 2-, 3-, and 4-syllable wordforms randomly generated using the thresholds 3 (Table 7), 2 (Table 8), and 1 (Table 9) respectively. Table 10 shows the filter factors observed for various combinations of wordform-length and CVCV violation threshold, and Table 11 gives the figures obtained by applying those factors to the relevant entries in Table 3. Most wordforms in Table 7 feel scarcely more plausible

7. The phrase "visual CVCV violation" may be misleading. The reason why the graphones listed above tend to reduce the plausibility of wordforms containing them may be, not that alternation of consonant and vowel letters is somehow "natural", but that long English words usually have classical derivations, and the reason why some sounds are spelled with digraphs in English is that those sounds did not occur in the classical languages and hence were not provided with single letters in the alphabet which we inherited from the Romans and, ultimately, from the Greeks. Be that as it may, experimentation shows that including this factor improves the alignment between numerical counts of "CVCV violations" and perceived implausibility of wordforms.

8. One might think that the threshold should be defined relative to wordform-length, with more violations acceptable in long wordforms. However, a little experimentation has suggested to me that absolute number of violations is the more important factor in deciding how realistic a graphone-sequence feels as a potential name.

than those of Table 5, where no constraint on CVCV violations was applied. But readers will agree, I believe, that on balance the wordforms become more plausible as names, as the CVCV violation threshold is reduced from three (Table 7) to one (Table 9).

Table 5

Trelsprels	*Threlceprelce*	sulCSiskhorp	*Sulchshiskhaup*
berswarks	*Birswarx*	TrarCtrondsprol	*Thrarchtrondsproll*
TreNkJond	*Threnkjond*	blabsweJgwanT	*Blabswedjgwanth*
dwoJspruls	*Dwodgesprulce*	swordzulkstam	*Swordzoolxtame*
swikwild	*Swickwild*	ganzTrulbskons	*Ganzthrulbsconce*
fargwuN	*Fargwung*	vanTsklartwunJ	*Vanthsclartwunge*
dwolksblel	*Dwolxblel*	wuskspektskrord	*Wooskspectscraud*
skerksspromp	*Skirxpromp*	sendglontsnaf	*Sendglontsnaff*
twYnsbulJ	*Twoinsbulge*	TwilSklerksnarg	*Thwilshclerxnarg*
skeldTeN	*Skeldtheng*	hilpbubsplal	*Hilpbubsplale*
smondtols	*Smondtolce*	snavmunJklarJ	*Snavmungeclarge*
flolTploNks	*Flolthplonx*	dwofzafskiT	*Dwofzafskith*
Colflif	*Cholflife*	golpmolnkworf	*Golpmolnquorf*
TwenzskoC	*Thwenzscotch*	flYztrikCab	*Floyztrickchab*
jampfokt	*Yampfoct*	CinstrolCbraNks	*Chinstrolchbranx*
glistpriNk	*Glistprink*	splilsmoJgipt	*Splilsmodjgipt*
TrizSroJ	*Thrizshrodge*	spolkspriNksdwerT	*Spolksprinxdworth*
sfiCwuT	*Sphitchwooth*	skilpgrolfsklid	*Skilpgrolfsclyde*
krosbon	*Crossbone*	tuntwelglarS	*Toontwellglarsh*
praSmarT	*Prashmarth*	sersSinCspem	*Sirceshinchspeem*

Table 6

TulT	*Thulth*	tub	*Tub*
haT	*Hath*	prost	*Prost*
swiJ	*Swidge*	Twenz	*Thwenze*
Traks	*Thrax*	lort	*Lort*
werz	*Wurze*	brun	*Broon*
skreg	*Screeg*	sklaz	*Sclaze*
swunC	*Swinch*	skulC	*Skulch*
splart	*Splart*	strad	*Strade*
jipt	*Yipt*	walks	*Walks*
brorv	*Brauve*	niz	*Nize*

Table 7

iJdrok	*Idjdroke*	huvmiNhiz	*Huvminghease*	ribelguntrig	*Ribbleguntrig*
lintmapt	*Lintmapt*	udkilmlid	*Eudkilmlide*	farsfamanwo	*Farcefaymanwoe*
martklel	*Martclele*	handgutdip	*Handgutdip*	gakudpizkrog	*Gacudpizcrog*
gespret	*Guessprete*	skakwabrov	*Scaquabrove*	ferpkopaljep	*Firpcopalyep*
otjek	*Ottyek*	brilkremun	*Brylcreamun*	sominswekert	*Sominswekert*
hilsrak	*Hilsrake*	povgolkdes	*Povgolkdess*	flavenhegulk	*Flavenhegulk*
melmhupt	*Melmhupt*	zazhotbeln	*Zazzhotbeln*	buvadwarblil	*Buvadwarblil*
flupleN	*Flupleng*	septkutvar	*Septcutvar*	tokripragzeg	*Tocripragzeeg*
huvgrop	*Huvgrope*	sladrugtos	*Sladrugtoss*	hataldfaghag	*Hataldfaghag*
Japkark	*Japcark*	boskrismov	*Boscrissmov*	metvodmakrek	*Metvodmacreek*
forvberd	*Fauvbeard*	gislusfult	*Gislussfult*	jezmukugfaN	*Yezmucugfang*
spunsmen	*Spuncemen*	sfedmegmer	*Sphedmegmere*	jodalsjegnot	*Yodalsyegnote*
mulglolf	*Mulglolph*	rugzalkdut	*Rugzaldut*	kodkakglefum	*Codcackglefum*
spalbzep	*Spalbzeep*	kimwokdeld	*Kimwokdeld*	tasukilsjof	*Tassukilsyoff*
zisdworv	*Zisdwarve*	zolkbupdun	*Zolkbupdune*	funedzumprus	*Fewnedzumprus*
lizgroln	*Lizgroln*	gultgumded	*Gultgumdeed*	spomevjipbop	*Spomevyipbop*
sukgreS	*Suckgresh*	vizumtiT	*Vizzumtith*	sputbubkapop	*Sputbubkapop*
zolprol	*Zollproll*	kotajelf	*Cotayelph*	bemrodlotpak	*Beamrodlotpack*
buntguks	*Buntgux*	Cugersbi	*Chugerceby*	rubdergsodav	*Rubdurgsodave*
swudgror	*Swudgroar*	dwabkobsol	*Dwabcobsole*	tiglidoTkim	*Tiglidothkim*

Table 8

zentjaf	*Zentyaff*	fiknusef	*Ficknewseff*	uhokefsfil	*Euhokephsphile*
kivswom	*Kivswom*	zizuskler	*Zizuskler*	nelwobjakos	*Nelwobyakose*
tusweJ	*Tusswedge*	zednotrap	*Zednotrap*	pudsogduguk	*Pudsogduguck*
twisjam	*Twissyam*	omdifki	*Omdiffky*	jamreljorug	*Yamrelyorug*
smongal	*Smongal*	suzweslu	*Suzewesslu*	hudupblenot	*Hudupblenote*
geptrep	*Geptrep*	pesarbrer	*Pessarbrer*	rosinilspos	*Rossinilsposs*
datgem	*Datgeam*	muspostan	*Muspostan*	bimnozlevok	*Bimnozlevoc*
baswon	*Bayswan*	hofilbzat	*Hoffilbzat*	nadefargwuf	*Naydefargwoof*
spakgas	*Spackgas*	snejaknam	*Sneyakname*	rabuforsnis	*Rabeuphorsniss*
futswol	*Footswoll*	tivmuprel	*Tivmuprel*	pahodlufbil	*Pahodluffbil*
hulvolp	*Hullvolp*	guvdwugag	*Guvdwugag*	ibviwetbi	*Ibvy-wetby*
gotrot	*Gotrot*	bonozpind	*Bonozpind*	tuJuzunfos	*Tujuzunfoss*
kugseJ	*Cugsedge*	jemstabeg	*Yemstabeg*	feklijafpul	*Feckliyaffpull*
lentsag	*Lentsague*	klofradup	*Clofradoop*	magpelgokot	*Magpelgocot*
lertpoz	*Lertpose*	nubipdwiv	*Nubipdwive*	egumvuhiln	*Eggumvuhiln*
febteN	*Febteng*	vukrabmif	*Viewcrabmiff*	pobetwufrog	*Pobetwoofrog*
fradhut	*Fradhoot*	ilswohov	*Ilcewohove*	diljawafdek	*Dilyawafdeck*
mubopt	*Mewbopt*	uvgevorg	*Euvgevaug*	dukrefizles	*Duckrefizzless*
trodwom	*Trodwom*	gamtumo	*Gamtumo*	fonmiruzjim	*Phonmiruzyim*
sanblal	*Sanblall*	totwozolf	*Totwozolph*	bafnerhozun	*Baffnerhosen*

Table 9

vinluk	*Vinluck*	gitretin	*Gitreatin*	mupogozbok	*Mupogozboke*
nufkos	*Nufcoss*	wuzmokor	*Wuzmocore*	fednefonon	*Phednephonon*
Coniv	*Chonive*	itpukas	*Itpucase*	gasivofdep	*Gasivoffdeep*
fasfib	*Fasfib*	lenekvot	*Lenecvote*	nikubuzvem	*Nicubuzveme*
nohilm	*Nohilm*	tuboskol	*Tuboscol*	pibewolger	*Pibewolgur*
rovkid	*Rovekid*	ruJefam	*Rudgeffam*	kubwihugak	*Cubeweeheugac*
wadgud	*Wadegood*	samudhom	*Sammudhome*	nafitumhap	*Nafitumhap*
asvos	*Assvoss*	hodzedil	*Hodzedil*	nelemhovep	*Nelemhovep*
mugluv	*Mewglove*	hefuzjad	*Hefuzzyad*	bulutrizoz	*Bulutrizose*
fozget	*Fozget*	wusitsob	*Wusitsobe*	kubulatag	*Cubulatag*
vegrot	*Vegroat*	dagitwik	*Daggitwick*	koskadopob	*Coscadopob*
bitril	*Bitril*	monefwes	*Monefwess*	gotigeslut	*Gotigeslute*
zuwoT	*Zoowoth*	runogfif	*Runnogfife*	mulgepizul	*Mulgepizzle*
laflis	*Laughlis*	havitrig	*Havitrig*	ihizakwez	*I-hi-zackwheeze*
okzib	*Oakzib*	sosguma	*Sosguma*	riwekuwam	*Ryeweekuwam*
fasner	*Fasner*	bagwulam	*Bagwoollam*	hihodniles	*Hihodnyless*
hubhus	*Hubhuss*	ekbakif	*Ekbakif*	dazfakivun	*Dazefacivune*
wikpad	*Wickpad*	hadozbis	*Hadozbiss*	usefulzid	*Eusephulzide*
hafhaz	*Halfhaze*	polakgev	*Pollackgeve*	tuzarebant	*Tuzarebant*
gimla	*Gimla*	betlukev	*Betlookeve*	kemavnusig	*Chemavneusig*

Table 10

	1 syll	2 sylls	3 sylls	4 sylls
threshold 3	0.85	0.13	0.0041	5.4e–5
threshold 2	0.69	0.038	0.00049	5.1e–6
threshold 1	0.32	0.0049	3.8e–5	2.1e–7

Table 11

	1 syll	2 sylls	3 sylls	4 sylls
threshold 3	17,400	55 million	35 billion	9.6 trillion
threshold 2	14,200	16 million	4.2 billion	900 billion
threshold 1	6,600	2.1 million	330 million	37 billion

To my mind the crossover from a point where the bulk of examples are too clumsy to be usable in practice, to a point where most examples are imaginable in use, falls between thresholds 2 (Table 8) and 1 (Table 9). (Perhaps, for disyllables, many of the examples at threshold 2 are plausible; but if names can be *n* syllables long, combinations of fewer than *n* syllables will never be numerous enough to affect the calculations significantly.) This is certainly not to say that all longer wordforms with more than one violation must be implausible. One can easily imagine a German manufacturer of specialist trousers marketing them in the English-speaking world as *Baffnerhosen*, for instance (see the bottom right-hand entry in Table 8). For that matter, we have seen that *Hampsthwaite* exists as a place name, and hence presumably could serve as a trade name of a quite traditional type, yet it scores five violations. But among all three- and four-syllable forms, I would argue that those with more than one violation but which are imaginable as names are quite rare.

Conversely I do not suggest that all forms with one or no violation would make good names. Traders want names to be not just memorable and pronounceable but euphonious; if they echo actual words, these should be words with positive (or at least not negative) associations. However, euphony is a matter of personal taste, and it is not clear that tastes in this area are widely enough shared or strong enough to be decisive against a wordform. To my ear, voiced obstruents and labial obstruents both tend to make for lack of euphony. The monosyllable /f@Up/, containing two labials, strikes me as notably blunt and ugly, yet *Fope* is the name of a manufacturer and retailer of elegant jewellery, which presumably wishes to be associated with the reverse of these qualities. The verb *meddle* has negative associations, but that evidently did not dissuade a startup group from naming their virtual health insurance card *Medlio* (see p. 184).

This reasoning suggests that the answer to the question of my title might be in the region of the figure in the lowest and rightmost cell of Table 11, namely 37 billion.

However, the decision to treat one CVCV violation as a cutoff was admittedly subjective, so I have approached the question in a second way as a cross-check. I randomly selected a sample of 239 proprietary drug names from the lists on the eMedExpert website (www.emedexpert.com), and noted how many of them contain various numbers of CVCV violations. The results are shown in Table 12.

Table 12

0 violations	56
1 violation	98
2 violations	71
3 violations	11
4 violations	3

The large difference between the figures for two and for three violations might suggest that this is where the crossover between plausible and implausible names should be placed, but that overlooks the fact that there are far more ways to construct graphone sequences containing more violations than fewer violations. What Table 12 is telling us is that each CVCV violation in a graphone string (including the first) reduces its plausibility as a name. The figure 98 is greater than 56, but 98 is a much smaller proportion of all pronounceable wordforms containing one violation than 56 is of all forms containing no violation.

If we accept the figures of Table 12 as an estimate of the relative numbers of acceptable names with different numbers of CVCV violations, then we might estimate the total number of acceptable names by assuming that *all* wordforms with zero violations are acceptable. The number of pronounceable wordforms of a given length in syllables and containing no CVCV violations can be calculated algebraically.[9] With one exception

9. The total number of pronounceable wordforms having *s* syllables is

$$(c + 1) \,.\, v \,.\, (cv)^{s-1} \,.\, (c - 2)$$

where *c* is the number of single consonants excluding /S C J N T/ (i.e. 17) and *v* is 5 as before. The terms $c + 1$ and $c - 2$ refer to the fact that a word can begin or end with a vowel, but cannot end with any of the consonants /h j w/.

which should probably be discounted,[10] all zero-CVCV-violation names in the sample contain four syllables or fewer. Possible wordforms one to four syllables long and containing no CVCV violations total 840 million; adding numbers in the proportions of Table 12 to allow for wordforms containing one or more violations gives us a total estimate of 3.6 billion plausible names.

Because the sample represents only drug names, this figure may well underestimate the total number of plausible names. We saw earlier that drug names tend to be chosen to suggest a "scientific" flavour, and this could militate against inclusion of some kinds of graphone sequence which would be perfectly acceptable for names to be used in other contexts. But on the other hand this calculation does suggest that the previous estimate of 37 billion, ten times larger, is unlikely to be too low. (Parenthetically it is interesting to note that these two estimates bracket Arthur C. Clarke's figure of "nine billion". If this was purely a guess by Clarke, it seems to have been a lucky guess.)

If the answer to the title question is "several tens of billions", or even if it is only "several billions", one might feel that humanity is in no imminent danger of running out of distinctive trade names.

However, available names run into billions only provided four-syllable names are acceptable. Drug names are often four syllables long, but laymen do not find such long names easy to remember. In many trade sectors I believe the preference might be for names no longer than two syllables, in which case Table 11 would suggest that the possibilities are a few million only. In the present context that is by no means a large quantity. It is far smaller than one well-informed estimate I have read of the total number of businesses in the world, namely "more than 235 million".[11] If this last figure is about right, then even allowing three-syllable names Table 11 would imply that there are only just enough possibilities for businesses to own one distinctive name each – in practice a business often needs to use many

10. The exception is *Phenylalanine Mustard*; *phenylalanine* has five syllables. But although the two-word phrase is evidently a proprietary name, *phenylalanine* is a formal chemical name, and such words belong to a system of their own in which commercial considerations such as memorability play little part. Many names of chemicals are much longer than five syllables. I do not see this single case as strong evidence for counting wordforms longer than four syllables as plausible trade names.

11. Worapong Smithirittha quoting Dun & Bradstreet data on Quora, <www.quora.com/How-many-companies-there-are-in-the-world>, dated 8 November 2014, accessed 28 November 2015.

names. And if the second calculation, based on the sample of drug names, were appropriate, then totals would be really tiny: 490,000 disyllables, or 42 million trisyllables.

In a legal context it is also relevant to consider that trade-name disputes are often not about separate businesses using identical names. Frequently the complaint is that a newcomer has chosen a name which differs slightly from that of an incumbent, but which is similar enough for the two to be confusable. My calculations have assumed that two names are distinct provided they differ by as little as one graphone, but we could also ask how many distinct names there would be if each pair had to differ in two, three, or more graphones, or in some given proportion of their graphones. I have not attempted to investigate the arithmetical consequences of requirements like those, but it is obvious that they would lead to figures much smaller than those of Table 11.

I conclude that, although possible names are certainly very numerous, they are not so numerous as to make the idea of "running out of distinctive names" merely fanciful.

And, more generally, this investigation demonstrates that there are new and worthwhile findings to be made using a linguistic training. Only, they are not scientific laws.

Envoi

In closing, I hope that this book will not be seen as merely negative and destructive. For those readers who happen to be linguistics teachers, that reaction would be understandable. (Perhaps they should consider doing what I did, and switching subject.) But, properly understood, this is not a negative book. The reason why "linguistics" is a delusion is that, in their cognitive life, human beings are creative – not merely "F-creative", in the terms of chapter 2, but truly creative.

Human beings are not things. Our thinking and our meaningful behaviour escape the fixed constraints that scientific theories must impose, as a requirement of being scientific.

I cannot tell whether what I have written is enough to convince readers of the truth of this message. What I do know is that any reader should want it to be true. We would be lesser creatures than we are, if linguistics were a science.

References

The purpose of a reference list is to help readers find the items listed, so where I am aware of a reprint that may be easier to access than the original publication, I list both. In some cases where an item is available online and I know the URL, I quote that also.

In the circumstances of modern publishing, listing place of publication of books is something of a ritual rather than a useful convention. I compromise by showing place, in brackets, only for publishers whose name does not include the place and where the publisher's sites listed in the prelims of the book do not include London.

Andoni Duñabeita, J. and E. Vidal-Abarca. 2008. Children like dense neighborhoods: orthographic neighborhood density effects in novel readers. *The Spanish Journal of Psychology* 11.26–35.

Annan, N. 1999. *The Dons: mentors, eccentrics and geniuses*. HarperCollins.

Anonymous. ca 1910. *Cassell's Lawyer and Business Man's Legal Handbook: a popular exposition of the civil, commercial, and ecclesiastical law of Great Britain, with such criminal law as affects the trader*, 3 vols. Cassell.

Baerman, M. 2011. Defectiveness and homophony avoidance. *Journal of Linguistics* 47.1–29.

Baker, M. C. 2015. Formal generative typology. In Heine and Narrog 2015.

Ballasy, N. 2010. White House science czar says he would use "free market" to "de-develop" the United States. Online at <cnsnews.com/node/75388>, accessed 2 January 2012.

Barsalou, L. W. 2005. Continuity of the conceptual system across species. *Trends in Cognitive Sciences* 9.309–11.

Barsky, R. F. 1997. *Noam Chomsky: a life of dissent*. MIT Press.

Bartley, W. W. 1978. The philosophy of Karl Popper, part II: consciousness and physics. *Philosophia* 7.675–716.

Baxter, W. H. 1992. *A Handbook of Old Chinese Phonology*. Mouton de Gruyter (Berlin).

Behme, C. 2014. *Evaluating Cartesian Linguistics: from historical antecedents to computational modeling*. Peter Lang (Frankfurt am Main).

Bergen, R. D., ed. 1994. *Biblical Hebrew and Discourse Linguistics*. Summer Institute of Linguistics (Dallas, TX).

Bergson, H. 1907. *L'Evolution créatrice*. Félix Alcan (Paris).

Berlin, B. and P. Kay. 1969. *Basic Color Terms: their universality and evolution*. University of California Press.

Bernstein, B. 1971. *Class, Codes and Control*, vol. 1: *theoretical studies towards a sociology of language*. Routledge & Kegan Paul.

Berwick, R. C. and N. Chomsky. 2011. The biolinguistic program: the current state of its development. In A. M. di Sciullo and C. Boeckx, eds, *The Biolinguistic Enterprise: new perspectives on the evolution and nature of the human language faculty*. Oxford University Press.

Biberauer, T., A. Holmberg, I. Roberts, and M. Sheehan. 2014. Complexity in comparative syntax: the view from modern parametric theory. In Newmeyer and Preston 2014.

Black, M. 1992. *A Short History of Cambridge University Press*. Cambridge University Press.

Blackstone, W. 1768–9. *Commentaries on the Laws of England*, 4 vols, 3rd edn. Clarendon Press (Oxford).

Blevins, J. and A. Wedel. 2009. Inhibited sound change. *Diachronica* 26.143–83.

Bloomfield, L. 1933. *Language*. Holt (New York).

Boas, F. 1911. Introduction to *Handbook of American Indian Languages*. Bureau of American Ethnology, Bulletin 40, part I, pp. 1–83. Reprinted in one volume with J. W. Powell, *Indian Linguistic Families of America North of Mexico*. University of Nebraska Press (Lincoln, NE), 1966.

Boeckx, C. 2006. Review of Postal 2004. *Journal of Linguistics* 42.216–21.

Boeckx, C. 2015. Linguistic minimalism. In Heine and Narrog 2015.

du Bois-Reymond, E. H. 1872. *Über die Grenzen des Naturerkennens*. Veit & Co. (Leipzig).

Boltz, W. G. 1986. Early Chinese writing. *World Archaeology* 17.429–32.

Boltz, W. G. 1994. *The Origin and Early Development of the Chinese Writing System*. American Oriental Society (New Haven, CT).

Boodberg, P. A. 1937. Some proleptical remarks on the evolution of Archaic Chinese. *Harvard Journal of Asiatic Studies* 2.329–72.

Boodberg, P. A. 1940. "Ideography" or iconolatry? *T'oung Pao*, 2nd series, 35.266–88.

Bottéro, F. 2004. Writing on shell and bone in Shang China. In Houston 2004.

Bouchard-Côté, A., D. Hall, T. L. Griffiths, and D. Klein. 2013. Automated reconstruction of ancient languages using probabilistic models of sound change. *Proceedings of the National Academy of Sciences* 110.4224–9.

Bybee, J. L. and C. Beckner. 2015. Usage-based theory. In Heine and Narrog 2015.

Cahill, M. 2014. Non-linguistic factors in orthographies. In Cahill and Rice 2014.

Cahill, M. and K. Rice, eds. 2014. *Developing Orthographies for Unwritten Languages*. SIL International (Dallas, TX).

Calvet, L.-J. 1998. *Language Wars and Linguistic Politics*. Oxford University Press.

Campbell, L. 1996. On sound change and challenges to regularity. In M. Durie and M. Ross, eds, *The Comparative Method Reviewed*. Oxford University Press.

Chalmers, D. J. 1996. *The Conscious Mind: in search of a fundamental theory*. Oxford University Press.

Chao Yuen Ren and Lien Sheng Yang. 1962. *Concise Dictionary of Spoken Chinese*. Oxford University Press and Harvard University Press.

Chipere, N. 2003. *Understanding Complex Sentences: native speaker variation in syntactic competence*. Palgrave Macmillan (Basingstoke).

Chomsky, C. 1970. Reading, writing, and phonology. *Harvard Educational Review* 40.287–310.

Chomsky, N. 1956. Three models for the description of language. *IRE Transactions on Information Theory* IT-2.113–24. Reprinted in Luce et al. 1965.

Chomsky, N. 1957. *Syntactic Structures*. Mouton (the Hague).

Chomsky, N. 1959a. On certain formal properties of grammars. *Information and Control* 1.91–112. Reprinted in Luce et al. 1965.

Chomsky, N. 1959b. Review of Skinner, *Verbal Behavior. Language* 35.26–58. Reprinted in Jakobovits and Miron 1967.

Chomsky, N. 1963. Formal properties of grammars. In Luce et al. 1963.

Chomsky, N. 1965a. *Aspects of the Theory of Syntax*. MIT Press (Cambridge, MA).

Chomsky, N. 1965b. Linguistic theory. Paper read to the Northeast Conference on the Teaching of Foreign Languages. Reprinted in J. P. B. Allen and P. van Buren, eds, *Chomsky: selected readings*. Oxford University Press, 1971.

Chomsky, N. 1966. *Topics in the Theory of Generative Grammar*. Mouton (the Hague).

Chomsky, N. 1968. *Language and Mind*. Harcourt, Brace & World (New York).

Chomsky, N. 1972. *Problems of Knowledge and Freedom*. Fontana.

Chomsky, N. 1975. *The Logical Structure of Linguistic Theory*. Plenum Press.

Chomsky, N. 1976. *Reflections on Language*. Temple Smith.

Chomsky, N. 1980. *Rules and Representations*. Blackwell (Oxford).

Chomsky, N. 1981. *Lectures on Government and Binding*. Foris (Dordrecht).

Chomsky, N. 1991. Linguistics and cognitive science: problems and mysteries. In A. Kasher, ed., *The Chomskyan Turn*. Blackwell (Oxford).

Chomsky, N. 2000. *New Horizons in the Study of Language and Mind*. Cambridge University Press.

Chomsky, N. 2002. *On Nature and Language*. Cambridge University Press.

Chomsky, N. 2005. Three factors in language design. *Linguistic Inquiry* 36.1–22.

Chomsky, N. 2007. Of minds and language. *Biolinguistics* 1.9–27.

Chomsky, N. 2009a. The mysteries of Nature: how deeply hidden? *Journal of Philosophy* 106.167–200.

Chomsky, N. 2009b. Noam Chomsky on language's great mysteries. Interview at <bigthink.com/videos/noam-chomsky-on-languages-great-mysteries>, recorded 18 August 2009, accessed 17 February 2015.

Chomsky, N. and M. Halle. 1968. *The Sound Pattern of English*. Harper & Row (New York).

Chomsky, N. and G. A. Miller. 1958. Finite state languages. *Information and Control* 1.91–112. Reprinted in Luce et al. 1965.

Chomsky, N. and M.-P. Schützenberger. 1967. The algebraic theory of context-free languages. In P. Braffort and D. Hirschberg, eds, *Computer Programming and Formal Systems*. North-Holland (Amsterdam).

Clarke, A. C. 1953. The nine billion names of God. In Frederik Pohl, ed., *Star Science Fiction Stories*. Ballantine Books (New York).

Cohn, W. 1988. *The Hidden Alliances of Noam Chomsky*. Americans for a Safe Israel (New York).

Cole, M. and J. 2006. Rethinking the Goody myth. In D. R. Olson and M. Cole, eds, *Technology, Literacy, and the Evolution of Society: implications of the work of Jack Goody*. Lawrence Erlbaum Associates (Mahwah, NJ).

Crafts, N. 1996. "Post-neoclassical endogenous growth theory": what are its policy implications? *Oxford Review of Economic Policy* 12(2).30–47.

Creel, H. G. 1936. On the nature of Chinese ideography. *T'oung Pao*, 2nd series, 32.85–161.

Creel, H. G. 1939. On the ideographic element in Ancient Chinese. *T'oung Pao*, 2nd series, 34.265–94.

Culicover, P. W. 1999. Minimalist architectures. *Journal of Linguistics* 35.137–50.

Culy, C. 1998. Statistical distribution and the grammatical/ungrammatical distinction. *Grammars* 1.1–13.

Dąbrowska, E. 1997. The LAD goes to school: a cautionary tale for nativists. *Linguistics* 35.735–66.

DeFrancis, J. 1984. *The Chinese Language: fact and fantasy*. University of Hawai'i Press (Honolulu).

DeFrancis, J. 1989. *Visible Speech: the diverse oneness of writing systems*. University of Hawai'i Press (Honolulu).

DeGraff, M. 2001. On the origin of creoles. *Linguistic Typology* 5.213–310.

Derrida, J. 1976. *Of Grammatology*. (English translation of 1967 French original.) Johns Hopkins University Press (Baltimore, MD).

Deutscher, G. 2000. *Syntactic Change in Akkadian: the evolution of sentential complementation*. Oxford University Press.

Deutscher, G. 2009. "Overall complexity": a wild goose chase? In Sampson, Gil, and Trudgill 2009.

Dixon, R. M. W. 1997. *The Rise and Fall of Languages*. Cambridge University Press.

The Economist. 2013. Has the ideas machine broken down? 12 January 2013, pp. 20–3.

The Economist. 2014. Bad characters. 23 August 2014, p. 52.

The Economist. 2015. Nine billion company names. 24 October 2015, p. 70.

Elliott, C. and F. Quinn. 2008. *English Legal System*, 9th edn. Pearson Longman (Harlow).

Evans, N. and S. C. Levinson. 2009. The myth of language universals: language diversity and its importance for cognitive science. *Behavioral and Brain Sciences* 32.429–92.

Evans, V. 2014. *The Language Myth: why language is not an instinct*. Cambridge University Press.

Evans, V. 2015. *The Crucible of Language: how language and mind create meaning.* Cambridge University Press.

Everett, D. L. 2005. Cultural constraints on grammar and cognition in Pirahã: another look at the design features of human language. *Current Anthropology* 76.621–46.

Faarlund, J. T. 2010. Review of Sampson, Gil, and Trudgill 2009. *Language* 86.748–52.

Feng Shengli and V. Yip, eds. 2014. *William Labov and William S.-Y. Wang: a dialogue on sound change.* Peking University Press.

Feyerabend, P. 1975. *Against Method: outline of an anarchistic theory of knowledge.* Verso.

Fiengo, R. 2006. Review of Seuren, *Chomsky's Minimalism. Mind* 115.469–72.

Fillmore, C. J. and C. Baker. 2015. A frames approach to semantic analysis. In Heine and Narrog 2015.

Fischer, K. 1992. Die Wissenschaftstheorie Galileis – oder: Contra Feyerabend. *Zeitschrift für allgemeine Wissenschaftstheorie* 23.165–97.

Fodor, J. A. 1975. *The Language of Thought.* Thomas Crowell (New York).

Fortson, B. W. 2010. *Indo-European Language and Culture: an introduction*, 2nd edn. Wiley-Blackwell (Oxford).

Frantz, D. G. 1978. Abstractness of phonology and Blackfoot orthography design. In W. C. McCormack and S. A. Wurm, eds, *Approaches to Language: anthropological issues.* Mouton (the Hague).

Fromkin, V., R. Rodman, and N. Hyams. 2010. *An Introduction to Language*, 9th edn. Wadsworth (Boston, MA).

Fykias, I. and C. Katsikadeli. 2015. The rise of "subordination features" in the history of Greek and their decline. In L. Kulikov and N. Lavidas, eds, *Proto-Indo-European Syntax and its Development.* John Benjamins (Amsterdam).

Gell-Mann, M. 1995. What is complexity? *Complexity* 1.16–19.

Gibbon, D., R. Moore, and R. Winski, eds. 1997. *Handbook of Standards and Resources for Spoken Language Systems.* Mouton de Gruyter (Berlin).

Gil, D. 2001. Escaping Eurocentrism: fieldwork as a process of unlearning. In P. Newman and M. Ratliff, eds, *Linguistic Fieldwork.* Cambridge University Press.

Gil, D. 2005. Word order without syntactic categories: how Riau Indonesian does it. In A. Carnie, H. Harley, and S. A. Dooley, eds, *Verb First: on the syntax of verb-initial languages.* John Benjamins (Amsterdam).

Gil, D. 2014. Sign languages, creoles, and the development of predication. In Newmeyer and Preston 2014.

Gilliéron, J. 1918. *Généalogie des mots qui designent l'abeille d'apres l'ALF.* Champion (Paris).

Goody, J. 1977. *The Domestication of the Savage Mind.* Cambridge University Press.

Goody, J. and I. Watt. 1963. The consequences of literacy. *Comparative Studies in Society and History* 5.304–45. Reprinted in Goody, ed., *Literacy in Traditional Societies*, Cambridge University Press, 1968, and in P. P. Giglioli, ed., *Language and Social Context: selected readings*, Penguin (Harmondsworth, Mddx), 1972.

Gordon, R. 2012. Is US economic growth over? Faltering innovation confronts the six headwinds. Policy Insight no. 63, Centre for Economic Policy Research, September 2012; online at <www.cepr.org/pubs/PolicyInsights/PolicyInsight63.pdf>, accessed 29 November 2012.

Graddol, D. 2004. The future of language. *Science* 303.1329–31.

Grice, H. P. 1975. Logic and conversation. In P. Cole and J. L. Morgan, eds, *Syntax and Semantics*, vol. 3: *Speech Acts*. Academic Press (New York).

Gross, M. 1979. On the failure of generative grammar. *Language* 55.859–85.

Halle, M. 1959. *The Sound Pattern of Russian*. Mouton (the Hague).

Hanks, P. 2013. *Lexical Analysis: norms and exploitations*. MIT Press.

Hannas, W. C. 1997. *Asia's Orthographic Dilemma*. University of Hawai'i Press (Honolulu).

Hannas, W. C. 2003. *The Writing on the Wall: how Asian orthography curbs creativity*. University of Pittsburgh Press (Philadelphia).

Hardy, G. H. 1940. *A Mathematician's Apology*. Cambridge University Press.

Haspelmath, M. 2015. Framework-free grammatical theory. In Heine and Narrog 2015.

Hayek, F. A. 1955. *The Counter-Revolution of Science: studies on the abuse of reason*. Collier-Macmillan.

Hayek, F. A. 1967. *Studies in Philosophy, Politics and Economics*. Routledge & Kegan Paul.

Heine, B. and H. Narrog, eds. 2015. *The Oxford Handbook of Linguistic Analysis*, 2nd edn. Oxford University Press.

Helpman, E. 2004. *The Mystery of Economic Growth*. Belknap Press (Cambridge, MA).

Henrich, J., S. J. Heine, and A. Norenzayan. 2010. The weirdest people in the world? *Behavioral and Brain Sciences* 33.61–83.

Hermann, E. 1895. Gab es im Indogermanischen nebensätze? *Zeitschrift für vergleichende Sprachforschung* 33.481–535.

Hill, J. 2007. Obituary: William Oliver Bright. *Language* 83.628–41.

Hockett, C. F. 1958. *A Course in Modern Linguistics*. Macmillan (New York).

Hockett, C. F. 1968. *The State of the Art*. Mouton (the Hague).

Hodgson, G. M. et al. 2009. Open letter to Queen Elizabeth II. Online at <www.feed-charity.org/user/image/queen2009b.pdf>, accessed 24 November 2016.

Hopcroft, J. E. and J. D. Ullman. 1969. *Formal Languages and their Relation to Automata*. Addison-Wesley (Reading, MA).

Hornstein, N. and D. Lightfoot. 1981. *Explanation in Linguistics: the logical problem of language acquisition*. Longman.

Householder, F. W. 1973. On arguments from asterisks. *Foundations of Language* 10.365–76.

Houston, S., ed. 2004. *The First Writing: script invention as history and process*. Cambridge University Press.

Itkonen, E. 1996. Concerning the generative paradigm. *Journal of Pragmatics* 25.471–501.

Jackendoff, R. 1993. *Patterns in the Mind: language and human nature*. Harvester Wheatsheaf (Hemel Hempstead).

Jackendoff, R. and E. Wittenberg. 2014. What you can say without syntax: a hierarchy of grammatical complexity. In Newmeyer and Preston 2014.

Jakobovits, L. A. and M. S. Miron, eds. 1967. *Readings in the Psychology of Language*. Prentice-Hall (Englewood Cliffs, NJ).

Johansson, S. 2005. *Origins of Language: constraints on hypotheses*. John Benjamins (Amsterdam).

Johnson, S. 2005. *Spelling Trouble? Language, ideology and the reform of German orthography*. Multilingual Matters (Clevedon, Som.).

Jones, D. 1944. *The Phonetic Aspect of Spelling Reform*. Simplified Spelling Society pamphlet no. 8. Sir Isaac Pitman & Sons.

Jones, D. 1967. *The Phoneme: its nature and use*, 3rd edn. (1st edn published 1950.) Cambridge University Press.

Joos, M. 1957. *Readings in Linguistics*. American Council of Learned Societies (New York).

Kahneman, D. 2011. *Thinking, Fast and Slow*. Penguin.

Kaplan, A. 2011. How much homophony is normal? *Journal of Linguistics* 47.631–71.

Kaplan, A. 2015. The evidence for homophony avoidance in language change: reply to Sampson (2013). *Diachronica* 32.268–76.

Karlgren, B. 1957. *Grammata Serica Recensa*. Museum of Far Eastern Antiquities (Stockholm).

Katz, J. J. and J. A. Fodor. 1963. The structure of a semantic theory. *Language* 39.170–210. Reprinted in Fodor and Katz, eds, *The Structure of Language*, Prentice-Hall (Englewood Cliffs, NJ), 1964, and in Jakobovits and Miron 1967.

Keightley, D. N. 1989. The origins of writing in China: scripts and cultural contexts. In W. M. Senner, ed., *The Origins of Writing*. University of Nebraska Press (Lincoln, NE).

Kennard, M. 2013. BB interviews…Noam Chomsky. *Beyond BRICS* 15 Feb 2013, online at <blogs.ft.com/beyond-brics/2013/02/15/bb-interviews-noam-chomsky/>, accessed 24 February 2015.

Kepser, S. and M. Reis, eds. 2005. *Linguistic Evidence: empirical, theoretical and computational perspectives*. Mouton de Gruyter (Berlin).

Kibrik, A. E. 1998. Archi (Caucasian – Daghestanian). In A. Spencer and A. M. Zwicky, eds, *The Handbook of Morphology*. Blackwell (Oxford).

King, R. D. 1967. Functional load and sound change. *Language* 43.831–52.

Kornai, A. and G. K. Pullum. 1990. The X-bar theory of phrase structure. *Language* 66.24–50.

Krugman, P. 2012. Is growth over? Online at <krugman.blogs.nytimes.com/2012/12/26/is-growth-over/>, accessed 15 April 2013.

Labov, W. 1975. Empirical foundations of linguistic theory. In R. Austerlitz, ed., *The Scope of American Linguistics*, Peter de Ridder Press (Lisse), and also published separately in 1975 by the same house under the title *What is a Linguistic Fact?*

Ladefoged, P. 1967. *Three Areas of Experimental Phonetics*. Oxford University Press.

Lakatos, I. 1970. Falsification and the methodology of scientific research programmes. In I. Lakatos and A. Musgrave, eds, *Criticism and the Growth of Knowledge*, Cambridge University Press.

Lakatos, I. 1976. *Proofs and Refutations: the logic of mathematical discovery*. Cambridge University Press.

Laurence, S. 1998. Convention-based semantics and the development of language. In P. Carruthers and J. Boucher, eds, *Language and Thought: interdisciplinary themes*, Cambridge University Press.

Li Xiaoding 李孝定. 1986. 漢字的起源與演變論叢 (*Papers on the Origins and Evolution of Chinese Script*). Lianjing Publishing Co. (Taipei).

Li, C. N. and S. A. Thompson. 1987. Chinese. In B. Comrie, ed., *The World's Major Languages*. Croom Helm.

Lin Dekang. 2003. Dependency-based evaluation of Minipar. In A. Abeillé, ed., *Treebanks*, Kluwer (Dordrecht).

Loewe, M. and E. L. Shaughnessy, eds. 1998. *The Cambridge History of Ancient China: from the origins of civilization to 221 B.C.* Cambridge University Press.

Luce, R. D., R. R. Bush, and E. Galanter, eds. 1963. *Handbook of Mathematical Psychology*, vol. 2. Wiley (New York).

Luce, R. D., R. R. Bush, and E. Galanter, eds. 1965. *Readings in Mathematical Psychology*, vol. 2. Wiley (New York).

Lyons, J. 1970. *Chomsky*. Fontana.

McBride, C., Xiuhong Tong, and Jianhong Mo. 2015. Developmental dyslexia in Chinese. In W. S.-Y. Wang and Chaofen Sun, eds., *The Oxford Handbook of Chinese Linguistics*. Oxford University Press.

Machamer, P. K. 1973. Feyerabend and Galileo: the interaction of theories, and the reinterpretation of experience. *Studies in the History and Philosophy of Science* 4.1–46.

McWhorter, J. H. 2001. The world's simplest grammars are creole grammars. *Linguistic Typology* 6.125–66. Reprinted in McWhorter, *Defining Creole*, Oxford University Press, 2005.

McWhorter, J. H. 2002. *The Power of Babel: a natural history of language*. Heinemann.

Manchester, C. and D. Salter. 2000. *Exploring the Law: the dynamics of precedent and statutory interpretation*, 3rd edn. Sweet & Maxwell.

Martinet, A. 1955. *Economie des changements phonétiques*. Francke (Bern).

Matthewson, L. 2014. The measurement of semantic complexity: how to get by if your language lacks generalized quantifiers. In Newmeyer and Preston 2014.

Mattingly, I. G. 1972. Reading, the linguistic process, and linguistic awareness. In J. F. Kavanagh and I. G. Mattingly, eds, *Language by Ear and Eye*. MIT Press (Cambridge, MA).

Miestamo, M., K. Sinnemäki, and F. Karlsson, eds. 2008. *Language Complexity: typology, contact, change*. John Benjamins (Amsterdam).

Nagel, T. 2012. *Mind and Cosmos: why the materialist neo-Darwinian concept of Nature is almost certainly false*. Oxford University Press.

Nevins, A. I., D. Pesetsky, and C. Rodrigues. 2009. Pirahã exceptionality: a reassessment. *Language* 85.355–404.

Newmeyer, F. J. and L. B. Preston, eds. 2014. *Measuring Grammatical Complexity*. Oxford University Press.

Nichols, J. 2009. Linguistic complexity: a comprehensive definition and survey. In Sampson, Gil, and Trudgill 2009.

Norman, J. 1988. *Chinese*. Cambridge University Press.

Norman, Y. 2009. *L'Influence de l'écriture sur la langue*. Doctoral thesis, Université de Paris III – Sorbonne Nouvelle.

OECD. 2016. *PISA 2015: results in focus*. Online at <www.oecd.org/pisa/pisa-2015-results-in-focus.pdf>, accessed 7 December 2016.

O'Grady, W., M. Dobrovolsky, and F. Katamba, eds. 1997. *Contemporary Linguistics: an introduction*. Addison Wesley Longman (Harlow).

Ohala, J. J. 2005. Phonetic explanations for sound patterns: implications for grammars of competence. In W. J. Hardcastle and J. M. Beck, eds, *A Figure of Speech: a Festschrift for John Laver*. Lawrence Erlbaum.

Ong, W. 1982. *Orality and Literacy: the technologizing of the word*. Methuen.

Peng Dan-ling and Jiang Hua. 2006. Naming of Chinese phonograms: from cognitive science to cognitive neuroscience. In Ping Li et al. 2006.

Perea, M. and E. Rosa. 2000. The effects of orthographic neighborhood in reading and laboratory word identification tasks: a review. *Psicológica* 21.327–40.

Piattelli-Palmarini, M., ed. 1980. *Language and Learning: the debate between Jean Piaget and Noam Chomsky*. Routledge & Kegan Paul.

Pielke, R. 2012. Is economic growth coming to an end? How Robert Gordon misreads the data and what it tells us about the dismal science. Online at <thebreakthrough.org/index.php/voices/roger-pielke-jr/is-economic-growth-coming-to-an-end/>, accessed 15 April 2013.

Pike, K. L. 1947. *Phonemics: a technique for reducing languages to writing*. University of Michigan Press (Ann Arbor).

Ping Li, Li Hai Tan, E. Bates, and O. J. L. Tzeng, eds. 2006. *The Handbook of East Asian Psycholinguistics*, vol. 1: *Chinese*. Cambridge University Press.

Pinker, S. 1994. *The Language Instinct: the new science of language and mind*. Penguin.

Popper, K. R. 1959. *The Logic of Scientific Discovery*. Hutchinson. (Translation of *Logik der Forschung: zur Erkenntnistheorie der modernen Naturwissenschaft*, Springer (Vienna), 1935.)

Postal, P. M. 2003. "(Virtually) conceptually necessary". *Journal of Linguistics* 39.599–620. A revised version is in Postal 2004.

Postal, P. M. 2004. *Skeptical Linguistic Essays.* Oxford University Press.

Postal, P. M. 2014. Chomsky's methodological fakery. *Lingbuzz,* January 2014 (ling.auf.net/lingbuzz/002006, accessed 3 February 2015).

Progovac, L. 2016. Review of Berwick and Chomsky, *Why Only Us? language and evolution. Language* 92.992–6.

Pulleyblank, E. G. 1995. *Outline of Classical Chinese Grammar.* UBC Press (Vancouver).

Pullum, G. K. 2011. On the mathematical foundations of *Syntactic Structures. Journal of Logic, Language, and Information* 20.277–96.

Pullum, G. K. and B. Scholz. 2002. Empirical assessment of stimulus poverty arguments. In Ritter 2002.

Putnam, H. 1973. Meaning and reference. *Journal of Philosophy* 70.699–711.

Quine, W. van O. 1951. Two dogmas of empiricism. *Philosophical Review* 60.20–43. Reprinted in Quine, *From a Logical Point of View*, 2nd edn, Harper & Row (New York), 1963.

Quirk, R., S. Greenbaum, G. N. Leech, and J. Svartvik. 1985. *A Comprehensive Grammar of the English Language.* Longman.

Ridley, M. 2011. *The Rational Optimist.* Fourth Estate.

Ripman, W. and W. Archer. 1948. *New Spelling,* 6th edn. Sir Isaac Pitman & Sons.

Ritter, N. A., ed. 2002. *A Review of "The Poverty of Stimulus Argument".* Special issue of *The Linguistic Review,* vol. 19 nos 1–2.

Romer, P. M. 1986. Increasing returns and long-run growth. *Journal of Political Economy* 94.1002–37.

Romer, P. M. 1990. Endogenous technical change. *Journal of Political Economy* 98.S71–S102.

Romer, P. M. 1994. New goods, old theory, and the welfare costs of trade restrictions. *Journal of Development Economics* 43.5–38.

Romer, P. M. 2015. Mathiness in the theory of economic growth. *American Economic Review: papers and proceedings 2015,* 105(5).89–93.

Rubinstein, W. D. 1981. Chomsky and the neo-Nazis. *Quadrant,* October 1981, -pp. 8–14.

Sampson, G. R. 1979a. *Liberty and Language.* Oxford University Press.

Sampson, G. R. 1979b. What was Transformational Grammar? (Review article on Chomsky 1975.) *Lingua* 48.355–78. A version is reprinted in Sampson 2001.

Sampson, G. R. 1980a. *Making Sense.* Oxford University Press.

Sampson, G. R. 1980b. *Schools of Linguistics: competition and evolution.* Hutchinson.

Sampson, G. R. 1982. The economics of conversation. In N. V. Smith, ed., *Mutual Knowledge.* Academic Press.

Sampson, G. R. 1987. Evidence against the "grammatical"/"ungrammatical" distinction. In W. Meijs, ed., *Corpus Linguistics and Beyond.* Rodopi (Amsterdam). A version is reprinted in Sampson 2001.

Sampson, G. R. 1989. That strange realm called theory. *Critical Review* 3.93–104. Online at <www.grsampson.net/ATsr.pdf>.
Sampson, G. R. 1994. Chinese script and the diversity of writing systems. *Linguistics* 32.117–32.
Sampson, G. R. 2001. *Empirical Linguistics*. Continuum.
Sampson, G. R. 2002. Exploring the richness of the stimulus. In Ritter 2002.
Sampson, G. R. 2005. *The "Language Instinct" Debate*, revised edn. Continuum.
Sampson, G. R. 2007. Minds in uniform: how generative linguistics regiments culture, and why it shouldn't. In M. Grein and E. Weigand, eds, *Dialogue and Culture*. John Benjamins (Amsterdam). A version is reprinted in Sampson and Babarczy 2014.
Sampson, G. R. 2013. A counterexample to homophony avoidance. *Diachronica* 30.579–91.
Sampson, G. R. 2014. Can we know how language began? *Language and Dialogue* 4.455–64.
Sampson, G. R. 2015a. *Writing Systems*, 2nd edn. Equinox (Sheffield and Bristol, CT).
Sampson, G. R. 2015b. Review of Newmeyer and Preston 2014. *Linguist List* 26.2028, online at <linguistlist.org/issues/26/26-2028.html>.
Sampson, G. R. and A. Babarczy. 2014. *Grammar without Grammaticality: growth and limits of grammatical precision*. De Gruyter (Berlin).
Sampson, G. R., D. Gil, and P. Trudgill, eds. 2009. *Language Complexity as an Evolving Variable*. Oxford University Press.
Sapir, E. 1921. *Language: an introduction to the study of speech*. Reprinted by Rupert Hart-Davis, 1963.
de Saussure, F. 1966. *Course in General Linguistics*. McGraw-Hill. (Translation of *Cours de linguistique générale*, Payot (Paris), 1916.)
Schuessler, A. 2007. *ABC Etymological Dictionary of Old Chinese*. University of Hawai'i Press (Honolulu).
Schütze, C. T. 1996. *The Empirical Base of Linguistics: grammaticality judgments and linguistic methodology*. University of Chicago Press.
Schützenberger, M.-P. 1963. On context-free languages and push-down automata. *Information and Control* 6.246–64. Reprinted in Luce et al. 1965.
Schützenberger, M.-P. 1996. Les failles du Darwinisme. *La Recherche* 283.87–90, January 1996.
Schweizer, P. 2005. *Do As I Say (Not As I Do)*. Broadway Books (New York).
Shu Hua and Wu Ningning. 2006. Growth of orthography–phonology knowledge in the Chinese writing system. In Ping Li et al. 2006.
Silverman, D. 2006. *A Critical Introduction to Phonology*. Continuum.
Silverman, D. 2010. Neutralization and anti-homophony in Korean. *Journal of Linguistics* 46.453–82.
Skinner, B. F. 1957. *Verbal Behavior*. Appleton-Century-Crofts (New York).
Smith, A. 1776. *An Inquiry into the Nature and Causes of the Wealth of Nations*. Edited by R. H. Campbell and A. S. Skinner. 2 vols. Clarendon Press (Oxford), 1976.
Smith, N. V. 1999. *Chomsky: ideas and ideals*. Cambridge University Press.
Snider, K. 2014. Orthography and phonological depth. In Cahill and Rice 2014.

Sokal, A. and J. Bricmont. 1997. *Impostures intellectuelles.* Odile Jacob (Paris). English translation published in Britain as *Intellectual Impostures*, and in the USA as *Fashionable Nonsense: postmodern intellectuals' abuse of science.*

Stockwell, R. P., P. Schachter, and B. Partee. 1973. *The Major Syntactic Structures of English.* Holt, Rinehart & Winston (New York).

Sweet, H. 1899. *The Practical Study of Languages.* Dent.

Tanenhaus, S. 2016. Noam Chomsky and the bicycle theory. *New York Times*, 31 October 2016. Online at <www.nytimes.com/2016/11/06/education/edlife/on-being-noam-chomsky.html>, accessed 15 December 2016.

Taylor, I. and M. M. Taylor. 1983. *The Psychology of Reading.* Academic Press (New York).

Taylor, J. R. 2012. *The Mental Corpus: how language is represented in the mind.* Oxford University Press.

Tennyson, A. 1842. You ask me why, tho' ill at ease. In Tennyson, *Poems*, vol. i, Edward Moxon.

Toolan, M. 2015. Review of Evans 2014. *Language and Dialogue* 5.471–84.

Tranter, N. 2001. Script "borrowing", cultural influence and the development of the written vernacular in East Asia. In T. E. McAuley, ed., *Language Change in East Asia.* Curzon Press (Richmond, Surrey).

Trudgill, P. 1989. Interlanguage, interdialect and typological change. In S. Gass et al., eds, *Variation in Second Language Acquisition*, vol. 2: *psycholinguistic issues*, Multilingual Matters (Clevedon, Som.).

Trudgill, P. 2011. *Sociolinguistic Typology: social determinants of linguistic complexity.* Oxford University Press.

UNESCO. 2006. *Education for All Global Monitoring Report 2006.* Online at <www. unesco. org/education/GMR2006/full/chapt8_eng.pdf>, accessed 14 August 2014.

Warsh, D. 2006. *Knowledge and the Wealth of Nations: a story of economic discovery.* W. W. Norton (New York).

Wedel, A., A. Kaplan, and S. Jackson. 2013. High functional load inhibits phonological contrast loss: a corpus study. *Cognition* 128.179–86.

Wedel, A., S. Jackson, and A. Kaplan. 2013. Functional load and the lexicon: evidence that syntactic category and frequency relationships in minimal lemma pairs predict the loss of phoneme contrasts in language change. *Language and Speech* 56.395–417.

White, M. G. 1950. The analytic and the synthetic: an untenable dualism. In S. Hook, ed., *John Dewey: philosopher of science and freedom.* Dial Press (New York). Reprinted in L. Linsky, ed., *Semantics and the Philosophy of Language.* University of Illinois Press (Urbana), 1952.

Wierzbicka, A. 1990. "Prototypes save": on the uses and abuses of the notion of "prototype" in linguistics and related fields. In S. L. Tsohatzidis, ed., *Meanings and Prototypes: studies in linguistic categorization.* Routledge.

Wierzbicka, A. 1996. *Semantics: primes and universals.* Oxford University Press.

Wilks, Y. A. 1975. A preferential, pattern-seeking semantics for natural language inference. *Artificial Intelligence* 6.53–74. Reprinted in K. Ahmad, C. Brewster, and M. Stevenson, eds, *Words and Intelligence I: selected papers by Yorick Wilks.* Springer (Dordrecht), 2007.

Wilks, Y. A., L. Guthrie, and B. Slator. 1999. *Electric Words.* MIT Press (Cambridge, MA).

Winn, C. 2005. *I Never Knew That About England.* Ebury Press.

Wittgenstein, L. 1953. *Philosophical Investigations.* Blackwell (Oxford).

Yeshaya, J. J. M. S. 2014. In the name of the God of Israel: Judeo-Arabic language and literature. In J. den Heijer, A. Schmidt, and T. Pataridze, eds, *Scripts Beyond Borders: a survey of allographic traditions in the Euro-Mediterranean world.* Institut Orientaliste de l'Université Catholique de Louvain (Louvain-la-Neuve).

Zhao Jing, Li Qing-Lin, and Bi Hong-Yan. 2012. The characteristics of Chinese orthographic neighborhood size effect for developing readers. *PLOS One* 8 October 2012. Online at <dx.doi.org/10.1371/journal.pone.0046922>, accessed 15 December 2016.

Index

www.ingramcontent.com/pod-product-compliance
Lightning Source LLC
LaVergne TN
LVHW010444080826
844660LV00026B/1212

* 9 7 8 1 7 8 1 7 9 5 7 8 1 *